Human Rights Journalism

Also by Ibrahim Seaga Shaw

EXPANDING PEACE JOURNALISM: Critical and Comparative Perspectives (*with Robert Hackett and Jake Lynch*)

Human Rights Journalism

Advances in Reporting Distant Humanitarian Interventions

Ibrahim Seaga Shaw

palgrave
macmillan

First published 2012 by
PALGRAVE MACMILLAN

Palgrave Macmillan in the UK is an imprint of Macmillan Publishers Limited,
registered in England, company number 785998, of Houndmills, Basingstoke,
Hampshire RG21 6XS.

Palgrave Macmillan in the US is a division of St Martin's Press LLC,
175 Fifth Avenue, New York, NY 10010.

Palgrave Macmillan is the global academic imprint of the above companies
and has companies and representatives throughout the world.

Palgrave® and Macmillan® are registered trademarks in the United States,
the United Kingdom, Europe and other countries.

ISBN 978–0–230–32142–7

This book is printed on paper suitable for recycling and made from fully
managed and sustained forest sources. Logging, pulping and manufacturing
processes are expected to conform to the environmental regulations of the
country of origin.

A catalogue record for this book is available from the British Library.

A catalog record for this book is available from the Library of Congress.

10   9   8   7   6   5   4   3   2   1
21 20 19 18 17 16 15 14 13 12

Transferred to Digital Printing in 2012

To my father Alhaji Mohamed Allieu Shaw of Blessed Memory

Contents

Figures and Tables

Figures

Tables

Foreword

Stuart Allan

Enshrined in the Universal Declaration of Human Rights (1948) is the basic premise that 'all people matter', a moral commitment to overcome the culture of 'othering' permeating everyday life around the globe. This premise, when considered in relation to the priorities and protocols of western journalism, throws into sharp relief the ways in which certain 'us and them' dichotomies, inflected in news reports, recurrently counterpoise the structural interests of 'people like us' against the suffering of strangers.

Journalists' routine, everyday choices about what to report – how best to do it, and why – necessarily implicate them in a discursive politics of mediation in what are increasingly globalised public spheres. This point is not lost on politicians, of course, anxious to make use of the news media for persuasive – or, more to the point, propagandistic – purposes. To take one example, Tony Blair, in the months leading up to his resignation as British prime minister, gave a series of 'legacy' speeches intended, in part, to help secure his place in the history books on his own preferred terms. In one such speech, delivered onboard the assault ship HMS *Albion* on 12 January 2007, he discussed the changing nature of the security challenges facing western countries in the post-9/11 era. Interestingly, singled out for attention in this regard were the problems posed by 'a completely new world of modern communication and media' for the armed forces. In Blair's words:

> [War] is no longer something read in dispatches. It comes straight into the living room. Take a website like Live Leak which has become popular with soldiers from both sides of the divide in both Afghanistan and Iraq. Operational documentary material, from their mobile phones or laptops, is posted on the site. These sometimes gruesome images are the unmediated reality of war. They provide a new source of evidence for journalists and commentators, bypassing the official accounts and records.

To Blair, such bypassing of official voices weakened the West's war against terrorists, for this type of material, in his estimation, contributed to public reluctance to support long military campaigns. LiveLeak's (www.liveleak.com) more controversial content has included digital photographs of torture in the Abu Ghraib prison, deemed too disturbing by news organisations to show, while the 'un-official' execution clip of Saddam Hussein (which, in contrast with the 'official' version, documented the chaotic nature of the scene) similarly became a prominent target of official condemnation.

Typically underpinning the public pronouncements of enthusiasts for what Blair called the 'unmediated reality of war' is a belief that these emerging forms of reporting upset habitual ways of seeing war, with profound implications for the formation of public opinion. From the perspective of officials, this communicative power is legitimate only to the extent that it respects their definitions. A more recent case in point concerned the whistle-blower Wikileaks website's posting of a video documenting the shooting of a group of civilians by US forces situated in a helicopter gunship hovering over a Baghdad neighbourhood. Sparking press attention around the world, the brutal rawness of the black and white footage – compounded by the harrowing exchanges between the air crew recorded on the audio track – proved acutely unsettling to viewers otherwise habituated to routine (effectively sanitised) renderings of the horrors of a warzone. US Defense Secretary Robert Gates admitted that the video made for difficult viewing. Asked whether he thought the events in question would 'damage the image of the US in the world', he replied that he didn't think so, insisting that videos such as this one provided an incomplete picture of what was happening on the battlefield. 'That is the problem with these videos,' he argued. 'You are looking at the war through a soda straw and you have no context or perspective.'

And herein lies one of the many virtues of Ibrahim Seaga Shaw's discussion, which shows us how journalistic decisions about context and perspective profoundly shape distant audiences' perceptions about the realities of conflict. In comparing and contrasting what he terms 'human wrongs journalism' with 'human rights journalism', he usefully pinpoints a range of pressing issues deserving of critical investigation. 'The human rights journalist is not only concerned about reporting human rights violations caused by direct physical violence in the sense of civil and political rights (negative rights/negative peace),' he observes, 'but also, and perhaps more importantly, those violations caused by indirect structural and cultural violence in the sense of economic, social and cultural rights (positive rights/positive peace).' Shaw's challenge to us, then, is to identify and critique the often subtle ways in which journalism is implicated in the structural imperatives of militarism, which more often than not underpin human rights abuse. That is to say, to find new ways to disrupt the ideological purchase of official truth claims, not least where the waging of war by 'us' against 'them' is effectively normalised to the point that peace-centred alternatives are trivialised, marginalised or excluded altogether as being less than newsworthy.

The perceptive analysis presented in these pages highlights the basis for a radical reconsideration of some of our most familiar assumptions. It does so in a manner alert to journalism's shortcomings, but also to its remarkable potential to foster points of emphatic connection at a distance. In this way, I would suggest, Shaw's intervention inspires us to reinvigorate our efforts to develop productive ways forward, to re-imagine new possibilities in the search for compassionate reporting, respectful of the human dignity of others.

Stuart Allan, Professor of Journalism, Media School,
Bournemouth University, UK

Preface

This is the first book to explore, exclusively and critically, the role of the media in the promotion and protection of human rights. Drawing on Kant's cosmopolitan principle of global justice and on case studies of the reporting of humanitarian interventions, especially in Eastern Europe and Africa, it argues for human rights journalism as a more radical alternative to mainstream journalism. This is because human rights journalism takes a more proactive approach in prioritising the deconstruction of indirect structural and cultural violence as the best way of preventing or minimising the incidence of direct political violence.

Yet, as the book goes to print (in the winter of 2011), the problem of human wrongs journalism, illuminated throughout its pages as the antipode of human rights journalism, continues to dictate the mediation of political protests, civil wars and humanitarian military interventions sweeping across the Middle East and Africa; in particular Libya, Syria, Yemen, Bahrain, Gaza and Ivory Coast. Questions are being asked, albeit not so far by the mainstream media, about the sudden frenzy of the international community, led by the big NATO powers, to intervene in Libya in the name of human rights promotion and protection – but not in Yemen, Bahrain, Gaza or the Ivory Coast. *Déjà vu*! A similar question is asked in this book – why NATO intervened in Kosovo and not in Sierra Leone, when the crises in the two countries peaked around the same time, in 1999, even when the situation was confirmed to be far worse in Sierra Leone.

Nevertheless, the conference in Bonn, Germany, 20–22 June 2011, organised by Deutsche Welle Global Media Forum on 'Human Rights in a Globalised World: Challenges for the Media', which I attended, indicated that, after all, it is not only bad news that greets the publication of this book. It showed that there are at least some media professionals who apparently share the central concerns expressed in this book, the timing of which is clearly appropriate. Among topics discussed in the plenary sessions was 'Advocacy versus Objectivity – Media and Human Rights'. This is one of the dilemmas facing journalists who have the moral obligation to be sensitive to human rights violations of all makes and forms, as discussed in this book. As I said in my contribution on a panel at a winter 2008 conference organised by the National Union of Journalists, 'New Threats to Media Freedom', journalists always walk a tightrope in striking a balance between 'objectivity' and 'advocacy'. At this event I recounted my experience in Sierra Leone as editor of the award-winning *Expo Times* newspaper in the mid-1990s, where I tried to be both an advocate and an objective journalist, depending on the circumstances, but had to pay a heavy price in threats, harassments and a number of spells in prison. I recalled how my advocacy for a peaceful resolution of the conflict between the rebels and the government was interpreted as a show of support for the former, which resulted, among other things, in my being arrested, charged with spying for the enemy and branded as a 'collaborator' of the military junta that temporarily ousted the civilian regime that was harassing me. In fact that experience, which forced me into exile in 1998, effectively marked the beginning of my scholarly interest in human rights-based journalism, and, by extension, of the motivation to write this book.

Ibrahim Seaga Shaw, PhD

Acknowledgements

I am first indebted to Christien van den Anker, Stuart Allan and Michael Palmer for their advice and encouragement as I researched and wrote this book. My special thanks go to Richard Lance Keeble, and also to Palgrave Macmillan's anonymous reviewer, both of whose comments and suggestions contributed to enriching the book's main arguments and focus. I am grateful to Jane Saville, James Pattison, Jake Lynch and Robert Hackett for their very useful comments and suggestions, which contributed to improving the quality of the arguments. I also acknowledge the support and patience of the Palgrave Media and Culture Commissioning editor, Felicity Plester, and her assistant Catherine Mitchell. I acknowledge with thanks the permission granted by *Ethical Space: The International Journal of Communication Ethics* to reproduce a substantial section of my article on 'peace journalism and global justice' (2009) – the case study of Sierra Leone in Chapter 6. Similar thanks go to Lisa Schirch for her permission to reproduce tables from her conference paper on 'Justpeace' (2002), and to all others whose names I have not mentioned here. I am grateful to Mike Jempson of Media Wise/UWE for all the support he gave me when I first moved to Bristol in 2006, and to my friends at the African Voices Forum, Exiled Journalists Network and Bristol Legacy Commission for their encouragement and support during the research and writing process. Finally, thanks go to Fatu for showing understanding and patience throughout my writing of this book.

1
Introduction: Background and Scope of Human Rights Journalism

In the last two decades the main focus of the theorisation of human rights journalism has been essentially two-fold: first, this type of journalism has focused on the role of the journalist in exposing human rights abuses, and, second, it has focused on free speech, which is in itself a human right. Rarely explored, if at all, is the conceptualisation of what I refer to in this book as human rights journalism as a normative journalistic practice, a rights-based journalism – a journalism based on the respect for human dignity irrespective of colour, nationality, race, gender, geographical location and so on. Despite the Universal Declaration of Human Rights (UDHR) in 1948 following the Second World War, it is the first two narrower interpretations of human rights journalism, and not the third, that have increasingly become central to efforts and challenges of making the last six decades the age of human rights. And I believe that this has been detrimental to fulfilling the declaration's aims. Indeed, as the United Nations (UN) celebrated 60 years of existence on 10 December 2008, the world body was criticised by international press freedom campaign organisations such as Reporters without Borders (RWB) for allowing post-Cold War politics to undermine efforts towards the realisation of most of the human rights principles, including the right to freedom of expression.

In this book I argue that progress would not have been slow with respect to the implementation of the UDHR if human rights journalism had been put at the centre of the global movement to make the world a better place. In this introductory chapter I will first discuss why the study of human rights journalism is important; and, second, I will conceptualise direct physical and indirect structural/cultural violence. In the discussion of these two sections of the introductory chapter, readers and other end-users are directed to the relevant corresponding details in the remaining chapters of the book; this will make it much easier for them to navigate through its contours.

1.1   Why is the study of human rights journalism important?

This book is important because it is the first one to focus exclusively on the conceptualisation of human rights journalism on the basis of the reporting of physical, structural and cultural violence within the context of humanitarian intervention. It aims to promote the understanding of the human rights-based approach to journalism, which claims that journalists not only hold the power to inform the public, connect people in different parts of the world and promote public knowledge and understanding of issues and events, but, more importantly, have the moral responsibility – as duty bearers – to educate the public, increase awareness in its members of their rights and monitor, investigate and report all human rights violations. This is, arguably, the first scholarly attempt to illuminate, in conceptual and empirical ways, how journalists can take on board as many perspectives as possible through in-depth analysis and can thus create a more informed and empowered public sphere. It is set to be an important contribution to the fast developing – albeit under-researched – scholarly interest in the role of the media in the promotion and protection of human rights, and in some ways to current debates in peace journalism.

Going by their profession, journalists have an ethical obligation not only to witness but also to report on human rights abuses of all makes and forms. These include not only political violence such as genocide, arbitrary arrests and detentions, extra-judicial killings, rape, ethnic cleansing and mistreatment of prisoners, but also, and perhaps more importantly, economic, social and cultural violence such as absolute poverty, famine, forced migration, forced labour, human trafficking, marginalisation or exclusion of minorities. Sadly, however, while some progress could be said to have been made in the reporting of issues of political violence such as civil and other wars of insurrection and in the attendant growing scholarly work in this area (Hallin, 1986; Shaw, 1996; Ginneken, 2001; Knightley, 1998; Carruthers, 1995, 2000; Hammond, 2000; Robinson, 2002b; Palmer, 2003; Allan and Zelizer, 2004; Nossek et al., 2007), such progress could not be said to have been made in the case of the reporting of issues of economic, social and cultural violence. One notable exception, however, was Herman and Chomsky's groundbreaking book *Manufacturing Consent: The Political Economy of the Mass*

Media (1988), which sheds light on the negative use of propaganda by the media towards undermining human rights protection. The theory of the propaganda model points to the existence of systemic biases in the mass media caused by structural economic factors. It sees the media purely as business enterprises, out there to make profit by selling their products (readers and audiences) to other business concerns (advertisers), rather than as providers of quality news for the public. The model identifies five factors (filters) that influence the selection and production of news: the wealthy elite owners, who are only interested in making profit; advertisers, who call the editorial shots; sources, which set the news agenda; sustained and intentional efforts (flaks) to manipulate public information; and the choice of 'good' (friend) or 'bad' (enemy), which is based on ideology (western/communist). When Herman and Chomsky empirically tested the model, they discovered a form of bias that consistently favours corporate interests.

Herman and Chomsky (1988) argued that the propaganda approach to the coverage of events and issues by the mainstream mass media, within the context of the five filters outlined above, points to a systematic and highly political dichotomisation style of reporting, aimed at serving important domestic political and corporate interests. This dichotomisation takes the form of choices concerning the stories reported and of ways in which the reporting itself is done in order to favour elite political interests. Thus the choice of favourable or unfavourable materials and the modes of reporting, together with the positioning, tone, context and fullness of treatment of these materials, vary in ways that serve political and economic interests. For example, only human rights activists and groups with little or no political leverage would show concerns for human rights violations in Turkey – such as the torture of political prisoners and the attack on trade unions – and call on the media to do something. However, this was not the case with the US government during the Reagan regime in the 1980s, which saw Turkey as a strong ally against communism and in fact supported the Turkish martial-law government since its coming to power in 1980. In line with the propaganda model, the US media followed the political lead of their government and thus considered the victims of human rights violations committed by their friend (the Turkish junta) as unworthy of media attention. On the contrary, the Reagan administration and elites of the corporate establishment welcomed protest over political prisoners and over the violation of the rights of trade union activists in Poland in 1981 as a noble cause. This was ostensibly so not because of their interest in human rights and democracy, but because they saw this attitude as a way of scoring political points against their ideological enemy, communist Poland. The US media seemingly toed the official line, as official sources in Washington provided press releases and opinion articles condemning human rights violations in Poland. The Polish dissidents became victims of human rights violations worthy of media attention and coverage, hence passing through the filters where their Turkish counterparts failed. It was as if the media had a clear instruction to focus on covering the victims of enemy powers and to ignore those of friendly powers (Herman and Chomsky, 1988).

Moreover, there are times when the abuses of worthy victims go beyond just passing through the filters to actually supporting sustained propaganda campaigns. A story of normally high political and economic interest is often dramatised and kept on the news agenda for some time. Take, for example, the shooting down of the Korean airliner KAL 007 in early September 1983 by the Soviets, which quickly provided the context for a sustained campaign of condemnation of a perceived ideological enemy. However, no such condemnation was forthcoming from the US administration following the shooting down by Israel of a Libyan civilian airliner in February 1973 by way of a 'cold-blooded murder' (Herman and Chomsky, 1988). Yet this differential treatment was explained by the *New York Times* precisely on utilitarian grounds: 'No useful purpose is served by an acrimonious debate over the assignment of blame for the downing of a Libyan airliner in the Sinai Peninsula last week' (Herman and Chomsky, 1988).

Although it is now over 20 years since the publication of the seminal work on the propaganda model by Herman and Chomsky, the five filters they talked about are as true today as they were in the days of the Cold War. One discernible difference, however, is that in this era of 'clash of civilisations', to quote Samuel Huntington (1996), the friendly/enemy country dichotomy is determined not necessarily by east/west/communist/capitalist ideologies but by who is on our side in the 'war on terror'. For example, while victims of human rights violations resulting from Ethiopia's 'war on terror' in Somalia since 2005 are not worthy of western elites and media attention, those resulting from Mugabe's high-handed rule in Zimbabwe are considered worthy to pass the filters of the propaganda model. Within the context of human rights journalism, all victims of human rights violations deserve equal media attention and coverage, if humanitarian interventions to prevent or address these violations are to be meaningful. Yet the implications of the media in the equation and the conceptualisation of a robust counter-hegemonic model to address them are relatively under-researched; hence, partly, why this book is important.

When talking about the academic literature on political violence, only the work of Martin Shaw (1996) came anywhere near calling for a more robust and pro-active role of journalism in the promotion of human rights and for the creation of what he called a 'global civil society', where people caught up in conflict situations are not represented merely as victims, but as participants. Martin Shaw concluded that 'Western dominated global media rarely take seriously the self-representation of individuals, communities and organisations in zones of conflict' and called for the development of 'a global civil society in which the globally vulnerable will be well represented' (Shaw, 1996: 182). Shaw and others, including Nossek et al. (2007) and Allan and Zelizer (2004), have all been concerned about how this may erode professional journalistic values. The national identity of the journalists always lulls them into prioritising 'our news' and relegating 'their news' to the backwater. Yet apart from being dated (and this is why the present book is partly intended to update the literature in this area), Shaw's work and those by Nossek et al. (2007) and Allan and Zelizer (2004) focus almost exclusively on political violence, with little or no discussion of the structural violence as an undercurrent of the conflicts they looked at. Martin Shaw fell short of this even in his more recent book *War and Genocide* (2003), where he called for a departure from 'humanitarian intervention' as military intervention 'to create access to aid'. In its place he suggested the more holistic approach of 'a military campaign motivated at least in part by concern to protect civilian lives, or create political conditions in which people may live in relative freedom and security'. It is the aim of this book to fill this gap in scholarship in the role of the media in the promotion or undermining of human rights.

Virgil Hawkins' conceptualisation of distant 'undetected wars' – such as the one in the Democratic Republic of Congo (DRC) – as 'stealth conflicts' and of the role of mainstream western media in the equation can also, arguably, be seen as an important academic intervention designed to illuminate the lack of human rights-based journalism practice. Hawkins (2008) talks about the DRC's 'stealth conflict' (DRC is on record as having the highest conflict-related deaths – 3.3 million – since the Second World War), like many others in the world, not only in the context of deaths caused by 'bullets and bombs '(direct physical violence), but also in the context of deaths caused by 'starvation and disease' (indirect structural violence). However, apart from stopping short of proposing an alternative form of journalism practice that can address the mainstream media deficit, Hawkins' reference to indirect structural violence as being the victim of 'stealth' has more to do with victims surviving or escaping direct physical violence already going on rather than with those who are not. Again, it is the intention of this book to address these gaps in the literature.

As this book is about the de facto role of the media in human rights promotion and protection, it is also important to recognise some of the literature that has contributed to the much wider debate on the mediation of distant human suffering. Hoijer (2004) sees the media coverage of distant human suffering as a driving force in the process of influencing both the public and the political elite to show compassion and do something about it. To illustrate her point, Hoijer points to the sustained television coverage of the shocking images of the senseless attack on Kosovo by Serbia, which forced the UN to impose sanctions on it (2004). There is therefore a clear nexus between the media coverage and the political reactions to distant suffering. In fact, as Hoijer et al. (2002) put it, media reporting can often be enmeshed in propaganda strategies. Pressure was brought to bear by the US authorities on the media to refrain from reporting civilian casualties during the invasion of Afghanistan by the allied forces to oust the Taliban regime as this was perceived to be undermining public support for the bombings (Hoijer, 2004). The CNN staff received instruction from its chairman to balance the reporting of victims in Afghanistan, if such news was going to be broadcast, with reminders to the audience of the victims of the terror attack on the World Trade Centre and in the Pentagon (Ottosen, 2002). In fact, Boyd-Barrett (2004: 438) proposed a sixth filter, which he called the 'buying out' of journalists by powerful state and private institutions, as an extension of Herman and Chomsky's five-filter propaganda model. Boyd-Barrett drew on the case of the 2003 US invasion of Iraq, and in particular on the complicity of *New York Times* (*NYT*)'s Judith Miller as 'conduit for stories originating in US military and intelligent agencies', which promoted the argument for weapons of mass destruction (WMD) in the hands of Saddam Hussein. Miller had strong connections with right-wing and pro-Zionist think tanks such as the American Enterprise Institute, the Hudson Institute, the Washington Institute for Near East Policy and the Middle East Forum. She was also a very good friend of Iraqi dissident politician Ahmed Chalabi, who provided her with a lot of distorted information, although she never quoted him. This distorted information later provided the context for many front-page *NYT* stories about WMD in the hands of Saddam's regime. Vann (2003) observes that, although Miller's reports were based on information provided by anonymous sources, which were later discredited, they ended up serving a political agenda by playing a direct role in campaigning for an illegal war in Iraq.

Wolfsfeld (1997) sees the rivalry among political stakeholders for control over the media as one among many complex battles for total political dominance. The extent to which politicians compete for media attention leaves the media with a lot of power, which could be better used in the interest of human rights promotion and for protection rather than to serve political elites. In his political context model, Wolfsfeld makes the case that politicians try to provide the media with something to think about and report.

It is clear that the mediation on suffering offers citizens and politicians alike the opportunity to empathise with the suffering of distant strangers, no matter the level of political influence on the reporting of different humanitarian crises (Hoijer, 2004). Yet Hoijer concludes that, in the critical media debate, it is quite common for suffering to be commodified by the media, to the extent that the 'audience become passive spectators of distant death and pain without any moral commitment' to change things for the better (2004: 527). The result is what Tester (2001) problematises as the 'compassion fatigue' of the audience, which easily gives up hope of changing things for the better after being constantly bombarded with gory images of human suffering.

In her groundbreaking book *The Spectatorship of Suffering*, Lillie Chouliaraki (2006) used the social theory model of the media to discuss the two narratives of how mediation can shape the cosmopolitan spectatorship of distant suffering. While the pessimistic narrative blames technology for eroding traditional public collectivities, the optimistic narrative takes advantage of the promise of technology to construct new collective sensibilities among media publics. The pessimistic narrative echoes the pessimism of Adorno, who alludes to the widening chasm between proximity and distance in the mediation of distant suffering in reference to Robin's eloquent paradox of *intimate detachment* (Adorno, 1938/1982: 270). The technology used by the media not only reduces audiences to being passive spectators, but in fact it entertains the myth that they participate in public life when they are simply, in Adorno's words, 'regressing in listening' or watching (Adorno, 1938/1982: 270). Chouliaraki notes:

The reason for this regression is that the very technological form of the medium 'sanitises' reality – that is, it cuts real life off from its raw sensations. The medium's sense of immediacy may be due to an ever-enhanced technical perfection, but, ultimately, it is these same technical determinants that deprive on-screen suffering of its compelling physicality and shift the fact of suffering into pixel fiction. (2006: 24)

This perceived sense of lack of authenticity in the images of violence screened, and the sustained manner in which their screening is done, often leads to 'compassion fatigue', thereby making audiences dismiss the images as normal happenings; hence they are under the impression that there is nothing they can do to change things. The second aspect of the pessimistic narrative is the domesticity of reception: spectators are less concerned, because they receive the spectacle of violence in the safety of their living rooms.

The optimistic narrative, on the other hand, is predicated on the anthropological idea that the media function as symbols that generate authentic sociability in two ways: a celebration of communitarianism – that is, the introduction of the spectator to a broad community of spectators; and the democratisation of responsibility – that is, the process of translating the mediated experience of the spectator into public–political consciousness. While the pessimistic narrative reflects the dialogic model, with the ethics of proximity as its public norm, the optimistic one reflects the dissemination model, with action at distance as its public norm. Although Chouliaraki agrees that cosmopolitanism more closely resonates with the disseminative conception of public life, she argues that 'this narrative also fails to tell us how television connects us with the "other" and how it may engage with distant suffering as a cause of action'(2006: 35). Chouliaraki's model of the social theory of the media was able to identify the problem of the mediation of distant human suffering but fell short of coming up with an appropriate solution to address it. Moreover, her interventionist approach was more reactive than pro-active, as the mediation or communication of emotional response was between the spectator and those suffering as a result of a distant violent spectacle, and not necessarily its ending or prevention. In other words Chouliaraki's approach was more geared towards mobilising public empathy through the media to address the needs of the victims of war than promoting a better understanding of the undercurrents of the war to encourage public support to help end it or prevent its escalation. What is more, the focus of Chouliaraki's model is on the cosmopolitan spectatorship of human suffering caused more by direct political violence – as for example in the case of 9/11, or in the stoning of a Nigerian Muslim woman from the state of Kano for committing adultery – than by structural or cultural violence. It is the aim of this book to fill these gaps in scholarship by proposing the all-embracing, cosmopolitan mediation of public life that I have conceptualised as human rights journalism. This is more pro-active and holistic in terms of capturing all forms of human suffering. It resonates with, and even goes beyond, what Hackett and Zhao (1998: 224) conceptualise as public communication for a sustainable democracy, 'which invokes not just the passive role of media reportage, [...] but the more active role of promoting communal dialogue about matters of shared concern'.

In his book *The CNN Effect: The Myth of the News, Foreign Policy and Interventions*, Piers Robinson (2002b) refers to the insights of a series of researchers and commentators on how historical frames of distance such as 'ancient ethnic hatreds' quickly become common, interpretative frameworks for journalists seeking to make sense of distant crises (see, for instance, van der Gaag and Nash 1987; Myers et al., 1996; Campbell, 1998: 51–4; Allen and Seaton, 1990; Beattie et al., 1999). However, Robinson (2002b: 29) refers to the critical media coverage of Kurdish refugees fleeing Saddam Hussein's Iraq as 'empathy and critical framing because the coverage encourages viewers to associate themselves with the suffering of people and criticises government inaction'. Alison Preston (1996) dichotomises media frames of human suffering into an empathy distance frame, which focuses on the banal images of the spectacle of violence, and an empathy critical frame, which focuses on giving its political context by explaining why the suffering is happening. It is these two binary frames that I conceptualised in Chapter 5 as the evocative and the diagnostic styles of reporting, respectively. Chapter 5 and Chapters 6–11 in Part II and Part III provide conceptual and empirical discussions of the foregrounding of evocative reporting (empathy distance framing) over that of diagnostic reporting (empathy critical framing) in the mainstream media, and implications for humanitarian interventions within the cosmopolitan context of global justice.

Van Ginniken (2001), Fowler (2001), Cohen (1963), Reese and Shoemaker (2001), Galtung and Ruge (1973), McNair (1994, 2000), Castells (2006) and a host of others have argued that there are also ideological and professional factors (mostly discussed in Chapters 3 and 4 of this book) that influence the selection and style of reporting distant human suffering. Castells adds factors associated with globalisation and identity as contributing to the choices constantly made by journalists on what to report and how to report it. Castells describes our world today as 'a network society' characterised, among other things, by a technological revolution, the transformation of capitalism, and the demise of statism, but he admits that the last 25 years have seen a surge of powerful expressions of collective identity that challenge globalisation and cosmopolitanism in favour of people's control of their own destiny. These expressions, which take diverse forms, include pro-active movements, such as feminism and environmentalism, which aim to change human relationships at their grassroots level. They, however, also include reactive movements, which choose to share a religious, family or ethnic identity. These particularist group identities are now often 'threatened under the combined, contradictory assault of techno-economic forces and transformative social movements' (Castells, 2006: 2). These paradoxical dichotomies of pro-active/reactive expressions raise the question of the nation-state based on the historical construction of a sovereign political democracy.

Castells sees the Seattle protests against globalisation in November 1999 as signalling 'the coming of age of a major social movement that opposes, on a global scale, the values and interests shaping the current globalisation process' (2006: 145). He describes the new social movement against globalisation as a deliberate attempt on the part of civil society to 'take over its institutions after the failure of traditional democratic controls under the conditions of globalisation of wealth, information and power' (2006: 147), and he notes that, instead of referring to the movement as the movement for global justice or the anti-capitalist globalisation movement, as preferred by social justice campaign organisations, the mainstream media refer to it as an 'anti-globalisation movement'. McNair (2006: 10) conceptualises this digital revolution as 'cultural chaos' for apparently 'challenging traditional boundaries between social classes, between white and black, homosexual and heterosexual, masculine and femine – boundaries which have directed the unequal allocation of economic and political resources for centuries'. McNair's vision of chaos emerges from what he considers as the 'unpredictability of events, multiplicity of news sources, and complexities of news processing' (Boyd-Barrett, 2009: 943). Yet Cottle (2008) problematises McNair's approach as reductionist, while welcoming its 'openness to complexity and contingency' (Boyd-Barrett, 2009: 943). However, Boyd-Barrett is also critical of Cottle's (2008, 2006) appeal to the 'public arenas' model based on the mediation of diversity and multiculturalism, since, as he puts it, this model underestimates how news content, especially international, originates from the same old gang of media conglomerates, with AP and Reuters as particular examples. Boyd-Barrett calls for greater attention to whether these cultural differences are impacting on the selection and framing of the news about the 'self' and the 'other' (Boyd-Barrett, 2009).

Although Castells (2006), McNair (2006) and Cottle (2008, 2006) talk a little about the contributing role of the alternative media and the inhibiting role of the mainstream media in the movement against global injustice, which is apparently caused by globalisation, there is little discussion (if any) on journalistic approaches to address the deficit. Moreover, while McNair (2006: 195) calls for media 'openness, honesty and transparency' and for 'proactive agenda setting' in the context of the 'persuasive strategy' to control the downside of the 'cultural chaos' (for instance, disinformation, hate speech and the like), he stops short of developing this into a conceptual counter-hegemonic journalism praxis. The filling of these gaps in the literature is the aim of this book, in particular of Chapters 4 and 8 and of all three case studies in Part III.

The aim of this book is to examine how the failure of the mainstream western media to practice human rights journalism has contributed to the general failure to achieve cosmopolitan-based human rights. While van den Anker (2005) points to the cosmopolitan concept of global justice as covering a wide range of issues, from global governance, conflict resolution and migration to poverty and global inequality, I would like to add to the list the concept of human rights journalism as an antithesis to human wrongs journalism. In fact I argue that the practice of human rights journalism is central to cosmopolitan-based human rights approaches to issues of global governance, conflict resolution, migration, poverty and global inequality. The relationship between cosmopolitanism and human rights journalism is conceptualised in detail in Chapter 8.

1.2 Direct physical and indirect structural/cultural violence: Towards a justpeace framework

In order to practise human rights journalism, journalists have to accept the responsibility to report all kinds of human rights violations, be these in the form of direct physical violence – such as genocide, arbitrary arrests and detentions, extra-judicial killings, rape, torture, ethnic cleansing and the mistreatment of prisoners – or in the indirect forms of cultural and structural violence – such as hate speech, racism, xenophobia, poverty, famine, corruption, colonialism, slavery, neo-colonialism, unfair trade, forced migration, forced labour, human trafficking, marginalisation or the exclusion of minorities. The central argument that cuts across this book is that, if the *indirect* forms of structural and cultural violence (discussed empirically in Part III) are managed pro-actively by human rights journalism, the *direct* forms of physical violence (discussed empirically in Part II) would be minimised or altogether prevented. This preventive or pro-active approach of human rights journalism resonates with what peace building scholar Lisa Schirch (2002) calls 'the justpeace framework'. The direct and indirect forms of violence draw on Lynch and McGoldrick's (2005) diagram of the typology of violence, which corresponds roughly to the three points of Galtung's ABC conflict triangle of attitude, behaviour and contradictions. Following in Figure 1.1 is Galtung's ABC conflict triangle:

> **Behaviour:** This is represented at the top of the triangle as direct/physical violence – hitting, beating, stabbing, shooting, bombing, raping, torture (VISIBLE VIOLENCE)
>
> **Attitude:** This is represented at the bottom left of the triangle as cultural violence – hate speech, persecution complex, myths and legends of war heroes, religious justifications for war, 'chosenness'/'being the chosen people', civilisational arrogance (INVISIBLE VIOLENCE – under the surface)
>
> **Contradictions:** This is represented at the bottom right of the triangle as structural violence – colonialism, apartheid, slavery, military occupation, corruption/collusion/nepotism, impunity, patriarchy, economic injustice (INVISIBLE VIOLENCE – under the surface)

For a more grounded conceptualisation of direct physical violence on the one hand and of indirect structural and cultural violence on the other hand, it is in order to explore the interesting overlaps of the political theories of journalism, human rights and peace. Each of these concepts reinforces the other. Communicating a message can serve both

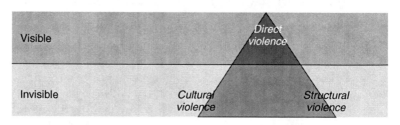

Figure 1.1   Galtung's ABC conflict triangle
Note: Galtung, J. (2004) 'Violence, War, and Their Impact: On Visible and Invisible Effects of Violence. Transcend: Peace and Development Network for Conflict Transformation by Peaceful Means.' Forum for Intercultural Philosophy 5 (2004). Online: http://them.polylog. org/5/fgj-en.htm.adapted from Lynch and McGoldrick (2005).
Source: Galtung's (2004).

as a means and as an end to the promotion and protection of human rights and peace. By taking part in an act of communication, one can contribute to the creation of peace, which can also be indispensable for human rights promotion and protection. Most cycles of violence (structural or physical), which have the knock-on effect of causing untold human rights violations, are caused by the simple lack of communication. The enjoyment of human rights, on the other hand, may lead to peace, while both human rights and peace combine to guarantee the freedom and security to communicate. There is therefore a clear nexus between peace and human rights, and between these two concepts and communication rights.

Schirch (2002: 210) asserts that it is possible for the words 'human rights' and 'peacebuilding' to be uttered 'in the same breath'. This view can hardly be contested, given the extent to which the concepts are interconnected. Schirch (2002: 16) traced the tensions between human rights and peace to a number of philosophical and practical differences. Schirch presents a chart (Table 1.1) that gives a snapshot of these tensions:

Table 1.1 Human rights, conflict resolution and justpeace building

	Human rights	Conflict resolution	Justpeacebuilding
Analysis of conflict	Conflict causes human rights abuses and human rights abuses cause conflict	Unmet human needs cause conflict	Unmet human needs cause conflict
Goals	Identify, stop and prevent human rights abuses	Help groups in conflict jointly identify and meet needs within a structured, problem-solving process	Focus on meeting the human needs and human rights of all groups through a variety of short-term, intermediate and long-term approaches
Stance or value framework	Advocates on behalf of victims and punishes human rights offenders; articulates and advocates a human rights value framework	Uses language of neutrality and impartiality to describe third-party intervener's commitment to not taking sides in a conflict	Uses a motto of "Impartial to People, Partial to Values"; defines values consistent with human rights documents

Table 1.1   (Continued)

	Human rights	Conflict resolution	Justpeacebuilding
Concept of justice	In most cases understands justice within the traditional legal/judicial framework where states or international bodies identify and punish offenders; focuses on the rule of law and equality before the law	Does not use the concept of justice in defining conflict resolution practice.	Understands justice within a restorative framework that centers on restoring victims and meeting their needs, holding people who have committed crimes accountable to victims needs, while also addressing offender needs
Coordination with other approaches	Little coordination with other approaches to conflict	Focus on bringing parties in conflict together to the negotiation or mediation "table"	Long-term framework that includes a variety of peace-building processes, including both human rights and conflict resolution approaches

Note: Table adapted with permission from Schirch (2002).

On the one hand, the work of human rights organisations is often interpreted as pleading against human rights violations and calling for the punishment of the violators. On the other hand, human rights workers aim to carry out their work according to standards of behaviour enshrined in the UDHR 'and use the legal system in the pursuit of a justice where offenders are punished for their crimes' (Schirch, 2002: 210). In human rights discourse, clear victims and offenders are identified, and that both victims and offenders cannot be equally held culpable of the acts of human rights violations.

On the contrary, conflict resolution approaches give equal attention to victims on all sides of a conflict, and all sides are mutually responsible for the task of addressing the problem. In other words, conflict resolution approaches to parties to a conflict care about the value of impartiality (neutrality), while approaches of human rights advocates care about partiality (bias). Hence conflict resolution practitioners prefer focusing on the process of bringing together people in conflict without the moral call of values or the announcements of victims' and perpetrators' judgements, fearing that these acts may discourage people from the parties in conflict from fully participating in the process. 'The goal of being a mediating "bridge" between groups in conflict, helping each to empathize with the other, to share perspectives on "truth", and work together to find ways of moving forward is often seen as incompatible with the goal of raising awareness and naming injustice' (Schirch, 2002: 210). The incompatibility between these two positions is so glaring that the human rights advocate might ask the peace worker: 'How can you work for peace without including a sense of justice for victims?' The peace worker might ask back: 'A peace without justice is better than no peace at all: How will we ever move forward if we insist on punishing offenders?' (Schirch, 2002: 210).

The concept of justpeace, which is a hybrid of human rights and peace, helps to provide answers to the questions posed in both fields. Justpeace goes beyond efforts to reduce direct violence. Justpeacebuilding efforts prioritise the proper transformation of principles and values over a long period of time through an organised system of distributive justice where resources and decision-making are shared. 'Moreover, the concept of justpeace builds on a restorative vision of justice, aimed at meeting basic human needs of both victims and offenders while holding the latter accountable for their crimes' (Schirch, 2002: 212). Justpeace is only possible where there are sustainable structures and processes that allow humanity to meet its basic human needs. Hence there are no contradictions between human rights peacebuilding goals within a justpeace framework. 'The field of human rights fits into a long-term plan for building justpeace by contributing analytical tools, value frameworks, and by playing a variety of roles in peacebuilding practice' (Schirch, 2002: 212).

Justpeace, unlike just war theory, prioritises conflict prevention or peacebuilding over and above conflict resolution, largely because of its sustainable approach of addressing the needs not only of the victims but also of the offenders of human rights abuses. In fact it is this focus on the basic human needs of all – victims as well as perpetrators of human rights violations – that makes the justpeace theory strongly resonate with Galtung's notion of a positive peace that deserves more attention than negative peace.

Peace as a concept is often interpreted differently, although the most common interpretation used in the human rights and international relations landscapes is that of 'negative peace', which means the absence of direct physical violence (such as is manifest in war). The negative peace theory is predicated on the simple belief that the presence of peace means the absence of violence (Barash and Webel, 2002). However, Galtung dismisses this interpretation of peace as too narrow and offers the argument that peace goes beyond just the absence of direct violence or war. He therefore develops the alternative conception of 'positive peace', which he describes as 'the best protection against violence' (Galtung, 1996: 32). Galtung distinguishes between direct physical violence, such as the violence manifest in wars and acts of genocide, and 'structural violence', for example the violence of exploitation, inequality, misery, poverty and forced migration. By developing the phrase 'structural violence', Galtung demonstrates that it is not only the harm inflicted by the pain of direct physical violence that needs to be deconstructed, but also, and perhaps more importantly, that inflicted by those indirect forms of political and economic exploitative, repressive structures. Galtung believes in sustainable positive peace, which can only be achieved by ensuring justice for all, since injustice leads to structural violence in the form of poverty, famine or forced migration, which may in turn lead to direct physical violence and human rights violations. Galtung argues that, to create a completely peaceful society, both these forms of violence must be eliminated (Galtung, 1996).

Galtung's holistic peace approach therefore favourably compares to the idea of a holistic human rights approach that sees all rights – be they negative civil and political rights (first-generation rights), positive economic, social and cultural rights (second-generation rights), both of which are enshrined in the 1966 twin covenants of the UN, or group rights (third-generation rights) like those adopted in the 1993 Vienna World Conference – as universal, indivisible, interdependent and interrelated. The twin International Covenants on Civil and Political Rights (ICCPR) and Economic, Social and Cultural Rights (ICESCR) of 1966, together with the Universal Declaration of Human Rights (UDHR) and the UN Charter of 1948, combined to form the foundation of the International Bill of Rights.

Civil rights include the right to life, personal liberty, security and integrity, privacy, fair trial and the right to marry. The first-generation rights covenant (ICCPR) also includes such political rights and freedoms as the right to vote and the right to participate in the conduct of public affairs and the right to freedom of expression, assembly and association. The second-generation rights covenant (ICESCR) includes economic rights such as the right to work; the right to just, safe and healthy working conditions; the right to form and join trade unions and the right to strike; social rights such as the right to health, social security and an adequate standard of living including food, clothing and housing; and cultural rights such as the right to education, to participation in cultural life and to self-determination. The twin covenants also include the right to equality and non-discrimination and the rights of special groups such as minority groups, children, women and aliens – although these rights, recognised as the third-generation rights, were not properly or strictly recognised by most nations of the world until the Vienna World Conference in 1993 (Nowak, 2005).

Human rights research scholars, however, disagree fundamentally on the negative and positive rights binary. While some see human rights as individual rights, otherwise called 'negative' civil and political rights, implying basic legal rights that all individuals must enjoy and that therefore deserve protection, some see them as group or collective rights, otherwise called 'positive' economic, social and cultural rights, implying moral rights that need to be provided to all. Another politically controversial area has been the question of who – the state or international community – is to be held responsible for the delivery of the negative and positive rights: while provisions are a bit clearer in the case of the former, they are not necessarily so in the case of the latter. Article 2 of the first-generation rights assigns every state the direct responsibility 'to respect and to ensure to all individuals within its territory and subject to its jurisdiction the rights recognised in this Covenant without any discrimination [...]'. Yet Article 2 of the second-generation rights holds the state responsible *only* 'to take steps, individually and through international assistance and cooperation, especially economical and technical, to the maximum of its available resources, with a view to achieving progressively the full realisation of the rights recognised therein' (Nowak, 2005: 194).

This rather problematic distinction largely called for by countries of the west recognises only civil and political rights as human rights in the real sense of 'legal and justifiably enforceable individual entitlements', while on the other hand economic, social and cultural rights were simply seen as 'programmatic rights without any immediately applicable, justifiable, and judicially enforceable corresponding state obligation' (Nowak, 2005: 194). However, the end of the Cold War rivalry between the west and the east apparently signalled the end of the division into negative and positive rights, which culminated in the 1993 Vienna World Conference on Human Rights Declaration. Nonetheless, despite progress made by this historic declaration in Vienna, the controversy, this time between two economic regional power blocs, north and south, over these two types of rights and over whether the state or the inter-national community should be held more responsible for their delivery, especially the positive kind, continues to this day. How, then, can we explain the role of mainstream journalism in perpetuating the contro-versy rather than helping to resolve it? Providing an answer to this question is one of the main preoccupations of this book.

The controversy over which form of peace – negative or positive – should be prioritised by scholars, journalists and state actors appears to be raging as well. While negative peace is conceptualised as an anti-dote of direct physical violence, positive peace is conceptualised as a way forward in tackling structural violence. The presence of direct phys-ical and indirect structural and cultural violence in society presupposes the existence of human rights violations. However, while social oppres-sion, which people experience as a problem of structural violence, may mobilise those who are normally non-violent to commit acts of vio-lence, such oppression 'is more difficult to notice than direct overt violence' (Larsen, 2009: 21).

Thus two fine parallels can be drawn here to support the human rights and peace nexus. First, there is the parallel between the more visible negative rights and the other, more visible negative peace (direct phys-ical violence), against which states and the international order are held responsible to protect all individuals. On the other hand, there is a par-allel between the otherwise less visible positive rights and yet another less visible positive peace (indirect structural violence), against which states and the international community are not necessarily legally held responsible to deliver. However, despite this distinction, along negative and positive lines, between peace and human rights, these two concepts reinforce each other in many ways. They are mutually dependent to such a degree that peace cannot be achieved if human rights are not protected and realised, while at the same time human rights cannot be protected if peace is absent. Achieving peace without human rights generally renders such peace as sterile (Ife, 2007).

Returning to the ABC conflict triangle of attitude, behavior and con-tradictions, Galtung provides a classic definition of the word 'violence' in peace research: it means anything that brings about a situation where 'human beings are being influenced so that their actual somatic and mental realisations are below their potential' (Galtung, 1969, cited in Lynch and McGoldrick, 2005: 59). Direct or visible violence is the name given to the more familiar form of violence. 'Violence is fomented by the imposition of singular and belligerent identities on gullible peo-ple, championed by proficient artisans of terror' (Sen, 2006: 2). *Direct* violence, physical and/or verbal, is visible as behaviour. However, as Galtung argues, human behaviour does not come out of the blue; there are roots. 'Two roots are indicated: (1) a culture of violence (heroic, patriotic, patriarchic, etc.), and (2) a structure that itself is violent by being too repressive, exploitative or alienating; too tight or too loose for the comfort of people' (Galtung, 2004: 1). Lynch and McGoldrick (2005: 59) describe structural violence:

> as a structure usually understood as a *system* of political, social or economic relations, creates barriers that people cannot remove – barriers to attaining food, shelter, education, jobs, security, or whatever. It may take visible forms such as 'whites-only' buses in Apartheid South Africa or in the US under Segregation, but it is usually thought of as an invisible form of violence, built into ways of doing and ways of thinking.

Lynch and McGoldrick (2005) identify two types of structural violence: first, vertical structural violence, which includes economic exploitation, political repression and cultural alienation; second, horizontal structural violence, which may keep together people who want to live separately or keep separately people who would like to live together (for example, Romeo and Juliet). Cultural violence essentially means cultural forms such as stereotypes and other loaded forms of communication, which 'justify or glorify violence' (Lynch and McGoldrick, 2005: 59); a person's potential risks being denied if that person is hit, shot or bombed. Lynch and McGoldrick (2005) argue that this painful effect of suffering can equally be felt by cultural and structural forms of violence – 'important component parts of the 'conflict picture' that can easily be blotted out by concentrating only on incidents of direct violence' (Lynch and McGoldrick, 2005: 59). Yet, as it turned out, the Lynch and McGoldrick empirical study was focused on 'how useful the concepts of structural and cultural violence of', for example, the Rwandan Genocide were 'in helping parties to a conflict think their way through to reconciliation'. The bottom line, according to the Lynch and McGoldrick (2005) argument, is that circumstances or situations, and not individuals, are to blame for conflict situations; this makes it justifiable, the argument goes, to tackle the circumstances or situations and not necessarily to attempt the demonisation of the parties to the conflict to resolve the conflict and promote reconciliation. It is thus evident that the focus here was on conflict resolution and reconciliation and not necessarily on conflict prevention, which is more important in the context of human rights journalism. Little wonder then that the Lynch and McGoldrick (2005) empirical analysis of the Rwandan Genocide focused more on the horizontal structural violence (the colonial legacy of 'divide and rule', as it relates to favouring the Tutsis against the Hutus) and largely ignored the vertical structural violence (economic exploitation, political repression and cultural alienation). Moreover, the empirical analysis of the cultural violence in the Lynch and McGoldrick study, for example the use of *bad language* or *hate speech*, tended to focus only on those of the local media, for example the newspaper *Kangura* and *Radio Télévision Libre Mille-Collines* (RTLMC) thus limiting this cultural violence to 'them' and ignoring completely the role of the mainstream media in the equation. This book seeks to address these gaps in the case study of the Rwandan Genocide in Chapter 7, where the focus is on both the vertical and horizontal forms of structural violence.

Furthermore, fundamentally lacking in the Lynch and McGoldrick (2005) study is a conceptualisation of journalism in the context of the links or overlaps between peace and human rights and, by extension, between positive peace and negative peace on the one hand, and between positive rights and negative rights on the other hand. This book seeks to fill these gaps by proposing human rights journalism as a complementary strand of peace journalism.

While I share the concerns of Lynch and McGoldrick over the somewhat problematic over-reporting of direct violence, as against cultural and structural forms of violence, I argue that it is when violence is allowed to canalise at will from the indirect cultural and structural forms of violence (positive peace) to the direct physical violence (negative peace) that it becomes more measurably biting and destructive, and that human rights journalism can be the effective alternative strand of journalism that can prevent this canalisation. This explains my reason for electing to look at some case studies of direct physical violence in Part II of this book and at other cases of indirect forms of structural and cultural violence in the final part – as a better way of gaining a proper understanding of the dichotomies of these two main forms of violence, and, above all, of learning to avert them at every stage.

In conclusion, I have demonstrated in this chapter how important human rights journalism is vis-à-vis the problematic mainstream journalism as well as vis-à-vis other alternative models of journalism. I have also explored direct physical violence and indirect structural and cultural violence within the context of Galtung's negative peace and positive peace respectively, to help readers to have a better understanding of the central concepts informing human rights journalism and human wrongs journalism. Human rights journalism is premised on the notion that the ideal cosmopolitan society is where peace and human rights co-exist; where the one cannot go without the other without creating an imbalance. This chapter has demonstrated how, on the one hand, human rights journalism resonates with Galtung's (1996) positive peace, which focuses on the pro-active tackling of indirect structural and cultural violence, and how, on the other hand, human wrongs journalism resonates very closely with negative peace, which focuses on the reactive tackling of direct physical violence.

I build on this argument by looking at the largely problematic media representation of direct political violence (human wrongs journalism), drawing on case studies from Sierra Leone, Kosovo, Somalia and Rwanda in Part II, and at the largely problematic media representation of indirect structural and cultural violence, drawing on case studies from the challenges of poverty alleviation in Africa and the myths and facts about asylum seekers and refugees in the UK in Part III. In Part I, I explore a much more detailed conceptual and theoretical framework of human rights journalism, as it relates to alternative models that also serve as counterweights to mainstream journalism.

Part I

Human Rights Journalism and Alternative Models: Critical Conceptual and Comparative Perspectives

Most scholarly work on the journalistic framing of distant humanitarian interventions has placed much emphasis on political factors, especially those relating to the question of national identity (Hallin, 1986; Carruthers, 1995, 2000; Shaw, 1996; Ginneken, 1998; Knightley, 1998; Hammond, 2000; Robinson, 2002b; Palmer 2003; Allan and Zelizer, 2004; Nossek et al., 2007), but less so on economic factors (Herman and Chomsky, 1988) or cultural (Carruthers, 1995, 2000). This book seeks to fill the gap through a conceptualisation of human rights journalism (HRJ) as the pragmatic way forward in overcoming the problem of political, economic and cultural framing of political violence and the human rights violations attendant upon it. Moreover, this brand of journalism can serve as the effective panacea to challenges of structural violence, which, if not prevented or tackled, have the potential to lead to direct physical violence.

Part I will discuss the theoretical and conceptual frameworks of human rights journalism in juxtaposition with mainstream and other alternative forms of journalism within the context of humanitarian intervention. The link between human rights journalism and humanitarian intervention is based on the premise that, if news consumers, including the political class, are provided with a better understanding of the structural reasons of various acts of violence by having the problem explained rather than sensationalised, they are more likely to empathise with the suffering people and hence to call for humanitarian intervention in order to end or prevent it. Sadly, however, this so far largely remains rhetoric, as the media and the political elite thrive by routinely invoking direct uncensored violence and not necessarily by promoting peace and human rights through pro-active illumination and by addressing indirect structural and cultural violence. This chapter deals, across four sections, with the following themes: a critical conceptual framework to human rights journalism; critical comparative analyses of human rights journalism and peace journalism, global journalism and human rights reporting; citizen, public and peace journalisms: towards the more radical human rights journalism strand; and the dynamics and challenges of reporting humanitarian intervention.

2
Human Rights Journalism:
A Critical Conceptual Framework

Human rights journalism is often associated with the reporting of human rights abuses, especially against the victims of political violence, and sometimes with freedom of expression, also a fundamental human right, which is enjoyed, denied or abused by journalists. While these two conceptualisations of human rights journalism are equally important, it is the third one, journalism for all human beings, regardless of race, nationality, race, gender or geographical location, that is the most important – and hence the focus of this book. Nevertheless, the first two conceptualisations of human rights journalism – free speech and reporting human rights conditions (good or bad) – are also very important as they are indispensable to the realisation of the third conceptualisation of achieving journalism for all. Moreover, the first two conceptualisations demonstrate the extent to which journalism or mass media are connected to human rights. The mass media–human rights nexus involves two different yet overlapping elements: first, the existence of independent and free media to communicate information to citizens, make them aware of certain human rights and claim them; and, second, the extent to which media organisations report on human rights situations such as cases of violation or protection. A country is generally said to respect and protect its people's human rights if it allows the two elements of the mass media and human rights nexus: free press and the unhindered reporting of human rights conditions (Caliendo, 2009).

Since the introduction of international human rights law, governments have signed many international treaties and conventions, with strong commitments to uphold the rights of their citizens and to protect them and others against genocide, torture and other crimes against humanity. Nevertheless, these commitments are yet to move beyond rhetoric, as nation-states have at the same time been busy jealously guarding their own sovereignty, cracking down on the slightest threat to national security or public order, and at best ignoring, or sometimes even sponsoring, genocide and other acts of violence – and above all violations of economic, social and cultural rights. As Pulitzer Prize-winning *Washington Post* foreign correspondent Glenn Frankel put it, 'the distance between what governments have pledged on human rights and what they actually do is a gasping chasm. It's here – in the gray zone between ambiguity and hypocrisy – that journalism lives' (Frankel, 2007). The challenge is how twenty-first century journalism can narrow the divide between the many pledges of human rights principles often made by world leaders and what happens on the ground. Human rights journalism, I argue, has the potential to address this gap.

This chapter is structured into three sections: exposing human rights abuses; free speech and human rights; and human rights journalism.

2.1   Exposing human rights abuses

Since journalists are often the first to bear witness to, and to report, serious human rights abuses, it is frequently their work that mobilises state actors to investigate. In the recent past, prosecutors have referred to media reports as evidence of their efforts to try war crimes suspects from Rwanda and the former Yugoslavia, and most recently from Sierra Leone and Liberia. Moreover, as Peter Spielmann, founder of the Human Rights Reporting Seminar at Columbia University's Journalism School, affirmed, the military assault by General Suharto of Indonesia on East Timor (in the late 1990s) benefited from fairly prompt and dramatic media coverage and the Australian government was impelled by the publicity to send a peacekeeping force that helped to disband the militia and to encourage the Timorese government to pursue a truth and reconciliation process.[1] 'Human rights give reporters a litmus test, a framework to work with', Spielman said. 'It gives you a broad perspective. When you get into these confusing individual situations, you have some principles to fall back on – some commandments as it were' (2008: 1). However, as Frankel (2007: 1) argues, human rights abuses are not confined to despots of the developing world:

> Western democracies, faced with perceived threats to their survival, have long been willing to abrogate rights. There is no more compelling contemporary example than the Bush administration's policies and practices in its declared Global War on Terrorism since the

9/11 attacks. In the name of security, the administration has sanctioned torture, extralegal kidnapping, secret prisons and collective punishment of non-combatants.

With the exposure of these violations in the media, though muted, official reaction was typical: denial, outrage, commissions of enquiry, selective prosecutions and, above all, promises to do better. This raises the question of the role of the media in the equation: to what extent did the mainstream western media contribute towards setting the agenda for the flawed war policy of President Bush? Exploring the role of journalists in exposing human rights abuses, Frankel points to 'how far reporters have come from the exquisite insensitivity of the BBC TV correspondent who once strode into a crowd of women and children in the former Belgian Congo and enquired: "Anyone here been raped and speaks English?" ' (Ibid.). (This famous quote of a query attributed to this BBC correspondent reportedly looking for sources during the crisis in Congo forms the title of the autobiography of distinguished foreign/war correspondent Edward Behr.[2])

Frankel, however, admits that 'they (reporters) are flawed watchdogs – unburdened by history or long attention spans, capable of wilful ignorance and self-aggrandizement' (Ibid.). Still, journalists, be they editors or correspondents, have a moral obligation to serve as honest and critical witnesses to the atrocities of war and other acts of genocide. Frankel acknowledges that this is more apparent than real in the reporting of most, if not all, of the world's hotspots such as El Salvador, South Africa, Zimbabwe, Rwanda, Bosnia, Sudan, Israel, Palestine, East Timor – to name a few. At the present time, nowhere is this more evident than in Iraq, Afghanistan and Somalia.

As David Dadge argues, while the US media performed excellently at giving a chronological narrative of the events of the 2003 US-led invasion of Iraq, they failed to investigate fully the justifications of war advanced by Bush, and in this way they also failed to live up to the expectations of the framers of the First Amendment, which is to hold the administration to account by asking difficult questions regarding these justifications in the countdown to the war itself (Dadge, 2006: 144).Yet, considering the thousands of human rights violations in Iraq since the invasion of 2003, it is clear that the media failed woefully in practising human rights journalism. This raised questions such as what really constitutes 'good' reporting of human rights issues. How should journalists and editors themselves judge the quality of their reporting in this area? What pressures and constraints do they face and how might they be managed better? In order to answer these questions, the International Council on Human Rights Policy (ICHRP) conducted a two-year study in 2002 involving interviews with over 70 journalists from several countries. The 154-page report of the research argues that, 'as human rights are integrated increasingly in policy frameworks, journalists have a professional duty to report on this subject with accuracy, fairness, consistency, and precise knowledge of human rights' (ICHRP Report, 2002).

The *Philippine Human Rights Reporting Project – Human Rights and Journalism* (2008) notes that, although reporting on human rights requires the same adherence to high standards as reporting on any subject, the great sensitivity of the risks involved in the reporting of political violence makes it necessary for journalists to be more 'careful and sensitive about the possible dangers and pitfalls' (www.rightsreporting.net). Any side may end up committing human rights violations in most conflict situations, and journalists often risk reporting more on abuses committed by one side, maybe because that side is perceived as the 'aggressor', or because there is more information about the alleged crimes against humanity committed by this perceived 'aggressor' side, or maybe simply because they belong to the 'other' side of those who have nothing to do with their (these journalists') national interests. Within the context of HRJ, the *Philippine Human Rights Reporting Project* (2008: 2) cautions that, 'although journalists must take care to distinguish between a policy of human rights violations and an isolated act of human rights abuse, they must be prepared to report any human rights violations by any group'. On a higher moral tone, the project adds: 'The underlying principle of human rights is universality: everyone is entitled to protection of life and freedom from abuse, regardless of ethnic origin, religion or gender' (ibid.: 2; see Chapter 3, Section 3.3 for the history of human rights reporting and how it is related to human rights journalism).

2.2   Free speech and human rights

The human rights-based approach to journalism, or human rights journalism, is a *sine qua non* for the realisation of human rights and democracy. It is often said that the media and human rights are mutually supportive, as one can hardly be realised without the other. Thus, while media serves as an important check on power and as an indispensable bulwark of human rights protection, it also relies on the protection provided by human rights in order to play that role effectively. Free speech is essential if other human rights are to be realised. State actors can only be held to account for their actions in realising the human rights of their people if there is freedom of expression.

Freedom of speech and expression does not belong to government but it is a fundamental human right, which owes its origin to life itself, as given by God – just as Jefferson declared: 'the God that gave us Life gave us Liberty at the same time' (Verghese, 1998: 31). Free speech has always been there since the existence of man, in fact long before it was enshrined among other rights in the Human Rights Charter of 1948, released after the end of the Second World War. 'It is the vital basis of society as it is the means by which the citizen holds all in authority accountable' (Verghese, 1998: 31). The first formal request for freedom of speech in recorded history was made by Sir Thomas More in front of the English Parliament and of King Henry VIII on 18 April 1523. However, one of the earliest and most striking defences of freedom of expression came in 1644, when John Milton published his *Areopagetica*, in defiance of a parliamentary attempt to block the publication of what was deemed as 'seditious, unreliable, unreasonable and unlicensed pamphlets' in England. Milton claimed that the facts must be considered from all sides for truth to be established; that censorship is inimical to progress; and that truth will defeat falsehood in open competition, with no single individual left to determine it. Freedom of speech, which is fundamental to the freedom of the press, has its roots in John Stuart Mill's *On Liberty*, in which freedom of speech is declared to be the basis for discovery of the truth (Mill, 1859). 'The protection of freedom of expression is a key element fo all modern human rights instruments' (Puddephatt, 2005: 27). Article 19 of the Universal Declaration of Human Rights (UDHR) affirms:

> Everyone has the right to freedom of opinion and expression; this right includes the right to hold opinions without interference and to seek, receive and impart information and ideas through any media and regardless of frontiers. (Article 19, 2002 cited in Puddephatt, 2005: 27)

Freedom of the press is often seen as the fundamental component holding in balance a delicate system of relations among the media, civil society and the state. Himelboim and Limor note that 'the media are obliged to provide citizens with the information necessary for informed social decisions, to serve as a conduit for all shades of public opinion' (2008: 235). It should be noted that free speech should be enjoyed not only by journalists or the elite political or corporate classes but by everybody (citizens and non-citizens), including vulnerable and marginalised people. Journalists are, however, the professionals entrusted with challenging the manipulations and falsehoods of the ruling and corporate classes: this is in addition to their information dissemination and education roles.

In theory, not only should all parties to a conflict allow journalists to work freely in conflict zones; all the political parties (ruling or in opposition) should also create the environment for journalists to carry out their work in the promotion and protection of human rights. Nonetheless, as Iraq, Yugoslavia, Palestine and other transition countries such as Sri Lanka, Sierra Leone, Liberia, Somalia, Ethiopia, Eritrea, Rwanda and Zimbabwe have shown, this is often not so in practice. Leading press freedom campaign organisations such as the Committee to Protect Journalists (CPJ), Freedom House (FH), and Reporters without Borders (RWB), the International Press Institute (IPI) and Article 19 have painted a very bleak picture of an ever-increasing spate of press freedom violations, especially in the form of the targeting and killing of journalists. Iraq alone accounted for the lives of more than 125 journalists and 50 media industry workers by 2008. 'This is by far the highest number for any conflict in the last quarter century. Staggeringly, it's believed to be higher than the combined media mortality rate for the Second World War and the Vietnam War combined' (Allen, 2008: 1). Journalists' death toll continues to rise; between 4 June 2008 and 23 October 2010, the International News Safety Institute has recorded 32 more deaths of journalists and other media staff, most of them in Iraq. What is even worse is that journalists are targeted not only in wartime but also in peace time, as we have seen in the case of Russia, where at least 21 journalists have been killed since 2006 – including, most infamously, Anna Politkovskaya. The case of this murdered Russian journalist is one among many others that show that journalists are also constantly targeted when investigating corruption or powerful vested interests, drug dealing or organised crime such as human trafficking. Politkovskaya had worked for the biweekly *Novaya Gazeta* since 1999. The circumstances surrounding her killing are shrouded in mystery. She was supposed to hand in an article, with photos, about torture in Chechnya, allegedly carried out by Russian troops, but unfortunately the article never reached the paper, as she was found murdered before she handed it in (www.rsf.org).

In recent years, free speech has come under fire not only in emerging democracies in Eastern Europe, South East Asia and Africa but also in western democracies in Europe and North America, especially the

US. Since 9/11 and the period leading to the US invasion of Iraq in 2003, dissent in the name of free speech was increasingly sacrificed on the altar of patriotism. During this period, journalists Dan Guthrie and Tom Gutting lost their jobs for writing critical articles about President Bush. Having succeeded in weakening dissent, the Bush government set about making the working environment more difficult for journalists. For example, Attorney General John Ashcroft supported the decision to instruct government departments to refuse to supply information to the media (Dadge, 2006). Furthermore, Defence Secretary Donald Rumsfeld was on record as having warned journalists that any criticism of their administration would be taken to mean aiding the 'terrorists'. It was therefore not surprising that, during the war in Iraq, in the spring of 2003 alone, 16 journalists, including translators and support staff, 'provided both the ink and their blood'. This was blamed on the so-called 'friendly fire' from US coalition troops between 22nd March and 9th May (INSI, 2003).[3]

Moreover, added to the list of casualties in the media was truth; truth, like free speech, and by extension human rights, gave way to patriotism following 9/11. A new alliance of willing fighters against terrorism rallied behind the US. Countries such as Uzbekistan and Turkmenistan, which hitherto were seen by the west as rogue states on account of the mass violation of their peoples' rights, including free speech, were suddenly welcomed into this new alliance, while Russia turned a blind eye to similar violations in its satellite state of Chechnya, and by Ethiopia in Somalia. Post 9/11 therefore quickly rendered rather hollow the prospects of building a world based on human rights. As Dadge puts it, 'rather than being upheld, human rights all across the world were being diluted, or in extreme cases, ignored altogether' (Dadge, 2004: 217). It was clear by this time that human rights had given way to politics proper. Information is power, and so states try to control it to make sure that they are in charge. Media and political science scholars have traditionally pointed to freedom of the press in any given society as a function of the relevant country's political ecology (Himelboim and Limor, 2008). Central to freedom of the press are free speech and freedom of information. Freedom of speech is 'grounded in a basic humanistic world view regarding human relations with society and the state'; a fundamental right largely taken for granted in the west (ibid.: 237). Thus, with their enjoyment of freedom of speech and freedom of information, journalists have a social responsibility to criticise those in power 'on behalf of citizens and society, effectively serving as their surrogates' (Hohenberg, 1978, cited in Himelboim and Limor, 2008: 237).

This thinking is largely informed by the social responsibility model (Siebert et al., 1963, 1956), which calls on journalists to serve as watchdogs of society on the basis of democratic principles such as their being transmitters of honest and fair information and opinions to help people hold their leaders to account for their policies and activities (Siebert et al., 1963/1956; Cater, 1957; Hohenberg, 1978; Cohen-Almaghor, 2001). However, the social responsibility model suffered a major setback with the introduction of the development media model, which became the buzz word in promoting good governance in the 1970s and 1980s. This model was forged out of a compromise between 'nation building', a 'free and unfettered press, especially during the immediate post colonial era in Africa and Asia' (Shaw, 2009: 500; see also Everett, 1962; Schramm and Lerner, 1976; McQuail, 1994; Bourghault, 1995). No wonder that the media and nation-state structures have been uneasy bed-fellows in both emerging and well-established democracies. However, scholars of the political economy model have shifted the focus of the criticism of press freedom regulation and censorship towards economic and financial conglomerates or corporate media organisations, seeing them more or less as behind-the-scenes manipulators, and in some cases predators, of press freedom (McChesney, 2004; cited in Himelboim and Limor, 2008). Scholars who have supported the political economy model over the more traditional social responsibility and development media models include Underwood (1993), McManus (1995), Limor and Nossek (2002) and Bagdikian (2004).

Yet there are many instruments in the Human Rights Charter that problematise the right to freedom of expression and they do so to the extent that some scholars such as Alexander (2005) have pondered whether there is any such thing as 'a right of freedom of expression'. Alexander's pessimism is rooted in the many limitations or trade-offs of free speech, as recognised, for example, in the First Amendment; such limits include the use of words or language that represent clear and present danger; hate speech or fighting words capable of inciting to violence; and expression that constitutes libel, slander, obscenity or anything that undermines public order. In fact Stanley Fish was even more categorical when he said: 'there is no such thing as freedom of expression and it is a good thing too' (1994: 102). Being able to speak without official or divine sanction and at the same time to ensure that this freedom does not impinge on, or affect, the delivery of the other rights and freedoms to others has been a subject of heated political debate in the last three to four hundred years. If a government insists on permitting only the expressions it believes to promote those values that it itself endorses, that government would not be seen as respecting the freedom of expression (Alexander, 2005). It has been an uphill task for states and civil societies to strike a balance between the right to freedom of expression and other rights such as equality, human dignity, privacy, security, national identity and so on. This raises another question: whether the right to freedom of expression can be traded off for these other rights. There is something of a dilemma here, because, while the UN system recognises free speech as necessary for protecting people from the whims and caprices of the state, at the same it agrees that free speech can cause some measure of harm to the public if it is abused.

Article 17 of the UDHR states: 'No one shall be subjected [...] to unlawful attacks on his honour and reputation [...]', while Article 20 states: 'Any advocacy of national, racial, or religious hatred that constitutes incitement to discrimination, hostility or violence shall be prohibited by law.' This article also requires that restrictions of freedom of expression are 'provided by law and are necessary for example for the protection of the reputation of others, privacy, national security, public order, public health or morals' (UDHR, 1948). Other instruments introduced include the McBride Commission, set up by UNESCO in 1977, which called for 'many voices, one world' in the context of the 'New International Communication Order' and of the 1978 UNESCO Declaration 'on Fundamental Principles concerning the Contribution of the Mass Media to Strengthening Peace and International Understanding, to the Promotion of Human Rights and to Countering Racialism, Apartheid and Incitement to War'.[4]

Some of these recent instruments have come to be used, and sometimes abused, by states in regulating or censoring the media. Political and moral inclinations for censorship are often informed by the thought that some ideas are so dangerous, subversive or incendiary that they must not see the light of day. Censorship is hence necessary because 'bad' words are embarrassing and rude; 'bad' words must be attended to or addressed in order for their spread to be avoided (the 'broken windows theory'); 'bad' words can quickly translate into action (Levinson, 2003). Yet, as Levinson argues, constraining or censoring freedom of expression is 'bad' because being able to speak our minds freely makes us feel good; much censorship looks irrational and alarmist; censorship is inimical to democracy; censorship backfires as opinions, tastes, social values and so forth change over time; and, finally, censorship does not work – it does not eradicate 'bad' ideas or 'bad' behaviour: history has shown that banning the 'unacceptable' only pushes it underground (Levinson, 2003). Striking a balance between enjoying and using freedom of expression for one's own good or moral well-being and making sure that other rights of other people are not undermined is therefore the greatest challenge facing free speech and, by extension, human rights. This is what Alexander calls 'evaluative neutrality', which he sees as the hallmark of freedom of expression – but he warns that 'no moral theory can support evaluative neutrality without generating a paradox' (Alexander, 2005: 185). Alexander argues that the great liberal freedoms – of religion, of association, of expression – are all deeply paradoxical, because they rest on the notion of 'epistemic abstinence' – the idea that a liberal government cannot impose its views of 'the Good' on dissenters; that, qua liberal, a government cannot know 'the Good'. Alexander sees the argument that liberalism cannot take sides as 'mission impossible'. He affirms that liberal government cannot help but be partisan, which means that liberalism construed as a governmental non-partisanship (or as a state of neutrality) towards religions, associations and expressions is an impossibility (Alexander, 2005: 185). He observes that any moral theory will take the view that certain interests should be seeking legal protection from acts that threaten them in the first place. He also argues that both the medium of expression and the messages conveyed may cause undesirable states of affairs and threaten interests worthy of being protected (according to moral theory); and, conversely, suppression of expression by virtue of reference to its content ('track one') or to its medium ('track two') may cause desirable states of affairs and safeguard interests worthy of being protected (according to moral theory) (Tribe, 1988). Therefore the government cannot permit the harmful expression without generating a paradox. It must instead demand suppression of the harmful expression and permit only expressions that are consistent with the goals of the theory. Yet this evaluative non-neutrality is the antithesis of freedom of expression. Laurence Tribe's track two branch of American First Amendment free speech cases covers regulations of expressive conduct enacted for reasons other than to affect what messages are conveyed and received. In other words, track two regulations are concerned exclusively with the non-communicative impact of the conduct being regulated. Track one regulations, on the other hand, are those enacted precisely in order to affect what messages are communicated (Laurence Tribe, 1988, cited in Alexander, 2005).

Little wonder, Alexander notes, that the theory of freedom of expression is premised on the idea that 'government cannot be trusted to regulate expression because', as he puts it, 'it is unduly error-prone in assessing [an] expression's harms and benefits, or because it has motives for regulating – notably, self-protection – that render it untrustworthy

in doing so' (Alexander, 2005). If freedom of expression is only important because of its consequences, those consequences that are valued
and disvalued will necessarily reflect partisan positions, not evaluative
neutrality. Any normative theory, liberal or not, will inevitably take
positions on what ought to be done. Thus the question of a middle ground is rather too problematic to be managed here. Exhaustive
though Alexander's analysis of the dilemma or limitations associated
with the principle of freedom of expression as a human right may
sound, his approach seems focused on the more traditional social
responsibility model (Siebert et al., 1963, 1956) and on the development media model (McQuail, 1994), where most of the blame for
these limitations is put at the doorstep of the political class. More
recent research has revealed the contrary about the political economy
model (Underwood, 1993; McManus, 1995; Limor and Nossek, 2002;
Bagdikian, 2004; Himelboim and Limor, 2008). Freedom of the press,
Himelboim and Limor argue, is susceptible not only to government-
imposed limitations (primarily in emerging or developing states) but
also to limitations imposed by media owners, because of economic constraints. In the western world, corporate media, and not governments,
are the real threat to press freedom (Himelboim band Limor, 2008:
239).

Therefore, since it is clear that neither the state nor the corporate
media can regulate free speech by way of protecting and safeguard-
ing other rights without being seen to be partisan or manipulative, the
onus of undergoing self-regulation and practising human rights journalism rests squarely with the journalists. As a result, while there is urgent
need to deregulate the media and to remove all state and market restrictions that unnecessarily hinder freedom of expression, there is equally
a need for journalists to take charge of their profession by practising
a journalism that is more accountable to the people for whom they
seek to make the world a better place. Practising human rights journalism, which is people-oriented rather than elite-oriented, is the way
forward in the promotion of free speech and human rights, because this
form of journalism ensures the following human rights-based scenarios: it offers more 'good' communication to offset 'bad' information;
it uses human rights-based limitations instead of political or market
manipulations; it tolerates dissenting views and marginalised voices, in
a truly democratic spirit of human rights; it encourages civil society to
offer human rights-based solutions and to demand action for problems
exposed by the media; it encourages global society to use the stick-
and-carrot approach in dealing with countries that persistently refuse
to respect free speech; and it encourages partnership between the state

and the media in the promotion of nation-building, good governance, development and global security in the cosmopolitan context of global justice.

2.3 Human rights journalism

In the first two sections of this chapter, I have tried to illuminate the two more traditional conceptualisations of what is today known as human rights journalism. This third conceptualisation calls for moving the parameters of human rights-based journalism beyond the role of journalism in exposing human rights abuse, which has resulted from more conventional political (physical) violent conflicts or from the discourse of free speech as a human right. It calls for the rarely explored third level, that of the more pro-active role of journalism as an agency that knows no borders, no race, no age, no gender and no class – a journalism with a human face and for the human race. This conceptualisation of journalism draws its inspiration from Article 1 of the UN Universal Declaration of Human Rights (1948): 'All human beings are born free and equal in dignity and rights.'[5] This declaration holds that every individual, as a human being, is entitled to enjoy certain rights regardless of his or her ethnicity, sex, colour, race, language, age, religion, political or other beliefs, national or social origin, property, economic status, disability, birth or other factors. These individual rights are considered inalienable; they cannot be taken away or violated. For journalism to be taken seriously, it must be seen to be helping, and not undermining or threatening, the enjoyment of these inalienable human rights by all human beings. This means that journalists should be able to select narratives and words that would impact positively, rather than negatively, on the people targeted as well as on those alluded to. *The Human Rights-Based Approach to Journalism Viet Nam Training Manual* affirms:

> Our views of history can be strongly influenced by journalists. Journalists carry the ability to inform the public, to connect remote worlds, and to shape an individual's knowledge and understanding of the world (we) live in. They have the opportunity to increase public awareness, to educate the public on their rights, and, above all, to help in monitoring human rights. (Beman and Calderbank, 2008: 7)

The key issue here is not necessarily whether journalists can inform the public and shape peoples' knowledge and understanding of what goes on around them. Rather the issue is whether journalists are really measuring up to these expectations. The truth is, as Parts II and III of this book demonstrate, most of what passes today as news and comments in the mainstream news media, especially in the west, is nothing but distorted versions of what is actually happening. This has the negative effect of misleading, rather than educating, audiences, and hence of making it difficult for them to understand the undercurrents of societal problems. If the people are not properly informed and educated about what goes on around them, this may impact negatively on the type of response they may formulate or support in tackling or coping with the issues raised. Since some of these issues may easily canalise, possibly first into structural, and later into direct or physical violence, 'journalists need to be able to draw upon a deep understanding of how conflicts develop and how people can respond to them in ways likely to reduce the risk of violence' (Lynch and McGoldrick, 2005: 91). This is more or less what Lynch refers to as a 'framework of understanding' (Lynch, 1998). However, as mentioned before, this is a largely normative theory, which mainstream journalists are yet to put to a proper test. Therefore, rather than contributing to the promotion and protection of human rights within the cosmopolitan context of global justice, mainstream journalism is promoting distortion, disinformation and, by extension, misunderstanding of the issues at stake. All this has the knock-on effect of encouraging negative manipulations and violent responses to tackling these issues, which in turn lead to more human rights violations. Truth, then, ultimately becomes the number one casualty, while the majority of vulnerable voices are caught up in the manipulation of the mainstream media and politicians.

'What you say is very interesting, but what is more interesting is what you do not say' (Lynch, 2008: XI). This is how Johan Galtung, eminent peace scholar, homed in on British Sky Broadcasting Head of News Nick Pollard at a Peace Journalism summer school at Taplow Court in the south of England in 2002. Galtung was, as a matter of fact, essentially dismissing Pollard's presentation in defence of mainstream reporting as nothing but 'war journalism' – just reporting the facts of the news, with little or no attempt to deconstruct them-style of journalism. Galtung proposed and coined 'peace journalism' as an alternative – a journalism that is not only about reporting the facts – say, political, economic, social or cultural acts of violence – but also, and arguably more importantly, asking questions about the reasons for these acts and how they can be prevented or managed with the minimum of suffering from the people (Lynch, 2008). This is what I have conceptualised as human rights journalism – a journalism with a human face, a journalism that cares for the people, one that prioritises them over capitalism and, above all, over the whims and caprices of political demagogues.

This raises the question of why journalists should contribute to human rights discourse. Journalists can use their much privileged access to news media sources and their professional ability to communicate, not only to report events as they happen, but also to deconstruct the news and add more in-depth analysis; this will then promote a better understanding of the undercurrents of the events and issues at stake and then encourage a human rights-based response to tackling or coping with them. 'Through analysis and the bringing together of multiple perspectives, journalists create the potential for a more knowledgeable, well-rounded and aware public. This increased awareness can lead to a stronger civil society and a more active population' (Beman and Calderbank, 2008: 7).

Many newspapers all over the world have the motto 'Eternal vigilance is the price of liberty' decorating their mastheads. Veteran media theorist Marshall McLuhan was smart enough to convert this adage in his celebrated work on the coming of age of mass media production and consumption by warning that 'the price of eternal vigilance is indifference' (McLuhan, 1965). McLuhan refers to this 'indifference' as 'compassion fatigue'. Human rights journalism – journalism with a human touch – can therefore serve as an effective panacea for the 'compassion fatigue' that makes consumers of mainstream news less concerned about the suffering of 'others' (McLuhan, 1965). This measured indifference to the plight of 'others' has in fact been identified as a negative consequence of reporting on humanitarian crises and human rights abuses. This brings to mind the rather lukewarm reaction of western audiences to the human suffering that resulted from the devastating floods in Pakistan in the summer of 2010. The western media's framing of the war on terror in Afghanistan has, for instance, largely portrayed Pakistan as a country harbouring Al-Qaeda terrorists and the Taliban. It could be argued that the rather tepid reaction of western audiences to the Pakistani floods to some extent resulted from this rather problematic media framing. It is, however, important to note that it is the dominant war journalism, based on the evocative style of reporting acts of violence, instead of the much preferred peace journalism or journalism with a human face, based on the diagnostic style of reporting, that drives the 'compassion fatigue' in the first place. If news consumers, including the political class, are provided with a better understanding of the structural reasons for the acts of violence, which the latter style is meant to supply, they are more likely to empathise with the suffering people and hence to call for intervention to end the violence and suffering. Yet, 'whereas in Kosovo the role of the critical and empathy framed media coverage in influencing military intervention by NATO on humanitarian grounds was very evident', Shaw argues, 'the mainstream media failed to perform a similar cosmopolitan role to save hundreds of thousands of lives in Ethiopia, Somalia and Rwanda'(Shaw, 2007: 366).

Critics of this conceptualisation of human rights journalism often point to its undermining of some of the important standards of professional journalism – especially objectivity, which emphasises neutrality and the simple separation of facts from opinion, as discussed in detail in Chapter 1. Yet human rights journalism can, but does not necessarily have to, be objective, since, as Lovasen argues,

> it has clear values of humanitarianism, truth, holism, and empowerment. It has its orientation on peace rather than war, on truth rather than propaganda, on people rather than elite, on solution and transformation rather than victory [...] is also proactive and asks questions of why violent acts are committed-before they are. And a core value is having a voice for all parties. (Lovasen, 2008)

Good media representation based on human rights can strengthen democracy and good governance, while bad media representation based on selective justice can undermine them. Thus the media representation of conflict and violence can affect international and/or local response to tackle or to cope with it. However, what permeates the news media discourse today is what I conceptualised in Chapter 1 as human wrongs journalism, which largely favours and reinforces the agenda of the ruling class as well as the corporate conglomerates. The problematic media representation of conflict and violence is two-fold: it consists, first, of the misreporting of conflict and, second, of the under-reporting or non-reporting of conflict. As Lovasen ponders: 'How the media presents [sic] conflict is one problem. The next is when conflicts are not presented at all [...] Why are some highlighted while others are not? What kind of criteria causes [sic] one news item to supersede another?' (Lovasen, 2008: 2). These questions are central to the challenges facing human rights journalism.

Going by professional journalism standards, it is inevitable that the work of the journalist is ruled by constantly making choices about what and how to report, what not to report, what to put in prime time or on the front page and what to put in other, less visible programmes or columns. The bottom line is, however, this: if a piece of journalism is to be considered human rights journalism, it must be informed by the values of human rights within the cosmopolitan context of global justice, and not by the manipulation of political or economic interests. Yet, as McChesney puts it, 'contemporary journalism serves as a tepid and weak-kneed watchdog over those in power, especially in the corporate sector. And it scarcely provides any reliable information or range of debate on many of the basic political and social issues of the day' (McChesney, 2002). Human rights journalism is therefore seen as the only way forward to rescue journalism from losing its real sense of purpose. In line with the human rights journalism ethos, Mustapha Masmoudi (1992: 43) argues as follows:

> The journalist's mission is to inform without reservation, without preconception and without harmful intention; ignorance generally being harmful, journalists should not resort to self-censorship except for a major cause and in extremely serious cases. They should especially seek to avoid the abuses of commercial exploitation.

Yet the status quo is arguably bad news; hence the urgent need for a change of direction. There has recently been a series of projects dedicated to doing just that. One such project is the Insyde's Media and Violence Project, set up in Mexico to discuss how the media portray events related to public security, penal justice, violence and other issues intertwined with the notion of human rights. This project describes good journalism – and, by extension, human rights journalism – as professional journalism that champions respect for human rights; it is rooted in the culture of justice and peace that will only see the light of day when 'the industrial routine of the news industry is revamped and the journalists [who] produce them [justice and peace] are fully qualified as professionals' (Klahr, 2008: 1). Another important project, Journalists for Human Rights (JHR) (www.jhr.ca/en/int_impact.php), was created in 2002 in Canada by Ben Peterson, recipient of Canada's Top 40 under 40 awards. JHR takes pride in empowering media, especially in post-conflict countries, to pressure state agencies to respect human rights and promote good governance. The Crimes of War Project (www.crimesofwar.org) offers more detailed explanations and case studies of reporting on humanitarian issues, particularly in conflict situations.

Central to the case for human rights journalism is its emphasis of the human angle of news media narratives. ' "Journalism with a human touch" means more than writing about people behind the story and the story behind the people. The human touch signifies compassion, a deep

sense of fairness, a concern for human dignity, a crusading tempera-
ment', says Mr Phillip Mathew, managing editor of the Indian magazine
The Week, while marking his publication's silver jubilee (Mathew, 2008).

Nonetheless, for human rights journalism to be taken seriously, it
must empathise with people not only when they are confronted with
the direct physical violation of their rights, such as in genocide, arbitrary
arrests and detentions, extra-judicial killings, rape, ethnic cleansing,
and mistreatment of prisoners, but also, and perhaps more importantly,
when they are confronted with indirect structural violations of their economic, social and cultural rights, including absolute poverty, famine,
forced migration, forced labour, human trafficking, marginalisation or
the exclusion of minorities. Thus, for journalism to be human rights-
based, it must be based on the holistic human rights approach informed
by first-generation rights (civil and political) and by second-generation
rights (economic, social, and cultural), both inspired by the Twin 1966
Covenants of the United Nations Charter. In fact, because human rights
journalism calls for a more robust pro-active (preventive) rather than
dramatic reactive (prescriptive) role of the media in humanitarian intervention, it is particularly concerned with getting the much neglected
second-generation rights (that is, positive economic, social and cultural
rights) in order to prepare the ground for the achievement of first-
generation rights (that is, negative political and civil rights). It prefers
to have as its point of departure the deconstruction of the underlying
structural causes of political violence – such as poverty, famine, exclusion of minorities, youth marginalisation, human trafficking, forced
labour, forced migration and so on – rather than merely the attitudes
and behaviours of the elite, which benefits from direct and uncensored
violence. Human rights journalism is simply predicated on the sustainable peace and human rights logic of the principle 'it is better to prevent
the escalation of violence than to try to stop it', as the latter situation
may lead to a cycle of violence and therefore to even more human rights
violations. Amartya Sen, 1998 Nobel Laureate in Economics, is on record
with the remark: 'There has never been a substantial famine in a country
with a democratic form of government and a relatively free press' (Sen,
2003, cited in Himelboim and Limor, 2008: 237). Human rights-based
journalism, made possible by a free and open media climate, gives early
warning of conflicts and other security threats. Sen credits India's free
and vibrant press for helping that country avoid major famines since
independence because their reporting stirred elected governments to
action when hunger reached life-threatening levels. Sen (1999) contrasts
this [much pro-active reporting of the Indian famine] with the massive

but almost unreported famine in China, during which Beijing's unaccountable authoritarian leaders faced neither domestic nor international pressures to save their citizens.

Sen's point about the free media helping to avoid famine and other humanitarian disasters ties in very well with his famous capabilities approach in economic development, which is based on empowering the people to take care of their own development. Equally, Sen's capability approach has close affinities with human rights education – another important strand of human rights journalism, which is specifically targeted at empowering people to take decisions and actions that impact on their lives directly. Human rights education is very closely related to the concept of community-based development work or participatory action research. 'The essence of these ideas is that the most effective means of enhancing people's capabilities is to facilitate their own social transformation through participation in the decisions that affect development' (Marks, 2005: 46).

In conclusion, I have tried throughout this chapter to demonstrate the importance of this third strand of human rights journalism over those of free speech and mere linear reporting of human rights violations, largely because of its solution-oriented and pro-active rather than problem-oriented and reactive approach. Human rights journalism compares and contrasts with peace journalism largely in the context of this pro-active and reactive journalism binary. Wenden argues, however, that there appears to be no recognition, in the peace education literature, 'of the need for educational activities that would develop the linguistic knowledge and related critical language skills for understanding how discourse shapes individual and group beliefs and attitudes and prompts social action' (Wenden, 2007: 165). To address this gap, Wenden proposes a framework for critical language education (CLE) that can be used to embed the linguistic perspective into peace education. Wenden's CLE framework has a lot in common with human rights education, and by extension human rights journalism, in as far as preparing a critically aware and active population is concerned. In fact, it is the journalism, human rights and democracy nexus that partly brings peace journalism, global journalism, public journalism and citizen journalism so close to what I have conceptualised here as human rights journalism. Where they agree and disagree, and how human rights journalism serves to fill the void created by these alternative journalism models, are matters that form the basis of Chapters 3 and 4.

3
Critical Comparative Analyses of Human Rights Journalism, Peace Journalism, Global Journalism and Human Rights Reporting

Having critically discussed the conceptualisation of human rights journalism (HRJ) as a distinct style of journalism based on cosmopolitan global justice, I will now proceed to focus, in this and the following chapter, on discussing how it compares to other, alternative genres of journalism, which serve as counterweights to mainstream journalism. This chapter is poised to show how the human rights-based approach to journalism makes HRJ stand out in the pack of alternative models, not only in helping to promote public knowledge and understanding of issues, processes and events but also in ensuring that journalists who follow it see themselves as having the moral responsibility – as duty bearers – to educate the public and increase its awareness of its rights; to monitor, investigate and cover all human rights violations; and above all to advocate pro-actively how to address or prevent them. This chapter takes the following structure: HRJ and peace journalism (PJ) within the justpeace framework; second, how it is different from global journalism; and, finally, its historical links with human rights reporting in the context of honest journalism versus objective journalism.

3.1 Human rights journalism and peace journalism within the justpeace framework

This section explores the links between justpeace and PJ on the one hand and between justpeace and HRJ on the other hand. Justpeace is seen as a holistic and practical framework, informed by the idea that war is not simply an isolated event but is very much rooted within the fabric of our societies and that this idea 'offers the hope that wars can be prevented from within by creating modes of negotiation and reconciliation practices to reduce and eventually end the necessity for violence' (Malone, 2004: 8). Ury (2001: 38) conceptualises justpeace as having a 'third side', that is, 'a kind of a social immune system that prevents the spread of the virus of violence'. Ury is very critical of Hobbes' view that human nature's inclination to war can only be restrained by a strong government. Going along with Frans de Waal (1990), who questions the myth that humans are innately aggressive, and with Ferguson (2002), who draws on archaeological evidence to prove that most of human history was peaceful rather than warlike, he ponders on how our ancestors were able to resolve conflict so successfully for so long (Ury, 2001). He comes up with an answer while researching Bushmen of Kalahari and observing the way in which family, friends and the extended community intervened to resolve issues between contending parties. There he discovers that conflicts never take place just between two adversaries, that is there is always a 'third side', 'which is made up of people from the community using a certain kind of power, the power of peers, from a certain perspective, which is a perspective of common ground; supporting a certain process, which is the process of dialogue and nonviolence; and aiming for a certain product, which is a triple win – a solution that's good for the community and good for both of the parties' (Ury, 2001: 73). Ury perceives conflict as a natural phenomenon and calls for a positive interactive dialogue rather than for mere opposition from external forces. He comes up with ten roles that 'third siders' can play in achieving justpeace (see Table 3.1).

Table 3.1 Ten roles 'third siders' can play to achieve justpeace

1)	Provider:	helping people meet their frustrated needs
2)	Teacher:	instilling skills or attitudes to defuse tensions
3)	Bridge Builder:	fostering good relationships across potential lines of conflict
4)	Mediator:	helping people reconcile their opposite interests
5)	Arbiter:	delineating the disputed rights
6)	Equalizer:	balancing the power between clashing parties
7)	Healer:	repairing injured relationships and defusing wounded emotions
8)	Witness:	taking heed and note of early warning signs of dispute
9)	Referee:	establishing objective rules for conflict
10)	Peace Keeper:	stepping in to separate the fighting parties, even physically

3.1.1 Defining Peace Journalism

Lynch and McGoldrick (2005: 5) define PJ as 'a set of tools, both conceptual and practical, intended to equip journalists to offer a better public service'. It is a journalism that helps reporters and editors alike to make informed choices of what stories deserve reporting and how this reporting itself is done to provide the society at large with opportunities 'to consider and value non-violent responses to conflict'. Lynch and McGoldrick (2005: 5) present PJ as playing the following three key roles:

1. It uses the insights of conflict analysis and transformation to update the concepts of balance, fairness and accuracy in reporting.
2. It provides a new route map tracing the connections between journalists, their sources, the stories they cover and the consequences of their journalism – the ethics of journalism intervention.
3. It builds an awareness of non-violence and creativity into the practical job of everyday editing and reporting (Table 3.2).

Like all alternative journalism models, PJ has both supporters and critics. By recognising the debates in favour of and against PJ, Lynch, in his book *Debates in Peace Journalism* (2008), critically engages the believers and practitioners of war journalism (WJ) to go along with the alternative paradigm of providing more diagnosis of conflict dynamics to help people to understand, and to encourage them to go for the win–win logic in finding solutions instead of just reporting the facts of violence within the context of the WJ option of win/lose, which often leads to more violence. The creation of an enabling environment by PJ that would help

Table 3.2 The Galtung peace journalism model

Peace/conflict journalism	War/violence journalism
1) Peace/conflict-oriented – pro-active: prevention win–win	1) War/violence-oriented – reactive: violence first zero-sum orientation
2) Truth-oriented – expose all truths	2) Propaganda-oriented cover up some
3) People-oriented – name all evil doers focus on all people suffering	3) Elite-oriented –'them' evil doers –focus on 'our'
4) Solution-oriented	4) Victory-oriented

Note: Galtung model adapted from Lynch and McGoldrick (2005: 6).

people consider non-violent approaches to ending violence resonates with the justpeace approach of the processing of dialogue and non-violence. Both have elements of critical conflict analysis and creativity that help in providing solutions to conflict. However, where justpeace goes further in the solution-oriented approach is where its own targeted end product is a triple win, that is, a solution that meets the needs of the two parties in the conflict and of the community as the 'third side'. Moreover, justpeace goes further in the people-oriented and justice-oriented approach by being attached to, rather than detached from, all the vulnerable victims of human rights violations. This is because, while justpeace is inclusive of all victims and offenders of human rights violations (making sure that the latter are also held accountable for their crimes) – and this includes the parties in conflict and the rest of the community – the people-oriented and justice-oriented approach is only concerned about the victims of the two parties to the conflict. In fact in some cases, such as the North Atlantic Treaty Organization (NATO) intervention for the liberation of Kosovo, advocates of PJ tended to be more supportive of the cause of the victims on one side of the conflict than of the cause of the victims on the other side (Lynch, 2007). Yet, as Lederach (1995: 20) puts it, justice is 'the pursuit of restoration, of rectifying wrongs, of creating right relationships based on equity and fairness'.

Defining human rights journalism

HRJ is defined as a diagnostic style of reporting, which gives a critical reflection on the experiences and needs of the victims and perpetrators of human rights violations of all types – physical as well as cultural and structural – in order to stimulate understanding of the reasons for these violations and to prevent or solve them in ways that would not produce more human rights imbalances or violations in the future. Moreover, it is a journalism that challenges, not reinforces, the status quo of the powerful dominant voices of society against the weak and marginalised ones in the promotion and protection of human rights and peace. It is, in other words, journalism without borders – a journalism based on human rights and global justice, a journalism that challenges political, economic, social and cultural imbalances of society at both local and global levels.

The HRJ strand of PJ is premised on the argument that, if journalism is to play any role in society, it should focus on deconstructing the underlying structural causes of political violence such as poverty, famine, exclusion of minorities, youth marginalisation, human trafficking, forced labour, forced migration and the like – rather than merely the attitudes and behaviours of the elite that benefit from direct and uncensored violence. In short, it calls for a more robust pro-active (preventive) – rather than dramatic reactive (prescriptive) – role of the media in humanitarian intervention. Unfortunately, however, the kind of journalism that is very dominant today is the human wrongs journalism (HWJ), a journalism that reinforces instead of challenging the problematic representational imbalances in society; it reinforces instead of challenging the concentration of power in the hands of the few resourceful people and political communities in global society.

Like PJ, HRJ resonates with the justpeace approach in the critical conflict analysis and creativity perspectives that are needed to help people actively participate in the resolution of violent situations. However, unlike PJ, HRJ resonates with justpeace in being more global, long-term, pro-active and sustainable approach as it provides a critical reflection of the experiences and needs of not only the victims but also the perpetrators or offenders, of human rights violations, and in this way ensures the prevention or resolution of all forms of future or present violence, respectively. Hence, HRJ has the potential to complement PJ to make it more global, long term, pro-active and sustainable in justpeacebuilding.

The orientation variables of PJ as outlined by Galtung (1992) and reproduced earlier in this chapter largely compare to those I have identified with HRJ as can be seen in my Table 3.3 below:

Table 3.3 Peace journalism and human rights journalism

Peace journalism	Human rights journalism
Peace/conflict-oriented: prevention/win–win	Non-violence/structural/cultural violence-oriented: pro-active/ preventing direct violence/triple win
Truth-oriented: expose all untruths	Human wrongs-oriented: expose all human wrongs
People-oriented: name all victims	People/human face-oriented/care for and empower all but biased in favour of vulnerable people
Solution-oriented	Holistic problem-solving: now/tomorrow and surface/hidden problems

On the other hand, the orientation variables or principles of WJ as outlined by Galtung (1992) also largely compare to those I have identified with HWJ as can be seen in Table 3.4 below:

Table 3.4   War journalism and human wrongs journalism

War journalism	Human wrongs journalism
War/violence-oriented: reactive/first zero-sum/win–lose orientation	Competition-oriented: violence/drama/evocative: solution after damage/ business profit or loss
Propaganda/deceit-oriented: expose 'their' untruths/lies and cover up 'ours'	Their propaganda/deceit/ conspiracy-oriented: talk about 'their' conspiracies to commit human rights violations and ignore 'ours'
Elite-oriented: focus on 'them' evil doers and 'our' victims/friend (good) enemy (bad)	Demonisation-oriented: focus on the human rights violations by 'them' 'others' or 'our enemies' and on 'our' or 'our friends' victims
Victory-oriented: peace = victory + ceasefire	Partial solution-oriented: focus on immediate physical needs only at the expense of long-term structural solutions

3.2   How human rights journalism is different from global journalism

While it is clear that HRJ is somehow similar to global journalism, there is a fundamental difference between the two concepts. In the discussion that follows, I will first explore the principal parallel that exists between these two concepts and then focus on their main difference. I first offer a brief conceptualisation of global journalism.

Global journalism is a concept that remains still largely under-theorised, despite the successive growth of contributions to its study since over a decade ago (Herbert, 2001; de Beer and Merrill, 2004; Berglez, 2007; Loffelholz and Weaver, 2007; Reese, 2007). Berglez (2008) has traced global journalism research to the fields of international communication and transnational communication, which discuss the links between news media and globalisation from political–economic (Boyd-Barrett and Rantanen, 1998; Hjarvard, 2001; Rantanen, 2007), news-cultural (Volkmer, 1999, 2001), news-discussive (Norstedt and Ottosen, 2004, 2005) and ethnographic (Bitereyst, 2001;Olausson, 2005) viewpoints.

Yet much more diverse perspectives have emerged in more recent research on global journalism. Its recent interpretations range from being seen as a survey of the whole gamut of global mass media and journalism cultures (Weaver, 1998; Herbert, 2001; de Beer and Merrill, 2004; van Ginneken, 2001; Loffelholz and Weaver, 2007) to being seen as a form of journalism ethics advising on how to avoid cultural stereotypes and west-centrism (van Ginneken, 2001); to being seen as a form of news reporting of military conflicts in different parts of the world (Seib, 2002); as well as to being seen as a newly developing newsgathering practice across national borders (Holm, 2001; Reese, 2007: 242; Berglez, 2008: 846). Berglez (2008) argues that global journalism suffers from a lack of empirical studies, largely caused by its lack of an elaborated definition as a news style, even where research exists on globalisation and on the language of news (van Ginneken, 2001; Fairclough, 2006). The conceptualisation of global journalism so far remains limited to transnational journalism, or, to put it simply, to foreign or international news. However, as Berglez puts it, 'global journalism as a news style is different from domestic and foreign journalism' (Berglez, 2008: 846). Berglez notes that, if globalisation is about ongoing global relations defined by capitalism, global journalism is about 'how people and their actions, practices, problems, life conditions, etc. in different parts of the world are interrelated' (Berglez, 2007: 151). Global journalism is normally generated when a journalist uses the global context of climate change to explain an environmental problem such as the South East Asian tsunami or hurricane Katrina. Another example of global journalism is where a journalist attempts to give the global context of the political crisis in the DR Congo by relating it to the unfair trade policies of EU countries.

Berglez (2008) sees global journalism as being endowed with a particular epistemology, defined as the global outlook – which is the direct opposite of the national outlook. While the national outlook puts the nation-state at the centre of things when framing social reality, the 'global outlook tries to understand and explain how economic, political, social, cultural, and environmental activities, processes, and problems in different parts of the world impact on each other, are interrelated or are similar'. Journalism with a global outlook facilitates understanding of how our lives in Copenhagen, Cairo, Sydney, London, Paris and so on are 'casually and dialectically intertwined' (Berglez, 2008: 847). This means using the global perspective to explain a local situation or vice versa, be it one of crisis or disaster.

This epistemological global outlook of global journalism is similar to the political context or the diagnostic reporting (critical empathy frame) epistemology associated with HRJ insofar as explaining the global undercurrents of crises in distant countries is concerned. However, one area where HRJ fundamentally differs from global journalism is where it goes beyond the global outlook in explaining crises in distant countries, to advocate a global ethics and a cosmopolitan global society. In other words, the explanation offered in the case of HRJ is not necessarily limited to the global context of distant crises or problems, but fundamentally skewed towards advocating a kind of pro-active intervention designed to address or prevent them in ways that would ensure the promotion and protection of sustainable peace and human rights. As Berglez (2008: 848) puts it, 'a global outlook is primarily a matter of understanding and seeking to explain complex relations across the globe, not to develop a universal (global) ethics'. As globalisation involves very complex relations between peoples, places and practices, global journalism, through the epistemology of global outlook, is the type of journalism that connects and covers these relations in the daily news.

3.3   The history of human rights reporting and how it is related to human rights journalism: 'Honest' journalism versus 'objective' journalism

Having discussed human rights reporting in the context of exposing human rights abuses in Chapter 2, I will now offer a historical outline and demonstrate how it is related to my conceptualisation of HRJ. The history of human rights reporting has largely been traced to that of reports of war. For his heroic traits of boldness, self-reliance and perseverance while reporting for *The World* in the late nineteenth century, Canadian foreign correspondent James Creelman is celebrated as the 'father' of human rights reporting and, by extension, of what has now gradually evolved as HRJ. In the age of mass newspaper circulation in America in the 1890s, foreign correspondents reporting from the world's hotspots were celebrated as heroes for their bravery in reporting human rights abuses within the context of the 'journalism of sensation' (yellow journalism), albeit 'amidst accusations of fabrication and exaggeration' (Moritz, 1997). Creelman prided himself as a 'yellow journalist' and saw the yellow press as a positive civilising force, one that helped to shape public events. Yet he noted in his memoirs: 'It may be that a desire to sell their newspapers influenced some of the yellow editors, just as a desire to gain votes inspired some of the political orators' (Creelman, 1901: 176).

The sensational style of reporting set the stage for foreign correspondents to go in search of violence. However, the dream of reaching journalistic stardom and recognition might tempt a sloppy reporter to fall for exaggerated rumours or fabrications. Yellow journalists are always on the lookout for eye-catching headlines and stories, and are under intense competition to attract mass readership; they go for 'drama and sensation to get notice, a by-line, a front page spot, or simply to keep a job' (Moritz, 1997). In Creelman's days, competition among newspapers simply meant that, to survive they had to focus on entertainment, drama and emotion. Creelman's reporting of the massacre of more than 2,000 Chinese civilians by Japanese soldiers at Port Arthur in China in 1894 earned him 'fame and international controversy'. He was accused of exaggeration and lacking balance, but his moral and journalistic positioning made him see no need for neutrality. His language was emotional and contained what passes today as 'editorialising'; it included his own personal views, 'emotions, or even actions' (Moritz, 1997: 6). However, as it was not normal in his time to break away from the mainstream ways of journalism, Creelman was often criticised even by some of his peers for putting too much of himself into a story: on many occasions he abandoned the objective stance to become part of the story when reporting the atrocities of wars such as in Cuba and Japan. His style epitomised the Victorian era yellow journalism concepts of how foreign correspondents might act as international 'watchdogs' to enforce western-style 'civilised' humane warfare. Creelman prided himself on being an activist. In his memoirs he recalled how he personally helped to lead an American charge against Spanish forces at El Caney when he returned to Cuba to cover the Spanish–American War in 1898.

Although Creelman is remembered as the father of human rights reporting, the style of attachment to the story, and thus of breaking from the morally traditional observer role, did not start and end with him. It can be likened to the cultural approach to the news that characterised the nineteenth-century American press, initially developed by James Carey (1989) and in more recent years by Michael Schudson (1995, 1998) and others, such as Ryfe (2006) and Shaw (2009). This type of reporting stressed the participation of ordinary people. Following Schudson (1995), Ryfe (2006: 62) affirms that these cultural conventions 'exhibit evidence of cultural norms according to which newspapers portrayed reality: norms which were part of a broadly shared sense that public life was for association, affiliation, and belonging'. Ryfe identifies four primary conventions of associational journalism that are unique to the nineteenth-century American press:

- Eyewitness accounts make for the most newsworthy and authoritative stories.
- A news story ought to be reported in the first person, or, where appropriate, in the third person.
- The more first-hand accounts of events a newspaper provides its readers the better, even if some of those accounts contradict the political views of the editor, or of one another.
- Events ought to be reported chronologically, as they happen in real time; and the distinctiveness of events is determined by the numbers, kinds and behaviours of the crowds that attend them. (Ryfe, 2006: 62)

This was no different from the mid-Victorian British Press in the nineteenth century, where newspapers 'contained leading articles propounding the official "line"; verbatim transcriptions of important speeches, strictly informative (not to say accurate) advertisements, and little else'. Views, rather than news, were the main preoccupation of this mid-Victorian press (Hampton, 2001: 217). Moreover, Shaw (2009: 498) argues that this form of nineteenth-century American and British journalism, which focused more or less on public life on the basis of a strong attachment to the people – which in a way inhibits the notion of objectivity, the hallmark of modern-day American journalism – was no different from the African journalism of belonging that we saw in the pre-colonial, colonial and immediate postcolonial periods. Like the yellow journalism of Creelman, the nineteenth-century American and British press and the African journalism performed a 'watchdog role while at the same time exhibiting a strong element of journalism of association, affiliation and belonging' (Shaw, 2009: 498).

However, human rights reporting did not end with the story of James Creelman. In her study of the political history of journalism, Geraldine Muhlmann (2008), for example, talks about the dominance of what she refers to as a 'unifying journalism', where the journalist often assumes the features of what she calls a 'witness–ambassador' in modern journalism. Muhlmann nevertheless recognises that, in the mist of this dominant 'unifying' journalism, ostensibly celebrating the triumph of the 'witness–ambassador' (objective journalist), who prioritises 'facts' acceptable to all, its opposite, the journalism of 'resistance' and 'attachment', which she refers to as 'decentring' journalism, is possible. She likened this decentring journalism to the new journalism that emerged in the US in the 1960s, 'on the border between the novel and journalism': a kind of a literary movement. This coincided with the emergence in 1965 of what Lionel Trilling called an 'adversary culture', which made modern literature become a vehicle of 'subversive intention', as readers were constantly urged to criticise the values and activities of the dominant culture of the day (Muhlmann, 2004: 135). This literary revolution increasingly saw the blurring of the line between the writer as a novelist and the journalist as a reporter. Thus both journalism and literature were liberated, which made the writer become a journalist and vice versa. The form of writing that emerged from this disappearance of the difference between reality (journalism) and fiction (literature) was writing in the first person, fully accepting the singularity of the point of view. The metamorphosis from fiction (imagination) to non-fiction (reality) then led to the emergence of the new journalism, where the journalist more or less became the 'observer–narrator'.

The French centre-left daily *Libération* was founded on 22 May 1973, in the ethos of this new journalism aimed at challenging the 'dominant journalism'. One of the founders of the *Libération*, Phillipe Gavi, declared: 'In a France occupied by "bastards", it was necessary to create liberation zones and support movements that emerged' (Muhlmann, 2004: 164). The idea of the new Libe (as the paper was popularly called) project was to provide 'another gaze' than that dominant in 'bourgeois' journalism. The paper posed a major challenge to the pseudo-objectivity of mainstream journalism, once again prioritising the notions of 'speech' and 'voice'. It signalled the end of the era of the singular dominant voice and the emergence of marginal voices. 'In fact there must be a return to questioning and to conflicting points of view – of the "I" – in order to fight against this consensual eye which claimed to unify an "us" by smoothing out disagreements' (Muhlmann, 2004: 165). The liberal French writer and existentialist philosopher Jean Paul Sartre was one of the four members of the editorial board of the *Libération*. Decentring journalism informed the editorial policy of the paper, as its journalists became more or less observer–narrators moving from the single dominant voice of the elites at the centre to the many voices of the suffering masses in the margins or on the periphery.

In the England of the mid-twentieth century, Muhlmann likened the decentring journalist of the *Libération* to the writer–reporter George Orwell (*nom de guerre* for Eric Blair), one of the greatest British novelists of his time. Orwell sought a different gaze at 'the others' (the colonised, the vagrants, the unemployed, men in war) and hence aimed at blurring the line between the 'them' and 'us'. He opted for the 'empathic gaze' as the best decentring approach, and he quickly became the archetype of decentring journalism. He believed that decentring was the real purpose of the activity of observing: if you did not decentre, you saw nothing, you were blinded by ideological constructions. Muhlmann moved this decentring discussion to encompass the reporting of the Vietnam War by Seymour M. Hersh and Michael Herr.

The then 32-year-old journalist Seymour M. Hersh, in three articles published in a series, revealed to the American public that, on 16 March 1968, a North Vietnamese village had been annilated by the First Platoon, under the command of Willam C. Calley of Charlie Company. This was in direct contravention of the Geneva Convention of 12 August 1949, which protects civilian victims in time of war. The decentring method Hersh used involves 'activating the voices of violence – of violence perpetrated. They suddenly bring this violence very close – we hear it, we can imagine it – without making it less mysterious.' The journalist urged these voices consistently to go further in order to shed light on this mystery they have in their mist. Hersh's question in the middle of his November 20 article, 'Why did it happen?', certainly goes beyond the traditional and simple process of reconstructing the facts, since it came on the heels of the revelation, made by soldier Michael Terry, of the 'fact' that they shot five enemy soldiers who were on the verge of dying. This article clearly shows that Hersh is already more interested in the representations and the language of those involved than in the 'facts'.

Twenty-seven-year-old journalist Michael Herr was sent to Vietnam in the autumn of 1976 by *Esquire magazine*. His book *Dispatches*, published in 1977, included some of the powerful articles he wrote at the frontline. Herr's writing hovers around the following question: 'Is a journalism of the *present of violence* possible?' In fact he sees the drama of violence in the present as contradictory, since the experience of the violence makes the dramatic aspect of it unlikely even when the violence itself is planned. Herr argues that, in the face of violence, the journalist is confronted with the dilemma of choosing between 'a protected gaze (opinion or view point) or the death of the gaze' (Muhlmann, 2004: 243). In other words, the journalist is forced to make a choice between decentring – that is, taking a position against evil – or remaining neutral – that is, focusing on the facts just as they are, without making any judgement. Herr argues that a reporter or journalist cannot capture the reality of war while remaining a mere spectator. He criticises himself for allowing the war to cover him while he went to report on it. He sees the 'information' as the place where the 'gaze' is overwhelmed by fantasy; the reporter becomes aware of the 'story' only when the violent drama has passed and the 'facts' of it are no longer relevant (Muhlmann, 2004: 247). Yet, although he admitted failure in reporting the Vietnam War, his intimacy with the soldiers was seen as one of Herr's strong points. His article 'Khe Sanh', reprinted in the *The New Journalism*, is one of the texts where he used dialogues most successfully in evoking 'empathy or intropathy' for the soldiers. However, Muhlmann argues that these incidents are largely seen as interludes 'outside the violence';'the horror is evoked only after the event, not in the present (p. 251).

As evident in the cases of Creelman, Orwell, *Libération*, Hersh and Herr, since the nineteenth century human rights reporting and war correspondence have been characterised by the dilemma that journalists face in having to choose between the more historical honest journalism (taking sides with the good and the human – 'reporting as I see it') and the more mainstream objective journalism (neutrality – 'reporting as it is'). The first approach focuses on the journalist as a moral witness of human rights violations who has a sense of attachment to the suffering of the victims, while the second focuses on the journalist as a witness of human rights violations who does not necessarily empathise with the victims. The debate between journalists as to which path to follow is nothing new. Another veteran British foreign correspondent, James Cameron, famously used the notions of 'honest' and 'objective ' journalism to explain a fundamental difference between American and British journalism. He noted that in the UK parliamentary debates are discussed openly, and the British press has the opportunity to reflect on them and to discuss them, whereas in the USA such discussions are limited to newspaper editorials with diverse opinions. Cameron said: 'British journalism at its best is literate, lightweight, and fundamentally ineffectual; American journalism at its best is ponderous, excellent, and occasionally anaesthetic. After working a great deal in both areas, it seems to me that Britain cannot match America's best but incomparably transcends America's norm' (Cameron, 1967). Recounting his experience in

Vietnam, Cameroun indicates his preference for honest journalism as against objective journalism:

> I had no professional justification left if I did not at least try to make the point that North Vietnam, despite all official Washington arguments to the contrary, was inhabited by human beings [...] and that to destroy their country and their lives with high explosive and petroleum jelly was no way to cure them of their defects ... objectivity in some circumstances is both meaningless and impossible. I still do not see how a reporter attempting to define a situation involving some sort of ethnic conflict can do it with sufficient demonstrable neutrality to fulfil some arbitrary concept of 'objectivity'. It never occurred to me, in such a situation, to be other than subjective, and as obviously so as I could manage to be. I may not always have been satisfactorily balanced; I always tended to argue that objectivity was of less importance than the truth, and that the reporter whose technique was informed by no opinion lacked a very serious dimension (Cameron, 1967)

Cameron clearly sees objectivity only as a dream or a 'mission impossible' for a journalist worthy of his name. Yet, when he demonstrated a sense of attachment to the suffering of the Vietnamese, he was accused by Washington of supporting the enemy. This shows the potential risks that journalists run when they decide to follow the path of honest journalism in the reporting of human rights violations.

I recall negotiating my path between these two complex and important binary notions of 'objective' and 'honest' journalisms while practising journalism in Sierra Leone in the late 1990s. The pacifist position of my newspaper, *Expo Times*, in calling for a peaceful resolution of the civil war, was unfortunately misunderstood by the Sierra Leone government, which was led by the then Sierra Leone Peoples Party (SLPP). They interpreted it to mean a declaration of support for the Revolutionary United Front (RUF) rebels and for all other international organisations (like the UK-based International Alert) that were involved in the peace process following the signing of the Abidjan Peace Accord in November 1996. In fact most of the organisations calling for a peaceful resolution of the conflict, including International Alert, were branded as supporters of the rebel cause. In addition to taking an honest position for a pacifist solution to the conflict, which was popular among the people, my newspaper's exclusive reports and commentaries, which reflected both the positions of the government and those of the rebel movement, were largely interpreted by the former as a clear-cut indication of support for the latter. Illustrative here is the publication of an opinion article of March 1997 that attacked the wisdom of arresting the rebel leader Foday Sankoh and of orchestrating a coup against him by the then Nigerian military dictator General Sanni Abacha and by former President Tejan Kabbah respectively, arguing that this was going to spell doom for the ongoing Abidjan peace process signed in November 1996. The author of the article, Gibril Gbanabome Koroma (now publisher and editor of the Canada-based Patriotic Vanguard), made it quite clear in the article that his intention was never to make a case for the rebel leader, who, in fact, was charged with destroying his home village Yonibana during the fierce fighting in the northern part of the country. Gibril's intention, as was clearly stated in the article, was to question the morality of what he termed an act of 'gangsterism' by then Nigerian dictator General Sani Abacha. Yet Gibril, deputy editor Charles Roberts and I were arrested and charged with spying for the enemy, and we were only released from prison on bail, three weeks later, following interventions from press freedom campaign organisations such as the Committee to Protect Journalists and Reporters without Borders.[1]

Carruthers (2000) alludes to the possibility of journalists trying to be both objective and honest in their reporting of humanitarian situations. She observes that most western media correspondents opted for objectivity during the twentieth century but refused to allow this option to create a confusion between their being honest and being objective. Yet Pedelty (1993) notes that although reports may strike a "balance" between different viewpoints, where journalists may appear to exhibit some level of detachment, objectivity often reproduces dominant understandings and values, while at the same time pretending to be free from any ideological influence in the manufacturing of the news. (Pedelty, 1993). However, Carruthers (2000) argues that common sense often dictates the distance journalists maintain between themselves and what they cover. In line with this thinking, she refers to the experience of freelance British journalist Richard Dowden, who described how a TV crew, bored of filming the sick, often asked relief agencies to help them to film dying Somalis. She added, however, that this kind of 'detachment' should not perhaps be taken as synonymous with objectivity (Carruthers, 2000). 'Conversely, whether commitment (or "attachment") and objectivity may co-exist has been the subject of much recent discussion, stirred especially by Martin Bell's interventions (1995, 1997, 1998)' (Carruthers, 2000; 240–241). Former Member of Parliament and BBC correspondent who covered the Balkan wars, Bell was accused by some – notably by Foreign Secretary Douglas Hurd – of belonging to the 'something must be done' brigade – a group of journalists, including *The Guardian*'s Maggie O'Kane, who openly supported pro-Bosnian intervention.

While Bell distances himself from crusading journalism, he reports: 'I do not believe that we should stand neutrally between good and evil, right and wrong, aggressor and victim' (The News World Conference November 1996). He called instead for a 'journalism of attachment, journalism which cares as well as knows', a call he has repeated in print and in radio broadcasts, and which has been widely debated (Bell, 1995, 1997, 1998, cited in Carruthers 2000: 240–241).

Bell's point touches on a central cord of the 'journalism of attachment' (honest journalism) against the journalism of 'detachment' (objective journalism), and in a way it sits with the notion of HRJ, a journalism with a human touch. However, Bell's argument raises the question of how one determines who is good or evil, right or wrong, victim or aggressor at any given time, as it could be morally problematic to support a victim today who becomes an aggressor tomorrow, or to support a victim today who was an aggressor of some sort yesterday.

Looking at this historical context, it is easy to see how human rights reporting has been a highly contested and controversial paradigm, and this largely because it is seen as a threat to 'business as usual' in journalistic practice. Small wonder that critics of HRJ often see it as a problem for some of the main standards of professional journalism – such as objectivity, which emphasizes the 'news as it is' only, and not the 'news as I see it'. What these critics fail to appreciate, however, is the fact that HRJ is the real panacea to the problems of mainstream reporting because, among many other things, it emphasizes both the 'news as it is' and the 'news as I see it', with special emphasis on or bias towards the marginalised and vulnerable voices who form the bulk of the victims of human rights abuses. Human rights reporting is often associated with HRJ insofar as the reporting of political violence or war is concerned. There is normally little or no problem with this association, although this book seeks to demonstrate that there is more to HRJ than the reporting of human rights violations. While human rights reporting is more or less limited to the reporting of direct physical violence such as civil wars, terrorism, torture in the context of civil and political rights (negative rights/negative peace), HRJ covers a much wider scope, encompassing both direct physical and indirect structural/cultural violence such as poverty, famine, human trafficking, unfair trade, forced migration and so on, in the context of economic, social and cultural rights (positive rights/positive peace). What appears problematic, nonetheless, is the association that is often made between WJ and HRJ in the narrow context of human rights reporting, since in the strict sense the former can undermine the latter in much the same way as PJ can.

In conclusion, I have tried to demonstrate in this chapter how HRJ is similar to alternative journalism models such as PJ and human rights reporting, and also where it differs from them. I have shown the characteristics that PJ shares with HRJ on the one hand, and with WJ and HWJ on the other hand. In short, I recognise the nexus between PJ and HRJ, whereas I problematise WJ as HWJ. In both cases, however, I identify fundamental differences in the context of Galtung's four categories for war and PJ: violence/conflict; propaganda/truth; elite/people; victory/solution (1996).

I affirmed that HWJ, which is dominant in mainstream journalism, is a journalism that reinforces, instead of challenging, the problematic representational imbalance in society; it strengthens, instead of challenging, the concentration of power in the hands of the few powerful people and political communities in global society. I noted that, although WJ is similar to HWJ in this respect, its focus is more skewed towards societal imbalances in terms of direct physical violence than of indirect structural and cultural violence. In a similar way, although I recognised the parallels between HRJ and PJ as counter-hegemonic journalism models, I identified the former as a more pro-active strand in addressing or preventing problems of structural and cultural violence that, if not tackled quickly, have the potential of causing direct physical violence and of perpetuating human rights violations.

In the case of what separates HRJ from global journalism, I go with Berglez's argument (2008) that the global outlook of the latter does not extend to moral ideas of a global ethics and of a cosmopolitan global (universal) society, based on equal rights in terms of treatment by, and access to, the media. I make the argument that HRJ on the other hand not only has a global approach to news production, but is fundamentally rooted in its (HRJ) human rights-based approach.

I argued that human rights reporting is often confused with HRJ insofar as the reporting of political violence or war is concerned; but, as this book demonstrates, there is more to HRJ than the reporting of human rights violations. The human rights journalist is concerned about reporting not only human rights violations caused by direct physical violence in the sense of civil and political rights (negative rights/negative peace) but also, and perhaps more importantly, those violations caused by indirect structural and cultural violence in the sense of economic, social and cultural rights (positive rights/positive peace).

4
Citizen, Public and Peace Journalisms: Towards the More Radical Human Rights Journalism Strand

This chapter explores links between public journalism and citizen journalism on the one hand, and, on the other hand, how these two notions and peace journalism (PJ) serve as counter-hegemonic models to mainstream journalism. The notions of public journalism and citizen journalism have generated debate among academics and journalists on two main fronts: first, which one is more credible in terms of reaching out to people marginalised by mainstream traditional journalism; and, second, which one presents patterns or styles of reporting that are more radically different from those of mainstream journalism? PJ advocates such as Galtung and Vincent (1992, 1996) and Lynch and McGoldrick (2005) have put the blame of misreporting and misrepresenting the world's crises squarely at the doorstep of war journalism, which prioritises violence. This is the opposite of PJ, which advocates conflict prevention and resolution. However, PJ has met with some scathing criticisms regarding its limitations in scope. In this chapter I make the argument that human rights journalism (HRJ) unravels the limitations of the three models insofar as bottom-up journalism and journalism based on the human touch are concerned. The chapter is divided into two sections. First it deals with the limits of public journalism and citizen journalism and with HRJ as an alternative paradigm; second, it discusses the limits of PJ and HRJ as a complementary strand.

4.1 The limits of public and citizen journalisms: Human rights journalism as an alternative paradigm

I will start this section by briefly looking at the limits of public and citizen journalisms within a comparative framework before discussing the details of these limitations in juxtaposition with HRJ as an alternative paradigm.

Although it officially emerged, or, more accurately, re-emerged in the 1990s, public journalism has its roots in nineteenth-century American and British press reporting, which Carey (1989) and Schudson (1995, 1998), and much later Ryfe, (2006), Shaw (2009) characterised as the 'cultural approach' to news. The 'cultural approach' to news production and dissemination is informed by the idea that 'the news expresses the structure of public life in another medium' (Shaw, 2009: 497). The nineteenth-century news of the American and British press 'tended to be reported by a great variety of people, often in the first person, and often through chronological narratives that stressed the participation of ordinary people' (Ryfe, 2006: 74). Shaw compares this nineteenth-century American and British journalism to the African journalism of belonging, which characterised the pre-colonial, colonial and postcolonial periods of the African continent (Shaw, 2009); this suggests that public journalism goes far beyond the nineteenth-century American and British press.

However, as Allan (1997: 319) warns, the mainstream western mass media are deeply embedded in the liberal democracy model's myth of 'objectivity' and 'impartiality', which is consumer- more than community-oriented, fundamentally departing from the nineteenth-century news culture of public life, which was characteristic of the nineteenth-century American and British journalism and, much earlier, of African journalism. It came as no surprise, therefore, that, when public journalism re-emerged in the last decade of the twentieth century, it did so by design rather than by default, as it had done in the nineteenth century and earlier. For, as Haas and Steiner (2006: 238) put it, public journalism

> emerged in the early 1990s in response to two widening gaps of 'crisis' proportions: between government and citizens, and between news organisations and their audiences. That is, declines in voter participation in political elections and, more generally, in civic participation in local community affairs, were often cited as evidence of widespread withdrawal by citizens from democratic processes. Similarly, scholars and journalists, having often criticized news organizations' horse-race approach to political campaigns, interpreted the public's apparent disinterest in voting as proving widespread public disaffection with mass mediated political discourse.

Small wonder, then, that many scholars such as Hardt (1999, cited in Haas and Steiner, 2006: 242) have criticised public journalism as being 'historically naïve, if not a cynical marketing strategy', given that its focus on audience concerns may boost the circulation and profits for the media owners and advertisers and not necessarily the citizens' democratic needs. Mainstream journalists for their part often dismiss it as a 'quasi-religious movement' advocated by preachers and gurus, while others simply see it as representing good journalism (Haas and Steiner, 2006: 239). Public journalism is defined as having two main goals: the first is to encourage news organisations to listen more closely to their audiences; the second is to make news organisations play more active roles in their communities (Platon and Deuze, 2003). What is more, prominent socio-historian Schudson (1999: 118) calls it 'the most impressive critique of journalistic practice inside journalism in a generation'. Yet, despite its counter-hegemonic role, public journalism has met with some fierce criticisms. Here I will only outline some of the most discussed scholarly and journalistic criticisms as identified by Haas and Steiner (2006). First, public journalism lacks historical perspective and a clear conceptual definition (Lambeth, 1998; Schudson, 1999; Zelizer, 1999). Second, it is merely a bundle of 'journalistic practices and techniques' that reinforces the elitism of the 'old journalism'. Third, it is a profit-oriented rather than a democratic project. Fourth, it lacks a coherent framework for defining the public and incorrectly presupposes consensus. Fifth, by failing to set the news agenda for the public, public journalism attracts criticism on the grounds that it is not formally accountable to the public. Finally, the professed problem-solving role of public journalists is often criticised by scholars and journalists as inappropriate because it tends to exaggerate their role as agents of political change and to compromise their neutrality (Peters, 1999; Schudson, 1999).

Citizen journalism is presented as the radical alternative strand to public journalism in that it is centred around people more than around elites; democratic more than profit-centred; less conceptually ambiguous; more partisan and empathic, more participatory, engaging and empowering; and more oriented towards problem-solving. Citizen journalism gives voice to the marginalised 'them'; hence Atton's phrase 'native reporting' (Atton, 2002: 112–7), a concept developed from Spurr's (1993) study of colonial journalism. This new journalism practice consists of activities that relate to political reporting; political web logs (Matheson and Allan, 2003) and the open publishing strategies of an international, revolutionary online news agency such as Indymedia or Independent Media Channel (IMC), which rely on news and opinions contributed by participants from a diverse range of social and political activists. Citizen media narrative practices emphasise 'the first person eye-witness accounts by participants, reworking of the populist approaches of tabloid newspapers to recover a 'radical popular style of reporting'; collective and anti-hierarchical forms of organisation [...] an inclusive, radical form of civic journalism' (Atton, 2003: 267). However, a parallel can be drawn here between this type of civic journalism of first-person, eye-witness narrative and the public journalism of the nineteenth-century American and British Victorian press, as well as the pre-colonial African journalism discussed earlier in this chapter. Platon and Deuze (2003) argue that the type of journalism offered through Indymedia websites worldwide can be traced back to traditional, 'old school' journalism, particularly as modernised in the twentieth century (Hallin, 1992), as well as to a history of 'alternative' media, as opposed to mainstream news media (Eliasoph, 1988; Atton, 2001); and that this type is theoretically rooted in more recent, innovative types of journalism, both in 'old' media – public or civic journalism – and in 'new' media – open-source journalism (Deuze, 2001, 2002). This apparent sense of shared history therefore creates a very strong parallel between public journalism and citizen journalism, and thus it often makes it very difficult to present the latter as a radical alternative strand. Besides, as we shall see later in this section, it is not without some fundamental limitations. Having briefly looked at public journalism and citizen journalism, I will now focus in the remainder of this section on discussing the details of these limitations side by side with HRJ, making a case for it as an alternative paradigm.

To underpin my argument that HRJ can serve as an alternative paradigm that can address the gaps or weaknesses of public journalism and citizen journalism, I will draw on the four main variables of the HRJ orientation listed in Table 3.3. These are non-violence/structural–cultural violence oriented; preventing direct violence/win–win; expose all human wrongs-oriented; human face-oriented/care for and empower all; and holistic problem-solving and now/then and surface/hidden problems. I will also draw on the five principles of the rights-based approach to reporting, namely linkages to human rights standards, participation, accountability, non-discrimination and empowerment, some of which feature among the HRJ orientation variables.

To start with, the claim that public journalism lacks historical perspective and a clear conceptual line, though rendered problematic by Haas and Steiner (2006), makes it difficult for it to be conceptualised as an alternative paradigm to mainstream journalism. I agree with Haas and Steiner's debunking of this claim as problematic on the strength of the historical work on the public sphere by Habermas (1989) and Fraser (1990); the earlier work on public opinion by Lippmann (1922); the account of nineteenth-century American and British press based on Carey's (1989) and Schudson' (1995, 1998) news as 'cultural life'; and that of pre-colonial African journalism (Shaw, 2009). Nonetheless, the criticism cannot be dismissed as entirely unfounded, especially the point about the lack of a conceptual definition. Advocates and critics of public journalism and citizen journalism are yet to agree on clear and widely accepted conceptual definitions of these two 'new' journalism models.

On the contrary, HRJ not only has been historically rooted in human rights reporting since the days of James Creelman, William Howard Russell and so on, but it is conceptually defined as a pro-active journalism that knows no borders, no race, no age, no gender and no class – a journalism with a human face and for the human race. This definition is largely inspired by Article 1 of the UN Universal Declaration of Human Rights (1948): 'All human beings are born free and equal in dignity and rights' (UN. Doc A/810).[1] The UN human rights doctrine that supports HRJ was itself introduced by the world leaders in 1948, with the aim of stemming the tide of human rights violations perpetuated during the Second World War. The human rights doctrine's underpinning of HRJ resonates with the latter's first non-violence/structural–cultural violence oriented variable, where everybody (the weak/strong/poor/rich) wins because the non-violent initiatives reduce the chances of clash or violence that leads to more human rights violations.

The second attack on public journalism as having structures that reinforce elitist rather than grassroots agendas was indeed also challenged by Haas and Steiner (2002) as not entirely true, given the consultations of ordinary people associated with it; but they recognised the apparent democratic deficit illustrated by the failure of public journalism to promote political knowledge and participation among people from different socio-economic backgrounds. Advocates of citizen journalism, however, claim that their own brand of journalism can overcome this democratic deficit of public journalism. They argue that in its case there is no danger of class exclusion from coverage or impact, since the structures and processes of news production are very much embedded in the normal life of the citizens in the driving seat (Rodriguez, 2001 cited in Atton, 2003: 267). Yet citizen journalists are not without problems in overcoming this democratic deficit. Low funds and the poorly paid or voluntary staff of citizen media 'might affect the ability to access a wide range of sources and make those experiments with news routines that have been so often associated with alternative media' (Atton and Wickenden, 2005: 351). Moreover, although Indymedia channels claim to be independent, 'they are not independent in the strictest sense of the word as the code and content of the news are made and regulated by people' often affiliated with many different movements, which contribute their own content (Platon and Deuze, 2003: 338). While blogs and other sites owned by community interest groups can engage people on defined sets of issues, such as robust criticisms of mainstream media content, they do not necessarily stimulate sustained debate, deliberation and action on a range of issues, especially ones that do not affect people directly or personally (instead they affect 'others'; Haas and Steiner, 2006: 252). What is more, as Caliendo (2009) argues, although there are certain aspects of free expression and access to information that do not necessarily relate to mass media, 'expression of individual rights and receipt of political information are virtually meaningless without the ability to print or broadcast ideas, as well as to receive information through mediated channels' (Caliendo, 2009: 1).

Conversely, there is no room for a democratic deficit in HRJ, because the latter is based on the notion of journalism without borders, be they physical or structural. This resonates with its third, human face-oriented variable, which focuses on care and empowerment for all. Humanitarianism and empowerment are among the four clear values of HRJ, the other two being truth and holism. The human rights-based approach principles of non-discrimination, equal participation and empowerment make it difficult, if not impossible, for the human rights journalist to practice instrumental and representational exclusion of the weak and poor people of society. In fact, if there is any bias, this will favour the weak and vulnerable by way of positive action; not be against them. The human rights journalist therefore has the moral responsibility to challenge, and not to reinforce, the existing individual, local and global imbalances (Beman and Calderbank, 2008).

The third problem is the location of public journalism in corporate, capitalism-driven media conglomerates. Its critics, including advocates of citizen journalism, say that this problem makes it difficult for it to operate outside their influence and manipulation. Since the alternative citizen journalists are not entirely free from the manipulation and hidden agendas of the individuals and interest groups involved in the news selection process, this makes the need for the conceptualisation of HRJ as a new all-inclusive alternative journalism paradigm even more fundamental. Whereas public journalism and citizen journalism are only concerned with engaging the public sphere, or various public spheres, into the news production and dissemination processes, HRJ is more interested in transforming mainstream journalism from its present passive and detached state into a more pro-active and caring form of journalism – one that places the participation and empowerment of all human beings at the centre of humanity. To achieve parity in human participation and empowerment, HRJ must draw on the other rights-based principles of non-discrimination and accountability and on linkages to human rights standards. Unlike the mainstream journalist, who is not that different from the public or citizen journalist in terms of being susceptible to the propaganda of the elite and corporate market classes, albeit on a relatively smaller scale, the human rights journalist goes in search of the honest truth and is overly sensitive to propaganda that will prevent him or her from exposing all the hidden agendas and causes of human rights violations. As HRJ is honesty-oriented, it is bound to be free from any economic or political manipulation; this freedom gives it the strength to expose all human wrongs. Despite the support public journalism enjoys from some media owners who are more sympathetic to the social responsibility role of the journalist than they are to the profit-oriented approach, Haas and Steiner (2006) recognise that public journalism is not very different from mainstream journalism in terms of being an easy bedfellow of market-oriented publics.

The fourth deficit of public journalism – its being oriented top-down rather than bottom-up – and the fact that it offers more generic interventions to address particular problems put it out of touch with the majority of vulnerable people. As public journalists follow more or less the same fundamentally elitist news values as their mainstream counterparts, their perspectives on reporting events or commenting on issues tend to be rather top-down and elitist. Citizen reporters or community correspondents occasionally use mainstream media as sources (Atton and Wickenden; 2005). Additionally, the personal and activist groups' websites sometimes have a close affinity with the sources of the often elitist political philosophy of their owners. This means that citizen journalists are not completely free from the elitist spin. The sourcing routines that assume 'power, legitimacy and authoritativeness' and are dominant in mainstream and public journalisms are also very present in citizen media – to go by the findings of the study by Atton and Wickenden (2005: 357). This deficit makes *SchNews* far removed from the idealised 'free space' (open space) theorisation of alternative media, at least as far as sourcing routines are concerned. 'The extent to which its journalists are deemed to be unproblematically "in solidarity" with their sources and the extent to which sources are deployed for ideological ends raise further questions about the critical practices of alternative journalism' (Atton and Wickenden, 2005: 358). Due to the fact that the over-dependence on official sources, which is one of the five filters of manipulation identified in Herman and Chomsky's (1988) 'propaganda model', is arguably recognised as a 'sub-set of a broader issue about media reporting routines (or ideas of journalistic professionalism)' (Boyd-Barrett, 2004: 448), it can be reasonably argued that public journalism and citizen journalism are no different from mainstream journalism in elitist sourcing routines, even where the first two share the first-person eye-witness narrative reminiscent of the nineteenth-century American and British press, as well as of pre-colonial African journalism.

At the other end of the spectrum, HRJ creates a mediation that is basically oriented towards humanity, whereby everybody is cared for and empowered with the knowledge and opportunity of becoming active participants in the kind of life they would like to lead. It is a form of journalism rooted in what Berlin (1969) and Ignatieff (1998) described as 'pluralism', which recognises that 'human goals are many [...] and in perpetual rivalry with one another' (Berlin, 1969: 171), and where 'the only moral political system was that which maximised liberty to allow individuals to make their own compromises among conflicting values' (Lee Plaissance, 2002: 216). Placing Berlin's claim in the context of the modern world, which is replete with ethnic or class conflicts, Ignatieff calls for a 'precarious equilibrium' and sees pluralism as the answer to all difficult conflict situations (1998: 217). Pluralism provides an atmosphere of what Carey calls 'democratic mediation', in which people need to transcend the 'narcissism of minor differences' and return to a common ground language, symbolic of our shared humanity (Lee Plaissance, 2002: 217). Human rights journalists are entrusted with the task of providing this democratic communicative space where the concerns of the majority of suffering publics are prioritised against those of the few affluent elites, and in this way achieve what Ignatieff calls a sense of shared human equilibrium (1998).

Moreover, HRJ's sense of attachment to all peoples or individuals suffering as result of the conflicts of the world makes it the appropriate alternative paradigm of a journalism that is truly accountable to the whole public, unlike mainstream journalism or public and citizen journalism. It therefore provides a well-measured answer to the fifth accusation directed at public journalism and citizen journalism – that are not accountable to the public. Human rights journalism's idea of getting involved in the story by telling it 'as I see it' (journalism of attachment), as opposed to telling merely 'as it is' (objective journalism), empathising with the vulnerable victims of conflict rather than the strong winners of it, a feature it shares closely with PJ, has made it the subject of fierce criticism from the so-called professional mainstream journalism. In this case, while HRJ is accountable to all the public (the strong and the weak), it is more accountable to the weak victims of human rights violations, who need help to catch up with the well cared-for public.

Finally, while public journalism and citizen journalism, like mainstream journalism, one way or another are weak in articulating the problem-solving role of the journalist, HRJ represents the perfect alternative in this respect. As I noted in Chapter 3, HRJ, very much like PJ, is not necessarily based on the so-called western professional journalism's notion of 'objective journalism', which simply emphasises the reporting of facts of violence or conflict as presented by all the factions; it is based rather on a notion of 'honest journalism' (the journalism of attachment), which goes the extra mile of analysing such facts in order to understand the causes and to prepare a peaceful and human rights-based response to solving the issues. Hence HRJ is a pro-active and holistic approach, oriented towards problem-solving and interested not only in the problems of today but also in those of tomorrow. These will arise if only the more obvious and superficial problems are tackled, whereas their less obvious causes and the hidden/structural undercurrents are ignored, so that they would manifest themselves in the fullness of time.

Whereas the problem-solving intervention of public journalism is focused more on the community, where journalists facilitate the efforts of citizens to identify problems and then to find solutions for them, citizen journalism has a much wider scope, using problem-solving intervention by mobilising civil society organisations and encouraging them to push for more activist intervention, as we saw in the case of Indymedia in Seattle. Since in citizen journalism most of the content consists of expressions of personal interests and feelings (OhmyNews) or in notices about highly local civic events (BBC Leeds), this brand of alternative journalism is lacking in global context or reach in problem-solving (Haas and Steiner, 2006). Like with traditional journalism, the reach of public journalism and citizen journalism is to a very large extent limited to the notion of a (particular) political community, whereas HRJ has a much wider global reach (as I discussed at length in Chapters 9, 10 and 11 of this book), owing to the fact that it covers 'universal' moral communities with a diverse history and culture – in short, cosmopolitan society as a whole. While political realists believe in the idea of 'particular' political communities, cosmopolitans believe in the idea of a 'universal' (moral) political community. Thus, while public journalism and citizen journalism are based on selective problem-solving, being limited more or less to the 'particular' political community – pretty much like mainstream journalism – HRJ is based on distributive problem-solving, open to the global human community as a whole. Such a community is inspired by the stoic idea of a human society where every human being – every life – is important, and hence worth protecting in the cosmopolitan context of global justice. HRJ is therefore a journalism that knows no borders.

Closely related to the criticism of the limited global reach of public journalism and citizen journalism is the point advanced by Glasser (1999) and Schudson (1999) – that they are largely or exclusively interested in the processes and not quite so much in the outcomes of citizens' interventionist discussions – another human rights deficit that HRJ readily fills. This is evident in the fact that HRJ is more interested in pro-active and sustainable rather than in reactive and ad hoc problem-solving approaches that aim to prevent, minimise or stem the tide of human rights violations. HRJ is not only interested in identifying the problem – which may for example constitute a human rights violation – but, more importantly, in diagnosing it; and its aim is to find out why it happened in the first place, in order to provide a solution not only 'there and now', but also 'there and tomorrow'. Moreover, in the process of diagnosing the causes of a problem, the human rights journalist can potentially draw on the support of citizens and experts alike, something that public journalism and citizen journalism shy away from doing.

Throughout this section I have tried to discuss the strengths and weaknesses of public journalism and citizen journalism, and I made a case for HRJ as a new paradigm to address the democratic deficit of mainstream journalism, which the first two proposed alternative models have so far failed to address completely. In the next section I will look at how, in a somewhat similar vein, the limits of PJ have rendered its pro-active and interventionist appeal too weak and ineffective for it to be an alternative paradigm of journalism, and how PJ needs to be complemented by HRJ.

4.2 Human rights journalism as a complementary strand of peace journalism

Galtung's PJ model essentially draws on a peace–conflict paradigm to counter-balance the war–violence model, with the main aim of moving from the current dominant culture of violence to a culture of peace. This call for a paradigm shift, coming on the heels of the end of the Cold War climaxed by the fall of the Berlin wall in 1989 and characterised by the outbreak of wars in the Balkans, the Gulf, Africa, South East Asia and more, was largely informed by lessons learned from the popular saying 'violence breeds violence' (Galtung and Vincent 1992).

HRJ complements the four orientations of the PJ model advanced by Galtung (1996)[2] and supported by Lynch and McGoldrick (2005), as represented in Table 4.1.

HRJ complements PJ by four other orientations, as represented in Table 4.2.

PJ, as Galtung (1992) notes, problematises mainstream journalism as war journalism mainly because it is problem- rather than solution-oriented; propaganda- rather than truth-oriented; elite- rather than people-oriented, and win–lose- rather than win–win-oriented (Lovasen, 2008). Lovasen (2008), of course going with Galtung, apparently used these orientations to justify the claim of PJ to have clear values of humanitarianism, truth, holism and empowerment. But this is a problematic claim. I make the argument that, despite ticking almost all the boxes of the above-mentioned orientations and values, PJ, as it stands, is lacking in the four others listed in Table 4.2, which typically reflect HRJ. To complement the orientations identified with PJ

Table 4.1 Peace journalism

win–win rather than win–lose oriented;
truth rather than propaganda;
people rather than elite; and
solution rather than victory.

Table 4.2 Human rights journalism

global (triple-win) rather than just selective (win–win) or win–lose
biased in favour of, rather than against, vulnerable voices,
pro-active (preventive) rather than reactive (prescriptive),
attached rather than detached to victims of violence and justice oriented

above, I argue that HRJ problematises mainstream journalism as human wrongs journalism not only because it fails to meet the four orientations mentioned in association with PJ in Table 4.1, but also because of its orientation towards selective justice rather than global justice; because it is biased against, rather than in favour of, vulnerable voices; because it is reactive (prescriptive) rather than pro-active (preventive); because it is detached rather than attached to victims of human rights violations – all of which are the antipodes of the four HRJ complementary orientations in Table 4.2. These four values advanced by Lovasen (2008) resonate somehow with the five principles of the rights-based approach to journalism: linkages to human rights standards, participation, accountability, non-discrimination and empowerment,[3] informed by negative and positive rights on the one hand and negative and positive peace on the other (Beman and Calderbank, 2008; Galtung and Vincent, 1992, 1996; Nowak, 2005). The four values and five principles of the HRJ also largely inform the justpeace-building approach advocated by Schirchs (2002).

It is clear that HRJ can, through the global, long-term, pro-active and sustainable approaches of justpeace, complement and strengthen PJ as a counter-hegemonic journalism practice. Drawing on these justpeace approaches, HRJ proposes a critical reflection on the experiences and needs of both victims and perpetrators of human rights violations and in this way prevent or end all forms of future or present violence. I will look at these justpeace approaches in the context of the critical debate of PJ involving the realist and human rights paradigms as well as the objectivity and advocacy journalism binary positions, respectively.

In the context of the realist and human rights paradigms, PJ advocates often fail to come to terms with the power relations, at both the national and the supranational levels, which tend to increase the powerlessness, helplessness, impotence and apathy of those whose mobilisation would best serve the peace efforts (Carrol, 1972; Ross, 2006). Carrol (1972) makes the case that a growing body of research fails to 'consider seriously the possibility that war is inherent not in human nature but in the power system of dominance in human relations' articulated through the nation-state. Yet PJ critic Thomas Hanitzsch (2007) considers news of the kind described by realists as 'socially constructed realities' (Schudson, 1998). Realists argue that, since journalists do not operate outside their immediate political, social, economic and cultural communities, it would be naïve to think that their reporting would not be influenced by them.

Kempf, however, disagrees with this realist view of the role of the media. In his synthesis of the arguments and counter-arguments in the PJ debate, Kempf (2007) defends Galtung's (2002) criticism that the mainstream media reduce conflict to a zero-sum game and Lynch's (2007) call on journalism to analyse and address its own role in creating realities. PJ is critical of the media on the grounds that they systematically conceal some specific facts, especially facts that favour the peace discourse, to promote others, for example facts that favour the war discourse. Kempf (2007) sees conflict as an interactive process involving three kinds of reality: first, the subjective reality of one party; second, the subjective reality of an opponent, both of which can interact internally; third, the kind of reality that can only be assessed from an external perspective. And he sees PJ as playing this third role, of an external perspective that shows how the two internal subjective realities interact with each other.

And yet the advocates of PJ are sometimes gullible – susceptible, that is, to manipulations of the realists who hide behind peace evocations to advance their political and economic agendas. Consider Nohrstedt et al.'s (2000) study of reporting violence in Kosovo, which found that international media engaged in nationalised propaganda discourse that uncritically incorporated the government's concept of 'military humanism' (391) to the extent that military violence as a rational solution to the Kosovo conflict aligned with the country's foreign policy objectives such as national security and trade . Issues of national interest and ideology often drive the US evocations of peace that are strategically employed by the US media not to support peace but to put a 'saintly glow' over American aggression (Herman and Chomsky, 1988: 14). Thussu (2000: 358) refers to such media representations of peace as defensive, because they only present peace as the military protection of 'our' borders against evil incursions. Politicians also hide behind peace initiatives to advance their political agendas. Marshall (1991) and Jones (2000, 2001a, 2001b) suggest that peace initiatives are a farce and a 'meaningless' 'charade', played out by politicians who seek the spotlight rather than substantive agreements. Peace initiatives are also used sometimes to play for time while political violence and human right violations continue unabated. Contextualising this politics of peace underpinned by political realism, which eventually leads to more violence and hence to further human rights violations, should also be a preoccupation of PJ scholars; but this is not what happens to date. As Ross (2006: 7) puts it, 'such representations of peace negotiations as a political game render the violence invisible', consistently reducing the real costs of conflict and ignoring human suffering. Ross warns against pursuing a 'peace frame' that continuously rely on elites, on media events and so on (Ross, 2006: 12).

The argument is often made by realists that, for intervention for peace and human rights promotion and protection to be effective, it has to involve the act of power, which involves sometimes taking sides, choosing which of the factions to support and imposing one's will by force (Brown, 2002). However, the problem is not so much taking sides in humanitarian intervention, be it by force or by peaceful means; rather it is siding with perpetrators of human rights abuses because of national interests. Sometimes inaction or tepid action in stopping or preventing human rights violations can be caused by the support that the violators may be enjoying from some big powers whose geo-strategic interests are taken care of as a kind of *quid pro quo*. Here the case of the French backing – through supply of logistics and through the Opération Turquoise, punctuated by evocations of peace in the western media – of the Habyarimana regime, whose militias turned out to be the perpetrators of the Rwandan Genocide, is illustrative. Also illustrative is the case of the Kosovo crisis, where peace evocations against the North Atlantic Treaty Organisation (NATO) intervention tended to gloss over the humanitarian suffering of the minority ethnic Muslim Albanian Kosovars, who were not all necessarily members of the rebel Kosovo Liberation Army fighting against the Serbian government of Milosovic. Peace journalists, like mainstream journalists, failed to contextualise these pretentious peace overtures in ways that would have helped to avert the killings in Kosovo and the genocide in Rwanda, even when PJ advocates had done a lot of work in promoting its ideal by this time.

However, peace advocates for their part always accuse human rights advocates of ignoring some humanitarian military interventions cloaked in human rights evocations. Lynch and Galtung (2010) alludes to Alan Kay's findings that public approval for the US use of force can reach 'consensus levels' if six 'screens' are passed, including the presence of allies to share risks and costs but also the apparent pursuit of a 'visionary objective' (2000). Hammond identifies 'humanitarian spectacle' as the correlate of this political condition, both feeding it and feeding off it: 'American military muscle was thus to be given new meaning in the post-Cold War era, no longer as a guarantor of the West's freedoms against the menace of communism but as the steel fist inside a humanitarian velvet glove' (2007: 38). Moreover, human rights have been exploited by warmongers in recent times – by Blair, to justify the invasion of Iraq; and even by the Sri Lankan government, which brazenly called the attack on the Tamils a 'humanitarian intervention' and then had itself congratulated for its 'achievement' at the UN Human Rights council (Lynch, 2010, Transcend website).

The concept of justpeace was invented as a direct response and antipode to Michael Walser's just war theory (1992), which is premised on the idea that there would be a time when a humanitarian military intervention can be justified as a 'last resort', if all the just war criteria – just cause, proportionality, least awful option, legitimate authority and low costs – were present.[4] Yet, as Malone argues, usurpation of the just war theory by political realism downplays the important principle of 'last resort', as it seeks to place 'war over and above negotiation and conflict resolution as a viable method for securing peace' (2004: 9). What is more, the just war theory is largely seen as a reactive doctrine consisting of a set of guidelines that are meant to prevent unjust wars on a largely ad hoc basis. Yet, as emphasis moves from 'just cause' (*jus ad bellum*) to 'just methods of war' (*jus in bello*), big political and military actors are increasingly hijacking the initiative whenever their geo-strategic interests are threatened. To the extent that the just war theory is often invoked by powerful states in the name of protecting and promoting human rights in some 'failed' or 'rogue' states, as we saw in the case of the two Gulf Wars, peace advocates have used it as a perfect punch bag in criticising what they generally refer to as the inhibiting role of human rights in peacebuilding.

However, if the just war theory is dismissed as a reactive zero-sum approach often used by powerful states in the name of human rights protection, the same cannot be said of the justpeace theory, which is made up of a pro-active set of activities that seek to prevent or reduce violence at the indirect structural or cultural level. Justpeacebuilding always regards conflict from a 'holistic perspective, as something that exists in all levels and arenas of human existence (Malone, 2004: 50). It caters for all humanity – the strong and weak, including vulnerable minorities such as women, children and strangers. Education and journalism can potentially build the awareness of people to challenge and resolve conflicts through non-violent means. However, because non-violence is considered feminist and less dramatic, it hardly catches the attention of the mainstream media. Little wonder that feminist peace activists are very critical of the just war theory for illuminating 'the gendered nature of war and the war system within which it is embedded, making the case that the just war theory's efficacy is currently compromised by its containment within the realist paradigm'

(Malone, 2004: 8). Feminist peace activists are often critical of peace advocates who ignore the role of women in justpeace-building processes (Tivona, 2011).

Unlike the just war theory, justpeace prioritises conflict prevention or peacebuilding over and above conflict resolution largely because of its sustainable approach of addressing the needs not only of the victims of human rights abuses but also of the offenders or perpetrators of these abuses, as well as of bystanders as third parties. And, since justpeace represents a common ground preferred by human rights and peace advocates on the one hand and by human rights and peace journalists on the other hand, justpeace has the potential to manage the divide between peace and human rights on the question of humanitarian intervention as long as this is done in a non-violent way. In any case, not all humanitarian interventions are necessarily violent. Moreover, the human rights paradigm of the justpeace global and long-term approaches can potentially complement PJ by expanding its horizon to make it encompass the more global triple-win (Ury, 2001), in which parties and non-parties in conflict, including victims and offenders, come out smiling. HRJ can therefore help PJ inculcate justpeace values of equality and interdependence based on the cosmopolitan justice of Kant (1963), Frank (2007) and Schirch (2002).

In the context of the objectivity and advocacy journalism binary, PJ continues to face the daunting challenge of relying on its critical conflict analysis approach on the basis of values (truth/honesty/ humanitarianism) that are at odds with those of mainstream 'professional' journalism, notably 'objective journalism'. Peace journalists must strike a balance between reporting and informing (objectivity) on the one hand and caring for humanity (advocacy) on the other hand. Are they getting the balance right? Or are they leaning more towards objectivity against advocacy – or vice versa? Both PJ and HRJ are putatively considered unlinear, that is, not based on neutral/objective journalism but on honest/subjective journalism. However, this is not always the case with PJ, which oscillates between the two kinds but tends more towards the objectivity standpoint. Perhaps the most illustrative case of this tendency of PJ is that offered by the Lee and Maslog (2005) and Lee et al. (2006) studies of the *Philippine Daily Inquirer* (*PDI*)'s coverage of political violence in the Philippines:

> The peace journalism framing is highly dependent on criteria of a less interventionist nature, for example, an avoidance of good/bad labels, a non partisan approach, a multi party orientation and avoidance of

emotive language. These four indicators, although important in the overall scheme of peace journalism [...] are mere extensions of the objectivity credo: reporting the facts as they are. These indicators do not truly exemplify a strong contributory, proactive role by journalists to seek and offer creative solutions and to pave a way for peace and conflict resolution. (Lee et al., 2006: 512)

By this display of neutral/passive stance, Lee and Maslog (2005) argue that the PJ practised by the *PDI* is conceptualised as the second strand of PJ, which is closely related to the 'classic' tenents of good journalism rather than to the first strand – which is the more radical interventionist approach, called 'advocacy journalism' (Hanitzsch, 2007: 3; Becker, 2002: 14). Lynch (2008: 149), however, weighs in on the two Lee and Maslog (2005) and Lee et al. (2006) studies, accusing each of them of having at least three out of the four least prevalent PJ indicators of active journalism identified by Shinar (2003), namely 'explore context', 'challenge propaganda' and 'make peace visible'. And yet, out of 368 articles, including those of *PDI*, content analysed by Lynch in his study over a month, starting from the point in June 2006 when Philippines armed forces were ordered to eradicate a group of armed rebels, only 41.2 per cent of *PDI*, which did better than all other international media, had the indicators of active PJ identified above.

Moreover, the percentage of the three indicators – avoiding emotive or demonising language (40.0 per cent), non-partisan (49.4 per cent), and avoiding labelling as 'good' and 'bad' (64.7per cent) of the *PDI* – shows that passive PJ was even much higher than that of the active PJ indicators of the same study as well as those of the passive PJ indicators in earlier studies by Lee and Maslog (2005) and Lee et al. (2006). Thus the low active PJ percentage and the very high passive PJ percentage in all the above studies raise the question of PJ's less interventionist or pro-active approach to justpeace-building initiatives. What is more, there can be a problem in measuring activist or advocacy journalism only in terms of the presence of indicators such as 'exploring context', 'challenging propaganda' and 'making peace initiatives visible', as we saw in the Philippine case study above. Rather, what is more important is that these indicators or issues are framed in ways that will not only illuminate the problems but also identify, recommend, advocate and mobilise actionable solutions to address them. The passive (neutral) PJ illustrated in the Philippine case study resonates with the 'impartial' conflict resolution approach, as opposed to the 'partisan' or value loaded human rights approach discussed in the first section of this chapter in reference to Schirch's (2002) justpeace model, which combines the two approaches.

Yet Kempf (2002) sees PJ as combining 'journalism with peace as an external aim' and rejects its advocacy explanation which means defending what one believes is right in favour of what he calls 'good' journalism, which he says has one aim: to represent reality accurately. Kempf (2002) presents objectivity, neutrality and detachment as means of reaching accuracy. While recognising the need to problematise the conventional journalistic appreciation of objectivity by way of liberating it (objectivity) from its shortcomings, Kempf cautions against turning away from it, as suggested by Lynch and McGoldrick (2005) or Hackett and Zhao (2006) warning that this may undermine the 'trust bonus' that PJ currently enjoys (Kempf, 2007: 7).

But, as I argued in Chapter 3, Martin Bell prefers this 'journalism of attachment' as the journalism that 'will not stand neutrally between good and evil, right and wrong, the victim and the oppressor' (Carruthers, 2000: 240–241). This position is sometimes misunderstood by some critics of PJ as a kind of 'legimation for biased coverage', 'war propaganda' (Kempf, 2007) and 'public relations' (Hanitzsch, 2007). This in itself is a very naïve criticism, as it seems to question the social responsibility or agency role of journalism per se. Kempf, like David Lyon, prefers to reserve the name 'good journalism' to describe the opposite of 'journalism of attachment' – journalism of detachment, albeit problematically. On the contrary, however, within the context of cosmopolitan global justice, good journalism is HRJ – a journalism that cares for all human beings, especially the more vulnerable people of global society.

This is in keeping with the advocacy journalism, which German political scientist Jorg Becker (2002: 14) sees as the political obligation of 'the media to participate and stand for peace of its accord' and – I will add – human rights. Becker looks to journalism not only to report reality 'as it is' but rather 'create reality, set examples and call for change' (Hanitzsch, 2007: 3). This is what Siebert et al. (1963, 1956) called the social responsibility of the journalism model; with their enjoyment of communications rights, journalists have a social responsibility to criticise those in power on behalf of peoples and societies, more or less serving as their watchdogs (Siebert et al., 1963/1956; Hohenberg, 1978; Cater, 1957; Cohen-Almaghor, 2001). Becker's call on journalists to uphold their moral responsibility of standing for peace is not just a call from a German thinker, but one that is grounded in international legal consensus enshrined in the Human Rights Charter. Article

3 of the 1978 UNESCO Declaration, for instance, states that 'the mass media have an important contribution to make to the strengthening of peace and international understanding and in countering racialism, apartheid and incitement to war' (UNESCO, 1980: 1). Article 19 of the 1948 UDHR stipulates that freedom of speech is to be enjoyed by all. To the extent that this responsibility is codified in the national constitutions of UN member states, it underscores how important it is in the scheme of the so-called 'good' professional journalism standards. In fact the MacBride UNESCO 1980 New International Communication Order Commissions Report sums up the relevance of this journalistic responsibility better: 'We live, alas, in an age stained by cruelty, torture, conflict and violence. These are not the natural human conditions; they are scourges to be eradicated. We should never resign ourselves to endure passively what can be cured' (Many Voices, One World, 1980: 177). To the extent that these human rights prescriptions resonate with the principles of the human rights-based journalism such as 'linkages to human rights standards', 'accountability', 'participation', non-discrimination and 'empowerment' (Beman and Calderbank, 2008: 24–26), they reinforce the social responsibility role of journalism as an agent of moral change. The social responsibility role of journalism, grounded in communication rights, underpins Nordenstreng's call for initiatives 'to systematically monitor what the media tell about the world with a view to improving media performance and contributing to media ethics' (2001: 1). Starkey (2007: 37) argues that 'holding governments to account is considered a legitimate journalistic activity', and it is a responsibility that most political journalists take seriously.

It is this social responsibility role that Lynch and McGoldrick (2005, quoted in McGoldrick, 2006: 4 and cited in Kempf, 2007: 3) allude to when they assert that journalists are responsible for how they report, and even for the creation of 'opportunities for society at large to consider and to value non-violent responses to conflict'. But Lynch and McGoldrick (2005) see this 'responsibility' not as an external goal imposed on journalism from outside, as, they argue, 'the obligation to create these opportunities results directly from the role assigned to journalism in democratic societies' (cited in Kempf, 2007: 3). Yet in a somewhat patronising response to Hanitsch's criticism of PJ as being an 'external goal' in the same light as advertising and public relations, Lynch and Galtung (2010: 91) contradictorily note that 'the external goal of peace is added instrumentally, to deliver more successfully on internal goals of accuracy and fairness'. HRJ, which, as an internal goal, consistently draws on the principles of the human rights-based approach to journalism mentioned above, can therefore potentially strengthen PJ's call on journalists to be socially more responsible in creating opportunities for the non-violent prevention or resolution of conflicts within the justpeace-building framework, without necessarily undermining the professional tenets of professional 'good' journalism, such as accuracy and fairness. In fact I argue that the internal goals of the HRJ principles assigned to journalism in democratic societies instrumentally reinforce professional journalism's internal goals of fairness and accuracy. In this respect Hanitsch's criticism of PJ as an external goal, which he compares to advertising or public relations, is untenable.

4.3 Conclusion

In conclusion, the problems of war journalism or mainstream journalism identified here are largely to blame for the under-reporting and/or misreporting of political and structural forms of violence – and, by extension, of human rights violations – that permeate today's news media. As Cottle argues, the alternative or 'corrective journalisms' discussed in his book *Mediatised Conflict* (2006), including the three kinds discussed in this chapter, have contributed insights and ideas towards a more radical conceptualisation, which I have called here HRJ, yet they have failed to provide such 'an encompassing conceptualisation of the complex communicative spaces of contemporary societies or how they could and should interact with these' (Cottle, 2006: 119). Hence, if there are problems with mainstream journalism largely informed as it is by the western liberal democracy model, and above all if the public journalism, citizen journalism and PJ models cannot sufficiently serve as a panacea, then it stands to reason that an alternative, or rather complementary, strand such as HRJ is required as a way forward in tackling these problems. This is the case I have tried to make as best as possible throughout this chapter.

HRJ complements the four orientations of the PJ model advanced by Galtung (1992, 1996) and supported by Lynch and McGoldrick (2005) – namely solution rather than victory, truth rather than propaganda, people rather than elite, and win–win rather than win–lose orientation – with four others, namely global rather than selective, biased in favour of rather than against vulnerable voices, pro-active (preventive) rather than reactive (prescriptive), and attached to rather than detached from victims of violence. With these complementary attributes of HRJ, PJ will be justified in laying claims to the four clear values of 'humanitarianism, truth, holism and empowerment' identified by

Lovasen (2008) in support of the Galtung model. These four values in a way resonate with the principles of the rights based-approach to journalism: participation, accountability, non-discrimination, empowerment and linkages to human rights standards informed by negative and positive rights on one hand and by negative and positive peace on the other hand (Beman and Calderbank, 2008, Galtung, 1992, 1996; Nowak, 2005, see also Shaw, 2011 for a detailed discussion of this connection). I argue that HRJ upholds the internal principles of human rights-based journalism, which encompass the tenets of professional journalism, to address the structural imbalances of global society at large and in this way to prevent or resolve direct physical violence within a justpeace framework.

When journalists employ human wrongs journalism (empathy distance frames), communication is bound to be manipulated in favour of the dominant classes of society. This will have the knock-on effect of discouraging advocacy or intervention, which, on the contrary, is encouraged by HRJ (diagnostic critical empathy frames). I now turn to the conceptualisation of the reporting of distant humanitarian interventions in the forthcoming chapter, where (among other things) concepts such as evocative reporting/empathy distance frames (human wrongs journalism) and diagnostic reporting/critical empathy frames (HRJ) are explored.

5
The Dynamics and Challenges of Reporting Humanitarian Interventions

For humanitarian intervention to be legitimate, and hence cosmopolitan, it must be apolitical; that is, it must not be influenced by issues of politics such as national or geo-strategic interests.[1] It must be based on human rights and global justice, not on politics. It must be seen to be free from all forms of historical baggage, be they political, economic or cultural. However, Africa is often seen in the West through the lenses of the sixteenth and seventeenth centuries, the days of the trans-Atlantic slave trade when Africans were largely seen to be good only as commodities to be sold.

The 1990s saw the notion of humanitarian intervention facing somewhat tough challenges, especially in Africa and the former Yugoslavia, which left human rights scholars to ask some difficult questions. Why do states intervene to address human rights violations in some countries and not in others, or when and how should they intervene, and when, if ever, should they not? What is considered as just war/intervention or unjust war/non-intervention, or why intervene in the former Yugoslavia and not in Africa? Or, to be more specific, why Kosovo and not Sierra Leone, when the conflicts in the two countries peaked almost at the same time in the late nineties? What are the implications of this politics of human rights for human rights journalism (HRJ), and more generally for human rights within the cosmopolitan context of global justice? In order to attempt a theoretical conceptualisation of possible answers to the above questions, this chapter covers the following three theorisations of reporting humanitarian interventions: the journalistic framing of humanitarian intervention in Africa; evocative versus diagnostic reporting; and political context and HRJ.

5.1 The journalistic framing of humanitarian intervention in Africa

In this section I argue that historical frames – stereotypical representations based on events, issues and myths located in the past – which are found often in news media discourse, can skew the way distant wars are perceived. This can have far-reaching implications for international humanitarian interventions within a cosmopolitan framework. Drawing on Alison Preston's typology of distance versus critical framing, I argue that the putative inertia of the international community to intervene on humanitarian grounds in order to end these crises was informed more by historical empathy/distance frames than by empathy/critical frames in the mainstream Western news media discourse. Alison Preston (1996) discusses two modes of reporting distance crises/wars/conflicts: first, *distance framing*, where the style of coverage creates emotional distance between the audience and the people suffering in a conflict; and second, *support framing*, where official policy is, in effect, deferred. Distance and support framing are implicitly supportive of a government policy opposed to military intervention and, as such, they either implicitly or explicitly promote a policy of non-intervention. On the other hand, critical empathy frames promote the policy of intervention because they help illuminate the underlying causes of the conflict and encourage human rights-based approaches to end it.

Media researchers have placed much emphasis on political factors, especially the one relating to the question of national identity (Allan and Zelizer, 2004), in shaping the reporting of distant wars. Others, such as Herman and Chomsky (1988), point to the importance of economic factors in the equation. While I recognise the importance of these factors, I argue that those associated with the cultural subjectivities of journalists in wartime contribute in a far more important way – by reinforcing the 'us' and 'them' binary, which has a knock-on effect on international response – towards ending human suffering in distant war-torn countries. As is demonstrated later in this chapter and subsequent chapters of this book, these historical or cultural frames largely explain the lack of concern for the protection of the fundamental human rights of people to live in peace in marginalised societies like those in Africa; and that concern is only manifested when the political and/or economic interests of the intervening country or agency are threatened. At stake here is the role of the media in the promotion of human rights. Hence the media, or what has come to be called 'the CNN factor' (Robinson, 2002b), makes up the fourth factor that shapes or influences the journalistic framing of humanitarian intervention.

In the context of journalistic framing, to frame means 'to select some aspects of a perceived reality and make them more salient in a communicating text in such a way as to promote a particular problem definition, causal interpretation, moral evaluation, and/or treatment recommendation' (Entman, 1993: 51–8). Entman, the leading scholar on news framing, referred to news frames as existing at two levels: 'as mentally stored principles for information processing and as characteristics of the news text'. However, Entman goes on to say that news frames also describe attributes of the news itself. 'Frames reside in the specific properties of the news narratives that encourage those perceiving and thinking about events to develop particular understandings of them' (ibid.). They are constructed and embedded in the key words, concepts, metaphors, visual images and symbols normally fore-grounded in a news narrative. Scheufele (1999: 103), however, sees news frames as 'lacking clear conceptual definitions and relying on context specific, rather than generally applicable operationalisations'. Scholars such as Iyenger and Kinder (1987), or McCombs and Shaw (1972), or Weaver (1987) have operationalised framing in line with other concepts such as agenda-setting and priming; Weaver in fact sees framing as an extension of agenda-setting. M'bayo et al. (2000) note that most mass communication researchers in the 1960s and 1970s, for instance Bernard Cohen, tended to attribute a good deal of power to mass media in the agenda-setting process. Mass media have the power to manipulate public opinion to the extent that it has come to be widely accepted that the event or issue that is constantly in the media domain at any given time is automatically considered to be the most important item occupying the minds of the public. In this way, mass media play an important role in setting the agenda of what the public is thinking and talking about. This is in fact what Piers Robinson called 'the CNN factor' (Robinson, 2002b). Yet the public, through public leaders and civil society, can also set the agenda for the media; this is what Virgil Hawkins (2002) calls the 'other side of the CNN factor'. As Rob Anderson et al. note, journalists, public officials and celebrities play an important role in setting the agenda for the news:

> By deciding what and who is news, the press emphasizes some values over others. We do not argue that news determines values, because media content must be analysed in the context of society, culture, and environment, yet news remains the most consistent source of information that people consider reliable, truthful, and accurate.

Therefore, its values certainly affect and reflect our values as citizens. In the world of news, people with power, authority, and celebrity prevail over the weak, disenfranchised, and unknown. The rich prevail over the poor, the official over the unofficial, the knowledgeable over the ignorant and the smart over the voiceless. The important prevails over the common, the unexpected over the routine, the dramatic over the casual, and so forth, through the list of attributes. The news also bestows authority and defines and bestows importance in some cases, while at the same time, it withholds authority and importance in others. (Anderson et al., 1994: 42–3)

The elite and the rich play an important role in the process of agenda-setting and, by extension, of framing. This is because their views more or less dominate the news media discourse. The poor and the weak are thus left in the margins of power play, which is central to the agenda-setting process.

In this book I am more concerned with framing as the construction of social reality, which draws on McQuail's observation that mass communication study is 'based on the premise that the media have significant effects' (McQuail, 1994). Media construct social reality by 'framing images of reality [...] in a predictable and patterned way' (McQuail, 1994: 331). Yet media effects are limited by an interaction between mass media and audiences. Media discourse is the process by which individuals construct meaning, while public opinion is formed as part of the process of meaning being developed and crystallised in public discourse by journalists. In the context of political communication, framing has to be seen and used on the basis of this social constructivism (Gameson and Modigliani, 1989). The frames of reference that readers and viewers use to make sense of, and discuss, public events or issues are set up by mass media discourse (Tuchman, 1978). They give the story a 'spin', taking into account their institutional constraints and professional judgements. It is, however, important to note that cultural and social factors impact in a very important way on the processing and interpretation of news by journalists and audiences alike.

Mainstream journalists tend to use frames whose logic is drawn from the most penetrated and unquestioned cultural values, myths, and ideologies – perspectives least likely to be challenged, or perhaps even identified, by audience and journalist (Hallin, 1986: 22–25). News frames that contain our most deeply held cultural subjectivities will therefore appear as 'natural' expositions of reality (Gitlin 1980: 6) – commonsense portrayals rather than constructed interpretative frameworks. Furthermore, the line between the historical framing of war and the cultural bias often demonstrated by western media journalists who cover distant wars is often blurred. The most commonly used historical frames in western media news discourse of conflicts or crises in Africa include 'historical baggage' (seeing Africa in the prehistoric era of exploration, or through the lens of the slave trade era of the sixteenth and seventeenth centuries): ethnic hatred (seeing Africa as only one country with many tribes fighting against each other) and a dark, primitive and hopeless image (seeing Africa as a 'basket case' where poverty and misery are rife, and where nothing can be done to change things) (Shaw, 2007: 356).

Historical frame, which former BBC Africa correspondent George Alagiah called 'historical baggage', often makes journalists in wartime see a particular war, or some aspects of it, through historical lenses. At the 'Reporting the World' Round Table in London (16 May 2001), New African Editor Baffour Ankomah explained Alagiah's reference to the 'historical baggage' factor: 'Africa is often perceived in the West through the lenses of the sixteenth and seventeenth centuries, the days of the trans-Atlantic slave trade when Africans were largely seen to be good only as commodities to be sold; it is for the same reason that the Western media see and present Africa as the 'dark continent' (Ankomah a, 2001: 3). Beau Riffenburgh (1993) went further down memory lane, to source the 'African historical baggage' to as far back as the exploration period before the birth of Jesus Christ. For example, he made reference to the great exploration of Africa and the Arctic, going back to ancient Greek literature. According to Riffenburgh, this great exploration began in 457 BC, when Herodotus sailed down the river Nile as far as the Aswan dam, adding that exploration is a memorable process of identification. Riffenburgh notes that the dominant Anglo-Saxon perception of the rest of the world as the 'other' owes its true origins to this historic adventure. For the eighteenth and nineteenth centuries explorers, he added, nature is viewed in terms of either the 'sublime' or the 'picturesque'. The notion of 'sublime', which influenced great philosophers such as Burke, Kant and Didérot, portrays things that are marvellous, surprising and impressive as well as ones that boost the spirit, such as divine glory.[2] Riffenburg notes, however, that the bottom line of Burke's interpretation of the notion of 'sublime' was terror when one is confronted with the unknown. According to Burke's classifications, no part of nature was more terrible or sublime than the Arctic.[3] Hence, in taking on board the 'sublime' and the 'picturesque' in the coverage of voyages of discovery, in novels and the arts, Riffenburg argues that the Anglo-Saxon public eventually developed a stereotypical representation of the north of Africa; hence the view that the use of clichés and stereotypes in news media discourse is far from being a new phenomenon.

This North–South cultural divide continued well throughout the slave trade, pre-colonial, colonial and postcolonial eras, with slight variations from one region to another. For some reason, Africa remains on the receiving end of some of the worst implications of this 'us' and 'them' cultural binary. As Kieh puts it, the 'sanctity of state sovereignty', informed by the primacy of the Westphalia Treaty of 1648, constrained international intervention in civil wars during the Cold War era (Kieh, 2000, see also Chopra and Weiss, 1992). The Westphalia norm was premised on the argument that states will invoke humanitarian reasons while pursuing other objectives through military intervention. The 1648 Treaty of Westphalia, signed at the end of the Thirty Years' War in Europe, was the agreement that made the principle of state sovereignty a fundamental basis of international relations, as it came to be enshrined later in the 1948 United Nations (UN) Charter. Yet, as Chris Brown (2002) points out, the primacy attached to state sovereignty in the Westphalia system was never as rigid as is often believed, and, even before North Atlantic Treaty Organisation (NATO)'s 1999 attack on former Yugoslavia, western states carried out numerous interventions before the twentieth century[4] However, the post-Cold War witnessed a paradigmatic shift as the international community began to relax the Westphalia doctrine to accommodate intervention in countries facing conflicts that involved serious human rights violations. Yet Africa witnessed the most devastating wars during this period. Post-independence Africa has been plagued by civil wars, military coups and other forms of political crises (Copson, 1996). Copson summarised the situation this way: 'During the 1980s, Africa was torn by nine wars, numerous other instances of large-scale violent conflicts, and a kaleidoscope of coups and demonstrations. Those hostilities exacted a great toll on Africa in terms of the destruction of human life, cultural damage, economic disruption, and lost investment opportunities' (Copson, 1996: 20). We saw how humanitarian intervention came 'too little too late' in Ethiopia, Somalia, Rwanda and elsewhere in Africa – after all the human suffering and deaths, which thus defeated its whole cosmopolitan purpose.

Martin Wight (1966, cited in Brown, 2002: 155), a leading international society theorist, argues that the norm of non-intervention is central to the Westphalia order, but that, in accordance with 'Western values in international relations', this norm may be breached in response to 'gross violations of human dignity'. Brown recognises the

historical grounding of Wight's proposition, but only with two important qualifications: first, Wight does not distinguish sufficiently between
relations among the core members of the system and their relations
with others; and, second, it is by no means clear that notions of
'human dignity' have remained constant throughout the last 400 years
(Brown, 2002: 155). Contributing to the historical context of humanitarian intervention over the last two centuries, Martha Finnemore
argues that 'this period has seen a change in terms of who is considered to be "human"' in the nineteenth century (Finnemore, 1966,
cited in Brown, 2002: 155); humanitarian interventions were carried
out by the western powers primarily to rescue Christian communities under threat from non-Christian rulers – for example, Greece in
the 1820s and the Maronite Christians of Lebanon in 1862–3. She
notes that, sadly enough, the often more obnoxious oppression of non-
European, non-Christian communities attracted much less attention –
especially, of course, when actually conducted by European states. She
argues that this trend has changed in the late twentieth century the
taxonomy of the 'human' is now considered to be genuinely universal, and interventions of this period are generally seen to be 'less overtly
ethnocentric' – warning, however, 'that those states with power to intervene are still disproportionately of European origin and still inclined
to regard oppression of fellow Europeans more seriously than that of
non-Europeans' (Finnemore, 1966, cited in Brown, 2002: 155).

Although, as Chris Brown notes, Finnemore's work represents a genuine advance on that of Wight, it fails to capture the ambiguities of the
way in which ideas of race and empire worked for the expansionist powers of the Westphalia doctrine, particularly the manner in which ideas of
racial inferiority and superiority actually proved compatible with some
kinds of humanitarian concern for the welfare of the so-called 'lesser
races'. As the principal motivation for calls to end the slave trade, Brown
refers to British internal politics – which aimed to satisfy the influential church and other non-conformist libertarian community leaders –
rather than to any genuine humanitarian concern for racial equality. He also points to the economic motive of 'undermining Britain's
competitors – such as Spain and Portugal, which were still reliant on
slave labour to power their economies'. Yet, as Brown argues, whether
or not these are the real motives informing humanitarian interventions,
the positive effects of these interventions would not be undermined
(Brown, 2002: 155–6). Brown disagrees with the view that intervention
to protect human rights can be taken to be non-humanitarian because
there is an implicit materialist motive driving it.[5]

It therefore stands to reason that, if humanitarian intervention is a 'coercive action' (Brown, 2002) taken by an external agency in a sovereign state with the expressed, but not exclusive, intention to protect the welfare of the members of that state, the inertia of the international community as far as Africa is concerned raises a fundamental question of global justice. International relations scholar Hedley Bull (1984) defines intervention as 'dictatorial or coercive interference, by an outside party or parties, in the sphere of jurisdiction of a sovereign state, or more broadly of an independent political community' (1984: 1). However, Caney (2000) dismisses Bull's words 'dictatorial' and 'interference' as being too pejorative and partial, and suggests instead 'coercive action'.

Humanitarian intervention itself can take either the form of aid programmes to help victims of war or various humanitarian crises or the form of military intervention for the protection and promotion of human rights – or, in some cases, both. If, as Simon Caney (2000) argues, military humanitarian intervention involving the international community can be justified to protect human rights, the question remains as to why there was a lack of political will on the part of the international community to act quickly in Ethiopia, Somalia, Rwanda, Liberia and Sierra Leone, compared to Kosovo and other parts of the world. John Stuart Mill's utilitarian argument of non-intervention provides that the Westphalia Treaty can only be broken in order to help a political community aggressed by another to seek liberation; in order to protect, by way of counter-intervention, the interests of a political community facing external aggression; or, finally, when the violation of human rights assumes unimaginable proportions, leading to genocide or massacre (Mill, 1859).

In defending the moral basis of humanitarian intervention, Terry Nardin (2002: 70) points to the more traditional interpretation of natural law or common morality, which sees humanitarian intervention 'as an expression of the basic moral duty to protect the innocent from violence'. As the realities of Kosovo and Rwanda dawned upon the world in the face of an increasingly weak UN system, the International Commission on Intervention and State Sovereignty (ICISS), an independent panel made up of scholars and political leaders and funded by the Canadian government, came up with a groundbreaking report called 'The Responsibility to Protect'. In this report the ICISS 'insisted that the primary responsibility for protecting civilians lay with the host state and that outside intervention could only be contemplated if the host proved either unwilling or unable to fulfill its responsibilities' (ICISS,

2001). Yet, as Bellamy puts it, 'the incorporation of the responsibility to protect into the outcome document of the 2005 World Summit has done little to resolve the challenge of preventing future Rwandas and Kosovos' (Bellamy, 2008: 167). Bellamy argues that, in the responsibility to protect doctrine, 'powerful states are no more likely to feel obliged to act to save distant strangers and there is no more likelihood of agreement about what to do in particular cases' – such as mass killings or ethnic cleansing – than they were in the case of Rwanda and Kosovo, respectively (ibid., p. 169). Bellamy calls on states to revisit some of the key questions the ICISS raised: '*who*, precisely, has a responsibility to protect? *When* is that responsibility acquired? *What* does the responsibility to protect entail? And *how* do we know when the responsibility to protect has been divested?' He warns that failing to do this risks the real danger of states hiding behind the language of the responsibility to protect to legally justify 'inaction and irresponsibility' (ibid.).

Thus, so far, the responsibility to protect doctrine is yet to bring a meaningful change in the norm of humanitarian intervention, in both a prescriptive and a permissive sense: prescriptive referring to the need to persuade powerful states to take responsibility to protect people whose human rights are threatened; permissive referring to the political costs of intervention in protecting people from extreme suffering without UN Security Council approval. Six years on since the doctrine was introduced, it has, importantly, entered the international diplomatic agenda and spearheaded the setting up of a 'Global Centre and network of regional affiliates committed to advocacy and research, and international coalition of non-governmental organizations (NGOs), a journal and book series, and a research fund sponsored by the Australian government' (ibid., p. 143). Moreover, it is now used by governments and humanitarian NGOs as a diplomatic language of emergencies, to justify 'behavior, cajole compliance, and demand international action' (ibid.). Yet, as Bellamy puts it, the responsibility to protect doctrine remains contentious in many areas. Critics still point to it being dangerous and imperialist, poised to undermine the sovereignty of the weak nations, with little consideration for the protection of the human rights of the most vulnerable populations. Another serious problem is that it is still being abused by the strong powers in their attempt to control the weak states that fail to cooperate in the furtherance of their geostrategic interests. For example, recently, the French in Myanmar and the Russians in Georgia used the doctrine to 'justify the actual or potential use of coercive force' when there was no clear evidence of the failure of those states to protect populations against acts of gross human rights violations – whereas neither they nor other big powers, attempted any such actions in Somalia, Afghanistan and Iraq, despite the recording of ongoing gross human rights violations of populations in these countries (ibid., p. 144).

What is more, the responsibility to protect doctrine is apparently silent about a more pro-active and preventive strategy, which is more human rights-based and therefore more in line with the approach preferred by HRJ. Within the context of HRJ, journalists also have a responsibility to help state and non-state actors to protect the rights of threatened distant populations, and at the same time to call to account countries that abuse the responsibility to protect doctrine in order to advance their national or geo-strategic interests, or countries that hide behind the somewhat ambiguous interpretation of the doctrine to legitimise non-intervention and irresponsibility.

Little wonder, therefore, that realists are sceptical of the motives of intervening states and, by extension, of the likelihood of genuine humanitarian intervention (Morgenthau, 1967: 430). Benn and Peters (1959: 361) argue that 'states rarely act out of altruism and contend that they will usually intervene to further their national interests rather than the fundamental rights of people abroad'. Brown describes the emphasis realists place on motivation as 'being little puzzling' and points to the widely held assumption that for 'an action to count as humanitarian it must be motivated unambiguously by genuine cosmopolitan values'. He, however, argues that the 'motives of state behavior should not actually undermine humanitarian efforts' (Brown, 2002: 154–155). Yet this is exactly what happened in the case of some of Africa's most serious conflicts: the hasty humanitarian backpedaling in Somalia and Rwanda when these 'motives' were no longer considered to be important deserve special mention. This raises the question of the cultural subjectivities of journalists whose framing of the humanitarian discourse in terms of 'their problems' (and 'not ours') factored in a very big way in this humanitarian U-turn. As Brauman and Backmann put it, the implication of the western media in these drawbacks in humanitarian intervention becomes even more glaring when the coverage of the crises in Yugoslavia and of the Gulf War by both state and private TV channels in the western countries is juxtaposed with coverage of the crises in Somalia and Rwanda, where even before the withdrawal of humanitarian efforts the focus was more on images of emaciated children than on massacres (1996: 24).

As Pattison (2010) notes, the problem of inconsistency in recent interventions has been the subject of one of the most frequent criticisms of humanitarian intervention. The NATO intervention in Kosovo, but not in Sierra Leone, Somalia, Rwanda (Shaw, 2007), or in the DR Congo (Damrosch, 2000), easily comes to mind. This selectivity gives the impression, albeit problematically, that 'some are more worth protecting than others' (ICISS, 2001: 150). This smacks of selective justice. 'If humanitarian intervention really is to be humanitarian, the objection continues, it has to be consistently applied whenever there is a serious humanitarian crisis' (Pattison, 2010: 170). In line with this thinking, Edward Luttwak (2000: 04) asks: 'What does it mean for the morality of a supposedly moral rule, when it is applied arbitrarily, against some but not others?' Pattison (2010), however, argues that there can be a problem with this criticism, because there can be cases where, for humanitarian intervention to be effective, the selectivity principle is 'desirable' and should be applied. He cites the case of two countries, Niger and Chad, facing crisis at the same time; and notes that it would be desirable for France to choose to intervene in Niger if it thinks this intervention would be more effective and less costly compared to that in Chad. However, he agrees with Tharoor and Daws (2001: 27), who caution that this does not suggest that we should ignore humanitarian crises where interventions will not be effective. 'Other measures of the responsibility to protect should be employed instead, short of military intervention, such as international criminal prosecutions and military, diplomatic, and economic sanctions' (Pattison, 2010: 170).

5.2   Evocative versus diagnostic reporting

5.2.1   Evocative reporting

The human interest frame or, better still, the humanitarian news discourse is mostly associated with the evocative style of reporting, which tends to sensitise public opinion on the suffering of the victims of conflicts or humanitarian disasters. The notion of humanitarian news discourse is grounded on the dramatic mediation on the plight of the poor victims of wars and other crises. The ultimate goal is to evoke public sympathy for these victims and to boost relief donations from rich western countries. In order to achieve this, human interest frames are often peppered with stereotypes and clichés that are emotive at best, if not pejorative in some cases (Philippe, 2001). Here the emphasis is more on raising awareness to boost aid programmes than to address human rights violations. In communicating the activities of humanitarian agencies, it is often difficult to draw a line between political and humanitarian discourses. Yet journalists covering humanitarian crisis are often influenced by the relief operations of these agencies. Simeant defines a humanitarian situation as one of 'emergency', where some urgent reaction is needed to save lives (Simeant, 2001). The mediation of humanitarian discourse is nothing new in journalism practice. Towards the end of the nineteenth century, one of the first American war correspondents, W. L. Stillman, is remembered for his articles published in the *Times*, which gave rise to what we know today as 'humanitarian discourse'. As Palmer 2003: 40–41) puts it:

> The emotion stimulated by this appeal to assist Christian brothers in distress, mobilized British prime minister Lord Beaconsfield Disraeli (1804–1881) to observe: "Britain (does not) necessarily have an interest at stake in Montenegro, but the government is obliged to take into consideration the enthusiastic support generated by the letters published in the *Times*"

However, going by Karl Marx's declaration that '[m]en can settle for only those problems they can resolve', former president and co-founder of Doctors without Borders Rony Brauman said: 'TV news gives us nothing but emotions that are supposed to move us' (Brauman and Backmann, 1996: 24). The production and transmission of such news are therefore inevitably subjected to an automatic selection process, made possible, according to Brauman, on two levels:

> On the physical level, the televised news is subjected to durable and rhythmic constraints which limit the coverage of more than two international crises per one newscast. On the symbolic level of the 'status of the victim' on the other hand power is seen as an effigy of unjust suffering and killing of the innocent. (Brauman and Backmann, 1996: 24)

Brauman noted that the idea of humanitarianism was born in the new atmosphere signalling the end of the Cold War, after the fall of the Berlin Wall in 1989. As soon as it became clear that the state was showing less interest in taking care of the victims of humanitarian crises, privately run organisations began gradually to step in to fill the void (Brauman and Backmann, 1996: 24). Thus, as state structures began to crumble one by one in the face of the new spirit of globalisation that followed the end of the Cold War, humanitarian organisations began to take centre stage in intervening in crises to halt human suffering. The 1980s therefore marked the effective beginning of the creation of many humanitarian agencies working in close collaboration with the media. Underscoring the link between humanitarian agencies and the media, Brauman notes: 'In the refugee camps in Cambodia and Afghanistan, in the hills of the planet where history itself appeared to have started the following three appeared in the wake of the crisis – the aid worker, the victim and the journalist [...] were all for better or for worse symbolically united in the cause of global humanity' (Brauman and Backmann, 1996: 33). Small wonder, therefore, that these humanitarian agencies exact a lot of influence in setting the agenda for western media journalists in their reporting of humanitarian crises. The fall-out has been an overemphasis of humanitarian discourse or evocative reporting, as against political discourse or diagnostic reporting.

Evocative reporting is that style of reporting which more or less concentrates either on spinning the national and geopolitical interests of the home countries of members of the western media or on the humanitarian angle of the news, with the primary aim of sensitising public opinion. It is the type of journalism that renders journalists largely gullible to manipulation by public and private individuals and corporations. Evocative or dramatic journalism encourages journalists covering distant conflicts or other humanitarian crises, for example in Africa, to focus on images of the emaciated child, images that contribute not only to misinforming the public but to distracting their attention from the real political issues – knowledge of which may be used to prevent or tackle the crises. Many obstacles no doubt stand in the way of normative journalistic practice. Pejorative and biased representation of the 'other' has always been at the centre of the problem. Evocative reporting largely draws on stereotypes that mirror human suffering, such as the images of emaciated children and the grim faces of mothers trying to calm them, with the aim of promoting humanitarian assistance. This type of reporting often ignores the political dimension of a humanitarian crisis, in particular the analysis of its causes, which is typical of diagnostic reporting. Evocative reporting is that type of reporting that is punctuated by stereotypical representations – by myths rather than facts; the bottom line here is not whether the piece of news is true, but whether it is emotionally strong enough to provoke a humanitarian discourse that is capable of mobilising the public to contribute more towards the efforts of the humanitarian agencies in saving the lives of the victims.

5.2.2 Diagnostic reporting

In a literary sense, when we talk about political discourse we are basically talking about communication involving the whole gamut of variables at the centre of the politics of a country; especially its nationalism, democracy, freedom of expression, rule of law and diplomacy. In a cognitive sense, political discourse means a political interpretation or context of a given event or phenomenon. As far as the humanitarian crises featuring in the mainstream western media – such as civil or inter-state wars in distant countries like Africa and Asia – are concerned, there is very little evidence to suggest the prioritisation of the political context or diagnosis of these crises. Martin Shaw proposes a two-fold solution to the problem of representing distant conflicts: first, the 'distant wars and the situations of those fighting' and suffering must be seen and ideologically represented as significant. For this to happen, information about, and images of, peoples' sufferings 'must be *shown* to other members of global society'. Second, those fighting and suffering must also be represented politically by ensuring that 'their needs and values' are forcefully articulated and advocated in the global arena (Shaw, 1996: 11). Shaw argues that, so far, participants and victims of distance violence are only represented *indirectly* by the western media, as part of the global civil society. He sees this as a problem, as it undermines the diagnostic angle of mediation, because this representation often fails to capture the exact perspective of the participants' and victims' needs, values and experiences. Shaw insists on the alternative paradigm, of allowing them to be actively involved in the communication of their own information and images so as to shed a proper light on the factors igniting or propelling the violence (Shaw, 1996). As this book intends to demonstrate, Shaw's alternative paradigm of diagnostic reporting or mediation still largely remains more normative than real. Shaw identifies two forms of diagnostic representation that he sees as mutually dependent: 'representation in the sense of knowledge requires political representation to be effective, and political representation requires information and imagery to inform it'. In other words, Shaw is saying that civil society needs to be properly informed about problems such as violence in order to be able to make and implement informed decisions in the political arena to change things, while at the same time civil society needs effective political representation to ensure that it is properly informed about these problems. Shaw points to civil society and the media as the two major institutional contexts corresponding to the two forms of representation. Civil society is in 'general the sphere of broad cultural, ideological and political representation of society', while 'communications media are the principal arena of informational representation in which images are produced, transmitted and consumed' (Shaw, 1996: 12).

Diagnostic reporting, while covering the national, geopolitical and humanitarian angles of the news, pays more attention to analysing its political context; that is, it puts emphasis on explaining why things went wrong up to the crisis, instead of just telling the story as it is. In other words diagnostic or political context reporting is a style of reporting that does not only speak about a given humanitarian crisis, but also attempts to reflect critically on the reasons of the crisis; and it does this in order to find a peaceful way out of it and to prevent something similar from happening in the future. It is largely in this respect that diagnostic reporting is similar to what Jake Lynch referred to as 'peace journalism', and to a very large extent to what I have referred to in this book as 'human rights journalism'.

Speaking almost the same language, Mathieu Brugidou describes diagnostic reporting as a deconstruction or analysis that helps us to get an idea of the reason why some situations or crises occurred; its imperative is, 'provide various descriptions but make sure there is an element of formatting to the narrative to make way for the introduction of an angle that is critically reflective of the political reality' (Brugidou, 1993: 40). To understand Brugidou's definition better, we need to deconstruct the journalistic messages that take on board to a sufficient degree the reflective dimension of a situation. Brugidou notes that this type of reporting can better be understood as the process of 'identifying the variables which condition the dimensions of a given text: relationship to sources, normative or non-normative posture, and emphasis on the narrative of the fact or putting it into perspective' (Brugidou, 1993: 40).

However, most journalists in the western media who cover wars or other humanitarian crises in distant countries (Africa, Asia) often focus only on the narration of events and issues, or at best on a dramatic evocative angle, and not necessarily on the political factors or contexts or processes that produced these situations in the first place. This lack of analysis in the reporting of distant crises by the mainstream media was the subject of an Organisation of Economic Cooperation and Development (OECD) forum panel discussion on the role of the media in development to which I participated – in Paris, in May 2005. A Danish journalist, Jan Lund, said that journalists can inform the public but don't have the time to educate it; 'in the digital media age people go elsewhere to find quickly the information you cannot give them'.

However, I countered that it is not enough to show images that may provoke people to send aid to victims of political violence; it is in fact more important to educate the readers by giving them the context of the news, to help them to understand why a given crisis is happening, so that they can influence policy decisions designed to address it and to prevent future crisis. Another panelist, Mr Guerrier of Radio France International, agreed that, while the media had work to do, perspective was needed. 'Feelings and emotions are key to (the) way we present news and how we provide accounts of events,' he said. Moreover, the response from the floor, which favoured the role of the media in defining the problems of the news, showed how popular the ideals of HRJ are to readers and audiences.[6]

It must, nonetheless, be recognised that, in the coverage of breaking news, journalists easily become vulnerable to drawing on sometimes problematic stereotypes for purely professional reasons, such as speed in the processing of news. Thus, in order to succeed in achieving diagnostic reporting – and, by extension, HRJ – journalists must attempt to strike a balance between this and the many demands of their professional practice, which also include the 12 news values outlined by Galtung and Ruge (1973).

Galtung and Ruge's 12 news values are widely accepted as critical factors that influence the journalists' selection of what event or issue to report and how to go about reporting it. However, while Fowler agrees that these 12 news values are worth studying in detail, he warns that it is 'worth reflecting' about the extent to which these factors are 'cultural' rather than 'natural'. The 12 factors are FI-*frequency* (how often); F2-*threshold* (volume or size of problem/casualties; F2/1-absolute intensity/F2/2-intensity increase (seriousness in terms of level and size, respectively); F3-unambiguity (news should not be confusing); F4-meaningfulness (news should be important); F4/1-cultural proximity (one should be able to connect culturally to what is happening); F4/2-relevance (something culturally far away can be relevant indirectly by virtue of some other interests); F5-consonance (events should involve people); F5/1-predictability (what is anticipated should come to pass); F5/2-demand (the piece of news should be eagerly awaited); F6-unexpectedness (no warning); F6/1-unpredictability (dramatic character); F6/2-scarcity (the piece of news should be about something that is very rare); F7-continuity (what is defined as news should continue as news for some time); F8-composition (meaning how readily available the information on it is); F9-reference to elite nations (that is, to important countries); F10-reference to elite people (that is, to important people); F11-reference to persons (that is, to people); and F12-reference to something negative (Galtung and Ruge, 1973; also cited in Fowler, 2001: 13).

According to Fowler (2001), there is enough evidence to suggest the extent to which the selection criteria for newsworthiness are, in Hall's words, 'socially constructed' (Hall, 1978, cited in Fowler). Thus social events exist only in the exact way they are formatted by the media; news production is first and foremost made up of representations largely reflective of social agents. As Nossek puts it, 'the journalist's definition of an event – as "ours" or "theirs" – determines whether the event is selected by the journalist and editor as news and how it will be covered' (Nossek 2007: 41). The challenge for journalists who wish to practise HRJ therefore largely depends on their ability to manage these cultural subjectivity factors in such a way as not to let them undermine the overall quality of their journalism, which is based on human rights and justice. As Brugidou affirms, only a journalist who is capable of embedding, in the news discourse, a strategic analysis that is based on a diverse range of facts will succeed in managing the balance between HRJ and their cultural subjectivities (Brugidou, 1993).

Moreover, it is important to deconstruct the ideological frames linked to stereotypical representations in mainstream media discourse to determine how they undermine the practice of HRJ. Stereotypical representations are often framed by the media drawing on clichés and other nuanced words that are capable of reflecting politically focused images. These clichés and expressions, like the masks in ancient Greek theatre, invoke positive or negative images of events and people, often without anything in return, and always as a substitute for credible information. A case in point is when veteran CBS television news presenter Dan Rather retrospectively alluded to the black civil rights movement and to the student demonstrations against the war as 'civil disturbances of the 1960s'. If he had explained them as 'movements for peace and justice' or 'demonstrations against military intervention and for racial equality', a different message would have been sent (Parenti, 1993). As Nobel Laureate for Literature, Wole Soyinka spoke as follows at the World Press Congress in the Japanese city of Kobe in May 1998: 'We are not necessarily asking for an equal attention of the world media but simply that we try to inject some minimum of common sense that the editorial space and time used to focus on events should be determined by reasoning' (Batumike, 2000: 60–61).

5.3 Political context and human rights journalism

Political discourses on given acts of violence that take place in distant societies must contain not only the dramatic images of the plight of the victims, but also reflections of the real experiences and challenges of these victims, as well as of the perpetrators of these unfortunate violent actions. This is in order to determine the underlying problems and their causes and to be able to formulate better and more constructive approaches towards resolving and preventing them from happening again in the future. It is only when journalists are able to achieve this that they can be said to be on the path of practising diagnostic journalism – journalism based on human rights and global justice, a journalism where every voice and every concern are equally important. Within the context of diagnostic reporting, all the concerns and factors, be they internal or external, behind, say, the deteriorating political situation of a given distant society must be taken into consideration. A deteriorating political situation or crisis can take different forms – such as civil wars, inter-state wars, state collapse, corruption, bad governance, poverty, forced migration, underdevelopment, exploitative policies of the rich and powerful over the poor and weak, and all others, which in the short or long term lead to violence and instability.

Unfortunately, however, the journalism that we know today is one that reinforces rather than challenges the concentration of power in the hands of the few powerful sections of society. This imbalance is even more evident in the face of humanitarian crisis where only the blood of the powerful is considered not worth shedding. In short, it is the journalism that reinforces the status quo of the powerful against the weak. As Sonwalker puts it, 'it nurtures and reinforces a power geometry that is inherently unfair – some versions of reality are routinely presented as *the* version of reality and the marginalisation of the life situation of some sections of society in news columns is routinely presented as normal' (Sonwalker, 2007: 247). Seib refers to this news selectivity as 'journalism of convenience' (Seib, 2002: 2, cited in Sonwalker, 2007: 247); but Sonwalker describes it as 'banal journalism' – 'preferring some events and issues to others, limiting the range of perspectives offered, reflecting the priorities of the dominant power groupings in society' (Sonwalker, 2007: 247; see also Sonwalker, 2005). Within the context of HRJ, justice and fair play must be the watch words, and if ever there is going to be any imbalance in the equation, then this must favour the weak and the vulnerable against the powerful, and not vice versa. Having said that, it is important to recognise that there have been some very few cases where the concerns of the weak have been to some extent advanced in the face of adversity within the context of HRJ, leading to some positive outcomes such as the military humanitarian intervention to create the Kurdish safe havens.

Media scholars have been preoccupied with the increasing role of the media in setting the agenda in most western capitals, sometimes canalising into massive international military and humanitarian interventions in some of the world's hotspots in the 1980s and 1990s. Martin Shaw, for example, argues that the 'virtually unprecedented proposal for Kurdish safe havens' was made possible by the often highly critical media coverage of Kurdish refugees fleeing from Saddam Hussein's forces (Shaw, 1996: 88). Robinson (2002b: 29) referred to these 'modes of reporting as *empathy* and *critical* framing, because the coverage encourages viewers to associate themselves with the suffering of people and criticises government inaction.'[7] Shaw saw this trend in the immediate post-Cold War period as the beginning of the emergence of what 'we may call *global civil society* in which members of global society' (Shaw, 1994: 132) are beginning to make the state system responsible the same way in which national civil societies had hitherto called for the accountability of the sovereign states. Hammond (2007: 8) refers to the creation of the Kurdish safe havens as the 'first of a series of humanitarian interventions which – as Western military forces were sent to deliver food to the starving in Somalia, to protect aid and keep the peace in Bosnia, and to restore democracy in Haiti – seemed to confirm the idea that foreign policy was increasingly driven by ethical and humanitarian concerns'. At the centre of the development of global civil society is what Shaw called the concept of *global responsibility*, citing the cases of western intervention to protect the Kurds and the Kosovars on purely humanitarian grounds (Shaw, 1996). However, as Hammond (2007: 8) puts it, radical critics have dismissed the claim of 'Western ethical and humanitarian concerns' as a mere ideological cover 'for the pursuit of hidden interests' (Ibid.: 9). Uwe-Jens Heuer and Gregor Schirmer (1998, cited in Hammond, 2007: 9) were, for example, critical of what they called 'human rights imperialism', because, on many occasions, 'the altruism of the intervening parties was a mere secondary phenomenon to crude self interested efforts toward the expansion of political and military power, spheres of economic influence, and the like'.

However, while the Westphalia norm of non-intervention did not hold sway for too long in the case of Yugoslavia, culminating into the NATO military intervention to stop the ethnic cleansing of the minority Muslim Albanians of Kosovo against the onslaught of the Serbian regime of Milosevic, it won the day when it came down to African countries such as Ethiopia, Somalia, Rwanda, Sierra Leone, Liberia and Sudan (Darfur). While international political and media pressure was exercised on world leaders to do something for the Kurds and Kosovars, this was hardly the case in these African countries. Moreover, media pressure was exercised on the US, forcing its 'ill-fated sortie in the Horn of Africa in 1992', when 'Operation Restore Hope' was dismissed as a major foreign policy disaster (Robinson, 2002b). How can we therefore explain the role of the media in the failure of the international community to avert total disaster in these distant countries in Africa?

While we should not be in a hurry to dismiss the more realistic interpretation of Western interventionism by Herman and Chomsky (1988) and by Hammond (2000: 365–86) as a mere continuation of traditional power politics in which the 'humanitarian' label is used as a smokescreen for the selfish pursuit of western interests, the mistake must not be made to narrow the global responsibility of the western media and leaders for failure in these African crises to the question of national interest. Even when the end of the Cold War was hot news, it was the consolidation of the victory of democracy and open markets as fronts for western countries' covert national and geo-strategic interests that quickly became the dominant paradigm in the mainstream news discourse of western interventionism; that (democracy and the markets) did not prevent the Western 'Big Brothers' from abandoning Ethiopia, Somalia, and Rwanda in 1984, 1992 and 1994 respectively.

5.4 Conclusion

To conclude, I have made the case in this chapter that, while it is important and in fact perfectly normal for mainstream western media journalists to cover national or geopolitical interest stories such as the evacuation of their citizens, trapped behind zones of conflict, or their killing by combatants, or other humanitarian crises like kidnappings and hostage-taking, it is equally important and normal, within the context of political or diagnostic reporting, for these journalists to reflect critically on their experiences and to explain the circumstances that produced these acts of violence in the first place. This is what I have conceptualised here as HRJ, which is informed by critical empathy frame, diagnostic reporting, pro-activism, interventionism and peace journalism. Sadly, however, the journalism that is dominant today is one that reinforces rather than challenging societal imbalances – a human wrongs journalism (HWJ), which Sonwalker refers to as 'banal journalism' (Sonwalker, 2007: 247). HWJ is informed by empathy distance frames, evocative reporting, re-activism, non-interventionism and war journalism. Below is Table 5.1 showing my HRJ model:

Table 5.1   Human rights journalism model

HWJ vs HRJ	
HWJ	**HRJ**
• Empathy/distance frame	• Empathy/critical frame
• Evocative reporting	• Diagnostic reporting
• Reactive	• Proactive
• Non-interventionist	• Interventionist
• War journalism	• Peace journalism

The above model underscores the importance of the role of the media in the promotion of peace and human rights. The existence of any solution presupposes the existence of a problem that solution is aiming to solve hence my reason for juxtaposing HWJ with HRJ in the table. The discussions of the role of the media – HWJ – in the failure of humanitarian interventions in Ethiopia, Somalia and Rwanda, and Sierra Leone will form the basis of the three chapters in the next part of this book.

Part II
Human Rights Journalism and the Representing of Physical Violence

This part presents three chapters that focus exclusively on case studies involving the reporting or misreporting of direct physical violence. Common examples of direct physical violence include genocide, arbitrary arrests and detentions, extra-judicial killings, terrorism, rape, ethnic cleansing and mistreatment of prisoners. The key argument of this book is that these direct physical forms of violence would be minimised, or prevented altogether, if journalists prioritised the reporting of indirect structural and cultural forms of violence such as poverty, famine, corruption, colonialism, neo-colonialism, unfair trade, forced migration, forced labour, human trafficking, hate speech, racism, xenophobia, marginalisation or the exclusion of minorities.

The case studies of direct physical violence I am looking at in this part include the 'us only' and the 'us/them' frames in reporting the Sierra Leone civil war; the framing of the Somali civil war in 1992 and of the Rwandan Genocide of 1994; and the ethnic cleansing in Kosovo and the North Atlantic Treaty Organisation (NATO)'s intervention. My aim in the next three chapters is to examine the extent to which human rights journalism was used or not in the western media reporting of the direct physical violence case studies and the attendant implications for human rights promotion and protection within the context of cosmopolitan justice.

6
The 'us only' and 'us + them' Frames in Reporting the Sierra Leone War: Implications for Human Rights Journalism

As Caney (2000: 131) puts it, humanitarian intervention so far essentially remains 'a "reactive" principle', which is adopted with hindsight – after people's needs or rights have been violated. This is exactly what happened in the case of the British 'intervention' in Sierra Leone. I argue that this largely explains the high failure rate of humanitarian interventions and the high preference for the military over the peaceful approach, especially to avert distant crises like those in Africa. To overcome this problem, I therefore go with Caney's 'strong case for tackling the roots of these problems and seeking to prevent them from occurring rather than responding to them once they have arisen' (Caney, 2000: 131, a view also shared by Parekh, 1997; Pogge, 1992: 100–1; Booth, 1995: 121). This chapter is important in three ways: first, it makes a contribution to the Galtung peace journalism model; second, it retheorises the binary notions of 'us' and 'other' or 'them' into 'us only' (patriotic/war/human wrongs journalism, which is evocative) and 'us + other' or 'them' (global/peace, human rights – journalism which is diagnostic); and, finally, it conceptualises the human rights journalism model as opposed to the human wrongs journalism model. It is structured into three sections: first, the limits of journalistic practice; second, human wrongs journalism frames in the coverage of the Sierra Leone civil war; and, finally, empathy distance frames versus empathy critical frames.

6.1 The limits of journalistic practice

My interest in this chapter is to explore the debate over the framing '"their" problem and "not ours"' in the context of the Sierra Leone civil war. Central to the limits of mainstream western liberal journalistic practice today is the inherent imbalance in the representation of the powerful against the weak, of the rich against the poor, of the middle elite class against the working class, of the citizen against the immigrant and so on. This imbalance can take various forms: between individuals in political communities or nation-states; between political communities in global society; or between individuals from two or more political communities in global society. This representational imbalance constitutes a denial of the human rights of the less powerful and of the poor, which can be a recipe for conflicts that may lead to further human rights violations. The Universal Declaration of Human Rights, adopted by the United Nations (UN) General Assembly on 10 December 1948, provides a minimum guarantee for each human being on the planet to be treated in accordance with the global standard of justice. This chapter aims to explore the role of the media in creating this representational imbalance in the context of the reporting of the Sierra Leone civil war. Although there is general disagreement over what factors influence these problematic representations, as discussed in the previous chapter, Cassara (1998: 478–86) suggests that 'factors of political power and conflict dominate news choices more than news selection because of economic or cultural ties' (cited in Herbert, 2001: 1).

Roger Fowler argues that there is 'an important *linguistic* consequence of the media's concentration on only one social category of accessed voice. Imbalance of access results in partiality, not only in *what* assertions and attitudes are reported – a matter of content – but also *how* they are reported – a matter of form or style, and therefore, I would claim, of ideological perspective' (Fowler, 2001: 22–23). Fowler talks about the notion of 'socially constructed news' by way of offering a cognitive commentary on Galtung and Ruge's 12 celebrated news selection factors: 'the commentary proposes that news stories are constructed on the basis of mental categories which are present in readers and built on by the media' (Fowler, 2001: 19). Fowler, however, identifies a problem with this cognitive account proposed by Galtung and Ruge: it says very little about the social, economic and historical determinants of the stereotypes in terms of which the news is to be understood. Take, for example, the twelfth of Galtung and Ruge's news factors – the reference to something negative: this is a culture-bound and not a natural factor, as there is no natural reason why disasters should be more newsworthy than triumphs. Moreover, natural disasters or bad news that are culturally remote, therefore lacking in Galtung and Ruge's factor 4–1, are not normally considered to be newsworthy.

It did not therefore come as a surprise when Channel 4 News International Editor Lindsey Hilsum said, at the 2006 International Press Institute (IPI) annual conference in Edinburgh, that it is normal that the media outlets in the West, like their counterparts elsewhere, should go for bad news more than for good news, and insisted that this is the way it is, whether people like it or not. In my contribution from the audience, I charged that it is not only that western media journalists care less about African news, be it good or bad, but also that, even when they show interest in reporting the bad news in Africa, such as conflicts, with Sierra Leone as a case in point, they only do so when their home government officials and/or troops become involved. It is illuminating that Ms Hilsum simply changed the topic. She countered that the duty of the journalist is to inform and raise public awareness of what is going on and not to bring about change. Yet a journalist from the *New York Times* disagreed with Ms Hilsum by highlighting the important role of the journalist in bringing about change in society. This raises fresh questions about the political economy of the media. How effectively, for example, can the media hold public officials to account, when the national and corporate interest stakes in news production are prioritised? Journalists in the West are quick to justify their role in making political accountability work only when dealing with issues about 'us' and not about 'them'. Yet it would make a great deal of difference if they were to decide to hold their home governments to account for failing to take prompt action, at least on moral if not on geo-strategic grounds, to end an African crisis. Questions of national identity and corporate interests always feature on the news agenda (Shaw, 2006).

The media, whether local or international, must be pro-active in mobilising world leaders to intervene and end, first by peaceful means and next, if necessary, by force, wars or conflicts in the context of the promotion of cosmopolitan values of global justice. One fundamental way this can be achieved is by emphasising the reporting of the political contexts of conflicts, and above all through empathy/critical frames rather than empathy distance frames. Human rights journalism prioritises the use of empathy/critical frames, which encourage caring and pro-active interventionist attitudes and approaches to promoting and protecting human rights.

Scholars of the political realist school do not, however, buy the idea of the existence of a genuine humanitarian intervention, that is, an intervention that is totally free from political or economic motives. Chris Brown (2002), for instance, points to geo-strategic motivations of securing Western Europe's hegemony over the rest of Europe as the primary reason for the NATO bombings of Serbia to protect Kosovo. Yet, as Hammond (2007: 9) argues, it has never been easy for critics of ethical intervention to argue convincingly that interventions in hotspots such as Somalia or Kosovo have indeed advanced the 'crude self-interest' of western powers. Moreover, in the case of East Timor, critics were found wanting when their criticism of self-interest as being the main motivation for the refusal of western powers to intervene was rendered shallow when Australia, which is part of the West, did intervene to establish a UN protectorate there in 1999, though critics such as Wheeler (1999) point to security concerns in the South East Asia–Pacific region as the primary reason for Australia's interest. While firmly criticising the West for contributing to the escalation of conflict in Yugoslavia, Pilger (1993) made the case for the need of another intervention by way of 'tightening sanctions against Serbia, extending sanctions to Croatia, arming the Bosnian Muslims, making better use of UN troops, and drawing up a new peace treaty' (cited in Hammond, 2007: 10). Critics of intervention and, by extension, supporters of sovereignty, on the other hand, argue that there is contradiction between the promotion of human rights and support for democracy and self-determination. Such criticisms largely informed the anti-war social movements against the US–UK-led interventions in Afghanistan in 2001 and in Iraq in 2003. Yet, as Chandler (2002: 109) argues, as far as democratic rights theorists are concerned, 'if a right could not be protected, or exercised, by its bearers then it could no longer be a right, an expression of self-government'. From the human rights perspective, therefore, any journalism that mobilises intervention – first by peaceful means and/or where necessary by force – genuinely to protect human rights is justifiably called human rights journalism.

6.2 Human wrongs journalism frames in the coverage of the Sierra Leone civil war

Drawing on a multidimensional exploratory discourse analysis based on the coverage of the Sierra Leone civil war between 1996 and 2001 by four western media journalists, I analyse the 'us only' and ' us + them' frames in the context of the 'empathy/distance' and 'empathy/critical' frames, respectively. I argue that the international community's putative turning its back on Sierra Leone (a move led by Britain – the Empire) was informed more by historical empathy/distance frames than by empathy/critical frames in the mainstream western media news discourse;

and I problematise these frames as human wrongs journalism frames. I argue that the British intervention, if any, came little too late in 2000, after thousands of innocent lives and property had been wasted. The question, for instance, of why Kosovo and not Sierra Leone warranted intervention, when the conflicts in the two countries peaked at around the same time (1998–1999), makes the socio-cultural environment in which journalists operate a key variable in distant wars and human rights violations. This chapter takes the form of a critical discussion of the prioritisation by the mainstream media of the empathy/distance frames (reflected by the evocative style of war journalism and human wrongs journalism) over the empathy/critical frames (reflected by the diagnostic style of peace/human rights journalism) in the western media coverage of the Sierra Leone civil war. Empathy/distance frames, conceptualised as evocative reporting, conjure up images of wars or other human rights violations that widen the gap between the concerns of the audience (in this case, the western public) and the plight of the victims, hence making the case for non-intervention. On the other hand, empathy/critical frames, conceptualised as diagnostic reporting, evoke representations that promote a better understanding of why the violations are happening and hence stimulate attachment and solidarity in the form of intervening to solve or prevent them.

Sierra Leone[1] witnessed one of the bloodiest civil wars in Africa, led by the Revolutionary United Front rebels between 23 March 1991 and 15 January 2002, when the war was officially declared over. Estimates put the death toll at about 160,000 people, hundreds of thousands of casualties and over 2 million displaced. Sierra Leone's former colonial power, Britain, did not come in to help to end the war until 2000, when it intervened apparently more to safeguard its business interests than out of any genuine humanitarian concern. The worst period of the war was the invasion of Freetown by the RUF rebels on 6 January 1999, which comprised two weeks of intense fighting for control of the country's capital that left thousands dead and hundreds mutilated.

The multidimensional methodological approach used here is based on an exploratory qualitative discourse analysis of data largely obtained through an in-depth interview with the four selected foreign correspondents: Alex Duval Smith (*Independent*), Sam Kiley (*The Times*), Anton La Guardia (*Telegraph*) and Steve Coll (*Washington Post*). This was a deliberate choice. First, this preponderance of British journalists is justified by the fact that the British press gave the most coverage of the civil war.

Second, Sierra Leone used to be a British colony and hence attracts more geopolitical interest from Britain than from any other foreign nation. Third, the choice of journalists from different newspapers is also aimed at helping us observe differences and similarities in their use of human rights journalism – or lack of it – in the reporting of the Sierra Leone war. Finally, the American journalist's discourse or reporting would help us to understand whether there were fundamental differences and/or similarities between him and his British colleagues in their use of human rights journalism– or lack of it.

Following Laurence Bardin (1996: 115–116), I employ a more qualitative type of content analysis juxtaposing some of the interview data from the selected journalists, coded according to the themes of the frames analysed, together with some data obtained from their reporting, in order to observe any differences. The Bardin (1996) approach is useful for deducing from an event a precise variable of inference, but it is not to be used for general variables. What characterises qualitative content analysis is that inference – whenever it is made – is grounded in the presence of an index (theme, word, personality and so on), not on the frequency of its appearance in every single communication process. Following Laramee and Vallee (1991: 271), a method called 'communication audit', based on interview data gathered from a professional group, is employed here. This method allows the process of collecting a large pool of information on the basis of a wide range of communication variables from a group of professionals working more or less as a pack. A combination of the in-depth interview data and some news media content forms the unit of analysis for this study. The multidimensional exploratory method employed here is largely inspired by the approach used by Mark Pedelty in his ethnographic study of a group of foreign correspondents who covered the war in El Salvador in the late 1980s (Pedelty, 1993).

6.3   Empathy distance frames versus empathy critical frames

Duval Smith (*Independent*): Alex Duval Smith's reporting of the Sierra Leone civil war framed war/human wrongs journalism more than peace/human rights journalism, although she made few attempts to avoid this. For instance, here we see her justifying Sandline's violation of the UN arms embargo:

Broadly speaking, Britain was on the side of the *angels*. Even though the Sandline arms had been shipped in breach of a UN embargo, President Kabbah had been elected by the people, then forced into hiding in neighbouring Guinea-Conakry while rebels *terrorised* his countrymen. His government was also that with which foreign diamond buyers were used to doing business. The Sandline arms (reportedly for use by a Nigerian-trained pro-Kabbah militia) have helped keep the president in power since he came back from the Guinean capital Conakry in February last year. (Smith, 10 January 1999)

Smith was Africa correspondent for *The Independent*, parachuting from her base in Johannesburg whenever there was an emergency. Here she uses empathy distance frames such as 'terrorists' and empathy critical frames such as 'angels' to portray the rebels and the Sandline mercenaries as bad and good, respectively. It is clear from her analysis that the British were supportive of the Sandline mercenaries. She reinforced this representation of the mercenaries as the 'good' in the interview I had with her in Paris:

Now my personal opinion about hiring mercenaries is not perhaps a typical one, and is not one that is probably shared by the British public, but I think mercenaries are professional soldiers, and I think it is acceptable, totally acceptable, for a government to hire them. In a way UN soldiers are mercenaries. So you have to ask first who is a mercenary. My personal opinion is that as long as they are accountable, then you can't stop them from being there. I don't find it surprising that mercenaries operate in Africa: they are hired by private companies, governments, and whole range of sectors, to do their dirty work. (Interview, 03 March 2004)

Another empathy distance frame employed by Alex Duval Smith was the ethnic/tribal factor, used in the context of the centre–periphery thesis, to explain the war.[2] This factor was problematic, as it was apparently largely informed by a historical baggage she developed from her reading of the *Heart of the Matter* by Graham Greene, former British colonial administrator in Sierra Leone.

Duval Smith's article in *The Independent*, 'Nostalgia Rises from Smoking Ruins of Graham's Hotel', dated 30 May 2000 was extensively sourced by a local man, Lloyd Parkinson, apparently from the Krio ethnic group (largely based in the capital, Freetown), who explains:

After independence, the ruling élite – the creoles who came back from slavery when British philanthropists established this Freetown – wanted to be like the white man. Our leaders have not changed. They want to be superior; they want to have all the wealth like the white man and to send their children to schools overseas. If we get rid of Sankoh, another one like him will come along and want all the diamond wealth.

Smith reinforced this thinking in our interview, by explaining the war thus:

A.D.S: I would say that the main cause was probably a combination of things; probably stemming from originally a disenfranchised youth in the rural areas feeling that it wasn't represented by the government of Tejan Kabbah [...], and partly a *tribal thing* because they were returnees, disenfranchised, freed slaves from [...] who were the people who returned as freed slaves?

QUESTION: The creoles?

A.D.S: Yes the creoles; so the problem of having a creole working class with whom the people upcountry didn't identify would be the root cause why a lot of people have become involved with the RUF; why the RUF appealed to them; then you have diamonds, rituals, financial insightments to [...] which allowed the rebels to raise money.

QUESTION: Did you by any chance reflect some of these points and arguments in your reporting?

A.D.S: I think I did over time; I don't think I did initially because I don't think I necessarily understood the situation then. And on my first visit it was the type of reporting that had to do with people having their hands cut off, it was not about the root causes of the war; and in any case in a newspaper article you only have room for that much when it is happening in front of your eyes. But, over time I hope I did reflect some of the root causes in my reporting, but it is normal for people of daily newspaper journalism not to have enough room for this while academics may have enough time to look at root causes of conflicts.

Indeed, despite her over-emphasis on historical and distant empathy frames, including the 'tribal factor', at the expense of critical empathy frames, Alex Duval made some attempt to blame the war on 'youth disenfranchisement'; at least she tried to give a critical empathy frame (diagnosis – peace/human rights journalism), hence justifying humanitarian intervention. She reinforces this frame in her article, dated 22 September 2001 when she writes about Koidu, a town rich in diamonds, where a young boy, Rahman, and a couple of others stood knee-deep in muddy water looking for diamonds – these were all over the place and yet could be hard to find:

> In the centre of the war-ravaged town, still rebel-controlled, a whole section of buildings has fallen down after diamond hunters looted their foundations. This is where 'conflict diamonds' come from – those gemstones that buy guns which fuel African wars. Rahman is at the begining of the chain – a long, long way from the 'civilized' world of jewellery shops. A middleman sent from Freetown pays him 500 leones (12p) a day plus a cup of rice. 'This is the only job around here because the war has ended our agriculture,' he says. (Smith, 22 September 2001)

In this article Smith factored in, albeit in an indirect way, the problems of corruption and bad governance, two factors featuring among the main causes of the war in the first place. It is probable that she could have done more in giving this diagnosis in the context of human rights journalism if she had not been clouded by the historical baggage (an empathy distance frame), which made her see the conflict as essentially a tribal problem.

Sam Kiley (*The Times*): Although Sam Kiley wrote many articles on this forgotten war, his reporting turned out to be more of the evocative (empathy distance frame) than of the diagnostic kind (empathy critical frame). Sam, a Kenyan-born British journalist recently turned freelance documentary film maker, served between 1997 and 2000 as an Africa correspondent based in Johannesburg and working for the *Times*. Like his colleague Duval Smith of *The Independent*, he used stereotypical representations such as *creatures, thugs, monsters, butcher* and the like to portray the RUF rebels as the bad guys – as he does in this article:

> Mr Taylor and his henchmen plan to get their hands on the country's enormously valuable resources of diamonds and rutile. They then propose to hand power to their *creatures* in the Revolutionary United Front (RUF). The RUF leader, Foday Sankoh, is on death row in Freetown for his past atrocities. There is a lot of competition for

the title of Africa's most *malevolent militia*, but in this crowded field the RUF stands out. Mr Sankoh's sidekick, Sam Bockarie, is a former hairdresser and professional disco-dancer turned *butcher*. (Author's emphases), (Kiley, 22 January 1999)

On the other hand, Sam Kiley paints the Nigerian Economic Community of West African States Military Group (ECOMOG) soldiers as the good guys in another article:

> In the wake of their campaign of atrocities, rebels are now being shot on sight, the day before, a close friend of the colonel, a major, was shot in the groin by a child. 'We're not bothering to take any rebels prisoner any more,' a Nigerian private said ... '*We lie in wait and grab the* killers *as they try to go in. They are taken down to the beach and we get rid of them,*' *the soldier said* [...]. (Kiley, 15 January 1999)

No special pejorative clichés or stereotypes are used here to describe the Nigerian soldiers as bad guys, despite the fact that they carried out many reprisal killings of rebels, suspected rebels and their supporters.[3] This is a case of war/human wrongs journalism *par excellence*, as emphasis is placed on violence, in a winner/loser situation where people kill each other for fun. This, in a way, reinforces the historical baggage of Africans killing each other as something normal – a kind of an empathy distance frame (evocative), hence discouraging any form of intervention or intention to put things right. Moreover, national interest (and not human rights) apparently depicted the Nigerian human rights abusers as the 'good' guys and the rebel human rights abusers as the 'bad' guys.

Sam Kiley's reporting, depicting the rebels as evil guys, was echoed in what he told me in an interview, although here he did admit that they had a legitimate right to fight, but observed that they were manipulated into a mad conflict by outside forces such as the Ukrainian mafia and President Charles Taylor of Liberia:

> If you gonna have a guerrilla movement you've got to have an ideology that is going to motivate it, if you don't have an ideology to motivate it you've got to recruit young men at the age where they can hardly distinguish between ideologies and just turn them into robots. You take a kid who is eleven, manipulate him to kill his sister, you know, you've got a kind of monster. That is exactly what they did. (Interview, 10 November 2003)

Anton La Guadia (*Daily Telegraph*): The reporting of La Guadia was similar to that of Sam Kiley, since they both featured more empathy distance frames than empathy critical frames. The framing of the RUF rebels as the bad guys and of the mercenaries (British Sandline) as the good guys is also very evident in La Guadia's despatches. For instance, he reported as follows on 14 January 1999 ('Sandline Should Have Been Left to Finish the Job'):

The scandal over private military consultants means few leaders are ready to turn again to companies such as Sandline, but the rebels are believed to have hired more obscure Ukrainian mercenaries with funding from Liberia. (La Guadia, 14 January 1999)

La Guadia, like Sam Kiley, blamed the war on Taylor and the Ukrainian mercenaries, while advocating the need to leave the British Sandline mercenaries to finish their job of dealing with the rebels. This was despite the 'arms to Africa' scandal, which involved their (Sandline) bursting of the UN arms embargo with the tacit support of the Kabbah regime in exile and of the British government. The portrayal of one set of mercenaries (Sandline) as the good guys and of the others (Ukrainian) as the bad guys – when all mercenaries are generally associated with war/human wrongs journalism (winner/loser binary), as opposed to peace/human rights journalism (win–win) – suggests that La Guadia was motivated by the British national interest (involving a British merce- nary company) rather than by any genuine humanitarian concern to end the war in Sierra Leone by non-violent means. La Guadia's report- ing was therefore informed more by the 'us only' frame (war/human wrongs/patriotic journalism) than by the 'us' + 'others' or 'them' frame (peace/human rights/global journalism). Moreover, this 'us only' frame was reinforced in another article, published later by La Guadia, where he weighed in on the rebel leader Foday Sankoh, whom he accused of lacking in ideology and of being only interested in the riches of the country:

He has used appalling brutality to cow civilians and recruit fighters, mined diamonds to pay for his war and relied on the world's lack of resolve to deal with another hopeless African war. It is easy to bargain with Mr Sankoh than try to defeat him [...] Now it seems that Sankoh is not content with merely sharing the spoils of the country's wealth – gold, titanium, bauxite and, above all, diamonds. Papa wants it all to himself. The Lomé agreement did not end the civil war; it was merely a pause in Sankoh's struggle for power. (La Guadia, 9 May 2000)

Note also La Guadia's allusion to 'another hopeless African war' – a historical baggage (empathy distance frame) portraying Africa as a continent ridden with senseless wars without end and thereby justifying non-intervention, as it sends the message that there is no point in trying to end something that would never end. Moreover, his critical reference to the Lomé peace agreement[4] shows his preference for war journalism to peace journalism and in a way reinforces the 'us only' frame, because the British government was not involved in the initiative. La Guadia echoed these empathy distance frames in an interview he granted me on 13 November 2003:

QUESTION: Were you by any chance influenced by the works of some historians or anthropologists before going to Sierra Leone, people like Robert Kaplan (1994) and Paul Richards (1996) for instance? I understand the article by Kaplan 'The Coming Anarchy' influenced many western diplomats and journalists.

LA GUADIA: Yes of course. I read the article by Kaplan. You are certainly influenced by the intellectual climate of the day; and the intellectual climate of the day was that this war is all about resources, this is a war over diamonds.

Q: But Kaplan was more or less blaming it on environmental problems based on the Malthusian theory of population explosion [...]

A.L.G: I mean yes, but there are lot of places in the world that are overcrowded but people still survive, okay; but part of that Malthusian argument is that what they are fighting over is for control of the resources such as diamonds. Yes you are influenced by that [...] Another thing, which possibly most British journalists might have been aware of, was Graham Greene's 'Heart of the Matter'; do we draw a big moral lesson from it? No. But you might use references to it.

Q: Maybe sometimes you are guarded by stereotypical representations, for instance?

A.L.G: Not directly [...] There is no doubt about it, we come from the West and report to a Western audience, to a British audience; just the selection of facts that would be interesting to them. You know

I'm not writing for an African audience. You would write about Sierra Leone very differently from the way I would.

It is interesting to note, from this interview, how the works of western intellectuals such as Kaplan and Greene impacted on the dominance of historical empathy distance frames in the reporting of Africa's wars by most western journalists. Also worthy of note is the influence of western audiences in the equation, which goes to reinforce war/human wrongs/ patriotic journalism ('us only') against peace/human rights/global journalism ('us and them') – which is the preferred alternative in the context of peace journalism and global justice, especially given the increasingly diverse and multicultural audiences we now have in western countries.

Steve Coll (*Washington Post*): Steve Coll's reporting in his groundbreaking special magazine feature 'Peace Without Justice: A Journey into the Wounded Heart of Africa' (*Washington Post* Magazine, 9 January 2000) stands out, being in sharp contrast to the reporting of the three British foreign correspondents in that it evokes more of the empathy critical frames than of the empathy distance frames. Of particular importance in his article is his criticism of Robert Kaplan's 'new barbarism' thesis, which argues that '[t]he war was a product of social breakdown caused by population pressure and environmental collapse'. In his controversial but highly influential article 'The Coming Anarchy: How Scarcity, Crime, Overpopulation, Tribalism and Disease Are Rapidly Destroying the Social Fabric of Our Planet', published in *Atlantic Monthly*, in February 1994, Kaplan had written:

There is no other place on the planet where political maps are so deceptive [...] as in West Africa [...] West Africa consists now of a series of coastal trading posts, such as Freetown and Conakry, and an interior that, owing to violence, volatility, and disease, is again becoming, as Graham Greene once observed, 'blank' and 'unexplored'. However, whereas Greene's vision implies a certain romance, as in the somnolent and charmingly seedy Freetown of his celebrated novel 'The Heart of the Matter', it is Thomas Malthus, the philosopher of demographic doomsday, who is now the prophet of West Africa's future.

Kaplan's thesis, based on the Malthusian theory of population explosion, influenced official thinking in Washington, as he is said to have circulated the article to all the US ambassadors serving in Africa and to all the senior government officials in the US government. In fact most of the western correspondents who covered the war and whom I had the opportunity to interview – including Sam Kiley and La Guadia, studied earlier – said that they had read that article before going to Sierra Leone. However, while most of them agreed with Kaplan's 'new barbarism' thesis, a very few ones, such as British Anthropologist Paul Richards and *Washington Post* Managing Editor Steve Coll, looked the other way. Richards was very critical of Kaplan (1994) – who had written that, throughout West Africa, drought and land hunger had driven young people to the teeming and only superficially modernised shantytown suburbs of the coastal cities. Spun off from a failing traditional society, these criminally inclined young migrants were 'loose molecules in a very unstable social fluid' (Kaplan 1994, cited in Richards, 1996: 15–16). Kaplan argued that the perpetrators of the violence in eastern and southern Sierra Leone lacked any clear political purpose. 'They were better pictured as criminals and bandits' (Richards, 1996: 15–16). Richards was simply not convinced that violence perpetrated by the rebels was for nothing. As he put it: 'The confused accounts of terrorised victims of violence do not constitute evidence of the irrationality of violence. Rather they show the opposite – that the tactics have been fully effective in disorientating, traumatizing and demoralizing victims of violence. In short, they are devilishly well-calculated' (Richards, 1996: 17).

Washington Post's Coll not only criticised Kaplan's thesis, but recognised its far-reaching implication for reinforcing the international community's abandonment of Sierra Leone in the hour of need:

> Was there really anything the United States or its European allies could have done to ameliorate Sierra Leone's violence? Perhaps – and it would not have involved a wrenching decision to put US or NATO soldiers at risk. But it would have required a view of Africa far different from the one that has shaped U.S foreign policy during most of the last decade. (Coll, 9 January 2000)

Coll wrote that American journalist Robert Kaplan's influential essay in the *Atlantic Monthly* set in Sierra Leone titled 'The Coming Anarchy', where he described the country as engulfed by 'an increasing lawlessness', came six years after the US troops' withdrawal from Somalia, where they sustained casualties in a humanitarian mission. Coll added:

> Kaplan's thesis that Africa was *drifting beyond governance* took hold with many members of Congress, diplomats and foreign policy analysts. It seemed to capture their own gathering revulsion and exhaustion with post-Cold War challenges America faced in the Third World, especially in violent corners of Africa. (Ibid.)

Steve Coll also challenges the empathy distance frames that often permeate mainstream media discourse as banal images of victims of war that only go to depict the hopelessness of the situation and hence invite distancing or withdrawal:

> But in Sierra Leone, outside engagement with the war came to be dominated by *pity-inducting, context-empty images of the limbless*, whether in media coverage or during visits by politicians to Freetown's rehabilitation camps for amputees. These *stripped-down, politics-free pictures of armless victims* helped to consign Sierra Leone's war to the *mental box* many Americans reserve for Africa. Few understood, for example, that most of Freetown's victims were as urban and middle class as Prestina's. (Ibid; author's emphases)

Steve Colls goes on to give the global political context of the abandonment of Sierra Leone within the cosmopolitan framework of global justice, hence completing the circle of the human rights journalism model:

> 'We are all *internationalists now*, whether we like it or not,' British Prime Minister Tony Blair said last year, explaining why the world intervened militarily to stop paramilitary bloodshed in Kosovo (as it would later in East Timor) [...] Blair sought to measure his *millennial ideas* by the world's conduct in Kosovo during the last year of the 20th century. But an African might want to measure them against the world's conduct in Sierra Leone during that same year of 1999. (Ibid.)

Coll echoed his refusal to buy Kaplan's historical baggage thesis in an interview he granted me on 4 May 2004:

In reality, I never agreed with Kaplan's thesis. In fact if anything I am concerned that it negatively impacted on Washington leading to lack of concern of the West for the terrible things that were happening in Sierra Leone. He turned out to be more pessimistic of the country's future. Although it is clear that Africa faces huge problems and challenges it is not in my nature to demonise or praise things but since I went to Sierra Leone and wrote that article I cannot remember supporting anything near the thesis of Kaplan's article. What I found on the ground was the total opposite to Kaplan's thesis. (Interview, 4 May 2004)

Coll was very consistent in his criticism of Kaplan's thesis, even after more than four years since he wrote the groundbreaking piece in the *Washington Post*.

6.4   Conclusion

This chapter concludes by making a case for human rights journalism and global justice as normative journalistic practice. It has attempted a multidimensional exploratory discourse analysis of the extent to which distance empathy news frames informed the 'I don't care' attitude of the international community in general and of the British government in particular and accounted for the delayed humanitarian intervention to end the 1991–2001 civil war in Sierra Leone on the basis of the cosmopolitan principle of global justice. The British intervention, if any, came 'too little, too late' in 2000, after thousands of innocent lives and properties had been wasted. Besides, despite anticipatory portrayals of the British army as 'a force for good' – a humanitarian military force (Dorman, 2010: 127, see also Elliott and Cheeseman, 2005) – when this army at last stepped in it did so in order to rescue some British troops held hostage by a breakaway rebel faction, the West Side Boys, around Okra Hill, some 40 miles from Freetown; and this, strictly speaking, did not qualify as humanitarian intervention. I argue that, for a proactive approach to humanitarian intervention to succeed, the media must equally employ a pro-active rather than a reactive approach in their reporting of conflicts and wars. However, as our exploratory discourse analysis of the reporting of the four western journalists studied shows, this is so far hardly the case.

The exception is the American journalist Steve Coll of the *Washington Post*, whose reporting stands out as a true reflection on the peace/human rights journalism frame, which is intellectual–contextual–diagnostic, as opposed to the war/human wrongs journalism frame, which is routine–factual–evocative. The latter was employed more or less by the three British journalists in the study: Alex Duval Smith (*Independent*), Sam Kiley (*The Times*) and Anton La Guadia (*Daily Telegraph*), although the first, Alex, did better than the other two in terms of reaching out to the peace/human rights journalism frame.

7

'Operation Restore Hope' in Somalia and Genocide in Rwanda

The argument, popular among media scholars and commentators, that there has been a significant change in war coverage over the years due to technological advances in the news production business brought about by globalisation, especially in the 1980s and 1990s, and by the end of the Cold War era, becomes problematic when the reporting, or non-reporting, of 'small' conflicts comes into the equation. Ecology, human rights and democracy are three political themes that have in recent years come to define the changing dynamics of journalism in the global context. These themes were each associated with seemingly universal values, beliefs and ideals that were perceived to be relevant to all countries of the world. Questions as to which values are more authentic have, however, informed tensions between the global and the local contexts (Volkmer, 2002). Alleged rights violations in China, or ecological catastrophes in South America, can potentially affect government policy and political activism worldwide; but there was no certainty that this would happen (Volkmer, 2002).

Questions of national and geo-strategic interests were as evident in the framing of wars in Crimea and Vietnam as they were in the framing of the Falklands, Serbia, Kosovo, Iraq 1 and 2, Ethiopia, Somalia, Rwanda and Sierra Leone wars. Moreover, this chapter, like the one before it, demonstrates reasons associated more with 'empathy distance frames' than with 'empathy critical frames', which delayed intervention from leading western powers in the so-called 'small wars' of Africa. On the question of over-reliance on official state or military sources as an explanation for this political framing, there is a good deal of evidence to suggest continuity rather than change from what I have referred to as 'human wrongs journalism'.

This chapter has three sections, which deal with post-Cold War politics; the 'Operation Restore Hope'; and genocide in Rwanda.

7.1 Post-Cold War politics: Human wrongs journalism and the cycle of violence

The proliferation of new information technologies in the 1980s provided new challenges for journalists, especially those covering the world's hotspots. The Tiananmen Square protests in China and the fall of the Berlin wall in 1989, which heralded the fall of communism, were instantaneously communicated to western audiences via TV channels, making television by far the most powerful news medium in the manufacturing of consent. However, recounting his experience, former Associated Press correspondent Mort Rosenblum admitted the downside of these new technologies: 'When communications were precarious, correspondents told their editors what was news. With satellite phones, editors talk back. They see events unfold on screens above their desk and filter them through their own cultural prisms. Reality is distorted by assumption and accepted wisdom back home' (Rosenblum, 1993). This encourages pack mentality[1] in the news production process, which deters journalists from going out for fresh angles, which bring diversity to the news.

On the upside, the new technologies appeared to reduce the latitude for calm policy deliberation, forcing policymakers to respond to whatever issue journalists focused on (Beschloss, 1993; McNulty, 1993, cited in Robinson, 2002b) – a perception reinforced by the end of the Cold War. It was assumed that journalists were freer not only to cover the stories they wanted but also to criticise US foreign policy. For the optimists of this technological revolution, the world had become like a 'global village' (McLuhan, 1965) in which the news media were helping to erode people's identification with the state and to 'mould a cosmopolitan global consciousness' instead (Carruthers, 2000).

Media researchers have recently been preoccupied with the increasing role of the media in calling the shots in most western capitals, sometimes canalising into massive international military and humanitarian interventions in some of the world's hotspots in the 1980s, 1990s and 2000s. For example, as Martin Shaw (1996: 88) put it, the 'virtually unprecedented proposal for Kurdish safe havens' was made possible by the critical media coverage of Kurdish refugees fleeing from Saddam Hussein's forces. We next saw how media pressure was brought to bear on the US, leading to its 'ill-fated sortie into the Horn of Africa in

1992', when 'Operation Restore Hope' was ultimately lampooned as a major foreign policy disaster (Robinson, 2002b). Chomsky (1999) and Hammond and Herman (2000), however, offer a more realistic interpretation of western interventionism, explaining it as a mere continuation of traditional power politics in which the 'humanitarian' label is used as a smokescreen for the selfish pursuit of western interests.

At issue here is the role of the media in reporting international conflicts. Conflict itself is seen as the fall-out of disagreement at the national and international levels, and the emergence, settlement, or abolition of conflict depends on communication between parties to the conflict, with the news media serving as one of the channels (Arno, 1984). It was assumed, implicitly or explicitly, that the clearer the communication between the parties, the easier it would be for the conflict to be resolved. International relations discourse of the 1940s and 1950s was conspicuously dominated by emphasis on open communication channels (Tumber, 2007). 'Lack of knowledge and stereotypical representation of the conflicting parties were identified as decisive obstacles toward the resolution of conflicting interests' (ibid., p. 24). A similar line of argument was followed by other scholars in the 1960s and 1970s; one of them, Jorgen Habermas, 'argued that enlightened, rational communication can be the panacea for human exploitation, ignorance, and repression' (Habermas, 1971, cited in Tumber, 2007: 24). All these accounts perceived conflict as the product of distorted communication.

More recent accounts have viewed the media not only as a transmitter of factual messages but as an important player in themselves, thereby moving from its more traditional role of neutral player between government(s), leader(s) and the public to a more structurally engaged role (Davidson, 1974) cited in Tumber (2007: 24). The key role of the media in the production and management of conflict can take two forms: either it 'makes' conflict – that is, scandal – or, in contrast, it operates as the public sphere assisting in the resolution (Arno, 1984: 2–3, cited in Tumber, 2007: 25). In the first case, the media are implicated in conflict disagreements by treating them on an individual basis; in the second, the media play a more structural role. Looking at the evolution of the news media as a channel of communication, it is clear that all the accounts of the last five decades agree that distorted or bad communication can produce rather than manage conflict. Distorted communication is bound to be produced when journalists employ human wrongs journalism (evocative, empathy distance frames) instead of human rights journalism (diagnostic, empathy critical frames). If one looks at the more recent accounts pointing to the metamorphoses of the media from a more passive role (journalism of detachment/objectivity/neutrality) to a more active one (journalism of attachment/subjectivity/honesty), one finds that the role of the media in making or producing conflicts has been more dominant than their role in managing them, especially after the end of the Cold War. Furthermore, since conflicts, especially the direct physical violent ones, are a recipe for human rights violations, any communication that produces them constitutes human wrongs journalism. On the receiving end of this type of journalism are mostly countries in the developing world, especially in Africa.

Following the Cold War era, the consolidation of the victory of democracy and open markets as fronts for western countries' covert national and geo-strategic interests quickly became the dominant paradigm in the mainstream news discourse of western interventionism. However, while this was true for central and Eastern European countries breaking away from the former communist bloc, it was not true for African countries, which either enjoyed the support of the former Soviet Union or risked sliding into the communist camp. At least in the case of Africa, the commitment was very limited. While it was recognised that winning the Cold War in central and Eastern Europe would cost money, such a calculation was never conceived of in the case of Africa. In fact, what we saw was a steady cut back of development aid from the US under Reagan and from the UK under Thatcher, two staunch anti-communist champions, to the developing world, especially Africa. Former BBC Africa Correspondent George Alagiah commented:

> The idea that Africa, the playground of the superpowers, might need extra financial help in its own journey out of Cold War rivalry was overlooked or forgotten. Basically, Africans didn't matter, or at least not as much as Europeans. Proximity, not principle, has too often driven foreign policy in the rich world. The short-term deployment of troops, such as in Sierra Leone, is not the same as a long-term commitment of money. So, while the carnage in Kosovo or the corruption in Moscow are put down to the inevitable teething troubles of the adjustment to the new world order, similar problems in Africa – and Somalia is but one example – are reckoned to be purely the product of Africa's apparently unique propensity for self-destruction. (Alagiah, 2001: 112)

Despite Alagiah's criticism of the West's relegation of Africa to the back-burner, with Somalia coming for special mention, the BBC was not free from blame in the rampant use of the empathy distance frames, which largely contributed to this abandonment in the first place. The Sri Lankan-born British journalist Alagiah, who spent his childhood in Ghana, appeared, however, more down-to-earth in his book *Passage to Africa* than when he was wearing the hat of BBC's Africa correspondent as we will see later in this chapter.

7.2 'Operation Restore Hope'?

US military intervention in Somalia, code-named 'Operation Restore Hope', stands out as another typical example where media coverage, especially American, tended to avoid the underlying political and social issues, preferring instead a discourse of simple humanitarianism that focused on the requirements of aid agencies and short-term relief. Preston refers to this type of framing as empathy distance framing, which emphasises 'the simple imperative of personal suffering' (Preston, 1996: 112). This type of framing is often invoked by policymakers in their attempt to justify intervention for the purpose of distributing relief aid to the desperately hungry and sick, who have been displaced by the crisis. This intervention was premised on the notion that Somalia's ills could be solved if only you could sidestep the 'rapacious' warlords and get food directly to the people who needed it. 'It was a bit like organising a soup kitchen for the homeless without stopping to work out why people are homeless in the first place' (Alagiah, 2001: 103).

Somalia has a history that is different from most other African countries in that it attained its independence in 1960 having a strong sense of national identity after the coming together of British Somaliland and Italian Somalia to form the Somali Republic. This unity was strengthened by the Somalis, 'who possess a common language and common culture, based on pastoral customs and traditions' (Meredith, 2005: 464). However, beneath what Meredith called 'passionate nationalism', there 'lay a complex society based on clan families, each one subdivided into sub-clans, extending all the way down to lineage segments consisting of close kinsmen and family groups. Somalis asked each other not whence they came but to whom they were related' (Ibid.: 465). During the Cold War era, Somalia changed hands twice; first in 1969, under the control of the then Somali leader Mohamed Sayid Barre, from the capitalist West led by the US to the East led by the former Soviet Union; and, second, switching back to the West after the Soviet Union switched sides and started backing Ethiopia in the mid-1970s. Barre's regime suffered defeat at the hands of Ethiopia under Mengistu Haille Mariam in 1978 and lost control of the Ogaden region, which went to the enemy. Following the fall of Barre's regime, Somalia fell into clan warfare, which has continued up to the present day, despite 'Operation Restore Hope' led by the US marines in 1992.

The UN Security Council (UNSC) authorised humanitarian intervention in Somalia in 1992 following reports of massive violations of human rights and widespread famine resulting from a civil war that began in 1991, after the demise of Said Barrie's regime (Manokha, 2008). The UNSC first established a peacekeeping force, the United Nations Operation in Somalia (UNOSOM) under chapter VI of the UN Charter. In December 1992 it authorised a US-led military force – the United Nations International Task Force (UNITAF) – under Chapter VII, which had a more robust mandate, 'to use all necessary means to establish as soon as possible a secure environment for humanitarian relief operations in Somalia' (cited in Manokha, 2008: 184). This resolution saw the landing of a US-led multinational force comprising 24,000 US troops and of 13,000 troops from other states in Somalia on 9 December 1992.

Although the resolutions did not specifically refer to human rights, the international human rights law was used to authorise force. Yet the situation in Somalia before, during and after intervention was widely seen as constituting large-scale human rights abuse, in particular political and civil rights abuse ranging from torture and mass killings of civilians to rape and mutilation. The most common explanation offered for this intervention is that news media coverage of suffering people mobilised US policymakers to intervene, hence making it a fine example of 'the strong CNN effect' and justifying the role of the media in manufacturing consent (Robinson, 2002b). In fact, President George Bush senior is said to have invoked this framing to justify his decision to send US troops to Somalia in his live televised address of 4 December 1992:

> The people of Somalia, especially the children of Somalia, need our help. We're able to ease their suffering. We must help them live. We must give them hope [...] Only the United States has the global reach to place a large security force on the ground in such a distant place quickly and efficiently and thus, save thousands of innocents from death. (Robinson, 2002b: 50)

The intervention, however, failed after the withdrawal of the US forces from Somalia following the death of 18 US Rangers in a battle at Mogadishu on 3 and 4 October 1993 (Manokha, 2008: 184). In fact many critics have argued that, while the apparent justification for the

US intervention was to provide safe humanitarian corridors for the delivery of emergency food aid to famine victims, the famine was actually finishing by the time of the intervention; the famine peaked again in August, but it was not until November that a decision was reached to send in the US intervention force under the aegis of the UN; unfortunately this came 'too little, too late' as the worst had already passed (Maren, 1997: 204). The question is asked as to what happened that led to the failure of the US-led intervention, despite all the talk of 'the CNN factor'. It stands to reason that, if 'the CNN factor' in the case of the backpedalling of 'Operation Restore Hope' was not a myth, the backpedalling itself and the ultimate failure of the intervention would not have happened. I argue in this chapter that the intervention failed because its motive had more to do with creating safe humanitarian corridors for the distribution of relief aid than with any genuine humanitarian intervention – first by peaceful means and second, if necessary, by force – to end the Somali crisis and to protect the human rights of the majority of people suffering at the hands of the warlords. This explains why, from the beginning, media coverage of the Somali crisis was dominated by superficial evocative empathy distance frames aimed at promoting only the 'us' and 'them' binary, where the short-term intervention to distribute relief to the wounded and dying was considered top priority. It was suggested that the media coverage of famine was misleading, as it tended to focus on isolated cases of individuals suffering and in that way it ignored the bigger political context of the Somali crisis (Hammond, 2007b). Most of Somalia was free from famine but politically unstable, and yet there was very little contextualisation of this in the western media (Maren, 1997). Anecdotal evidence rather suggests that the media merely focused on sensational and evocative images (Carruthers, 2000: 240). Alex De Waal and Rakiya Omaar, both of *Africa Watch* – and later *Africa Rights*, which they founded following their sacking from the former – accused the media of producing 'disaster pornography' (Hammond, 2007b). This is human wrongs journalism as opposed to human rights journalism, which emphasises the diagnostic empathy critical frames that promote a sense of genuine humanitarian solidarity. The human wrongs journalism (evocative, empathy distance frames) that accounted for the failure of 'Operation Restore Hope' was caused by political, economic and cultural factors.

Virgil Hawkins (2002) defines the CNN factor as a concentrated and emotion-based media coverage of a select conflict, packaged in an oversimplified 'morality play' format of good versus evil, which evokes an emotional response among the citizens of a distant country, forcing that country's government to take interest, and perhaps intervene in some form in the conflict. Yet, in the case of Somalia, the CNN effect, emblematic of the power and influence of the new media, which makes the war correspondent of recent years more of a 'hero' than his/her predecessor, has been overly exaggerated. Drawing from subsequent research (Gowing, 1994; Strobel, 1997; Robinson 2002b), Robinson argues that 'substantive military intervention, even during the 1990s (with Iraq 1991 and Somalia 1992 coming in for special mention), remained driven by geostrategic reasoning rather than any kind of media pressure or CNN effect' (Robinson, 2004: 108).

In the first place, politics, and not any genuine humanitarianism, was the key driver of the US-led intervention in Somalia. According to Cusimano, there was an inbuilt political agenda that is at stake in this media influence. She argues that senior aides claimed that Bush believed the Somali situation presented him with the opportunity to 'exit in glory' and 'leave office on a high note' (Cusimano, 1995: 8 cited in Robinson, 2002b). Four alternative explanations, not necessarily connected to media influence, were offered. First, the outcome of domestic political and interest group pressure; second, the idea of humanitarian intervention in a 'failed' state conformed with Bush's internationalist 'New World Order' vision in which the international community had a duty to uphold international law'; third, Bush's own Christian principles, which led him to do something to save lives; and, finally, the Bush administration's desire 'to deflect congressional pressure to intervene in Bosnia' (Robinson, 2002b: 51). As we can see, although all but one of these alternative justifications of the intervention had clear-cut political agendas, it is clear that the key motives that mobilised the US-led military intervention in Somalia were not entirely humanitarian.

Thus, dismissing the CNN effect on 'Operation Restore Hope' as nothing but a myth, Robinson argues that 'the decision to deploy [...] US troops in Somalia was not prompted or "caused" by media attention to the starvation in Somalia, adding that in fact, the media did not pay any significant level of attention until after Bush had decided to send in US troops' (2002b: 62). He points to other factors – such as aid agency, congressional lobbying and President Bush's own personal conviction – as more plausible explanations for the intervention. I therefore go along with Robinson's argument that, if the media played only a supportive rather than a pressuring role in what ostensibly turned out to be an easy case for the CNN effect, the question is raised as to the validity of the CNN factor thesis in the case of 'Operation Restore Hope' in Somalia. As Hammond (2007b) notes, many studies have shown that the link between media coverage and US official policy on Somalia was pretty much the opposite of the so-called CNN factor thesis, as coverage simply followed rather than influenced the dominant elite official line (Livingston, 1997; Mermin 1999; Robinson 2002b). Hawkins refers to this as the 'Reverse CNN Factor' – the phenomenon by which the government influences the media, as opposed to the media influencing the government (Hawkins, 2002). Hawkins alludes to the arguments by Hallin (1986) and Bennett (1990) that the content of the US media is a reflection of the agenda and of the range of debate among elites in the US government: that the media 'index' the news according to government viewpoints. Due to budgetary constraints and the credibility of sources, news organisations tend to rely heavily on elite sources, mostly government officials in domestic capitals, for context in their reporting. The consequence of this is 'an increase in the power of the government in choosing what will or will not become news, and a dominance of government spin on the news' (Hawkins, 2002: 227).

In fact, while there is little evidence to support the claim of the CNN factor influencing US official policy to embark on 'Operation Restore Hope' in Somalia, there is more to support the less popular claim that media coverage led to the sudden US withdrawal from Somalia, as evocative images of corpses of US rangers being dragged through the streets of Mogadishu were constantly splashed on western TV screens. US President Bill Clinton was widely reported to have been put 'under intense pressure to pull American troops out' (*Independent*, 5 October 1999), and he had already indicated that 'he intended to withdraw' (*Times*, 4 October 1993).

Robinson, however, warns that, if the 'CNN effect' was a myth in the case of Somalia, it was for real in Bosnia, since, 'by emphasising the failure of the West and empathising with the expelled population of Srebrenica, news media coverage was of a critical "do something" nature' (Robinson, 2002b: 51). The theoretical insight provided by the 'policy–media interaction' model is that, under these conditions, media coverage is likely to have influenced the policy process, causing a strong 'CNN effect' to occur and helping to produce a decision to intervene in order to defend Gorazde (Robinson, 2002b: 82). The question is then raised as to why the CNN effect turned out to be real in the case of Bosnia and not in that of Somalia.

Writing with hindsight, Alagiah notes that knowing the difference between good men and bad men and understanding the bridge that separates right from wrong is indeed the stuff of moral certainty. He blamed the Americans for failing to grasp the fact that the break-up of

Somalia was a political problem, as much a part of the fall-out from the Cold War as Bosnia was. 'In Bosnia, the warlords were treated with caution, if not respect' (Alagiah, 2001: 105). Alagiah also blamed the failure of the US-led intervention on the deliberate slighting of the UN contingent, made up of mostly Pakistani troops on the ground, when they landed. At least one Pakistani soldier confided in him, saying that this was due to racism. On the humiliating exit of the US troops, Alagiah said:

> America [...] had only itself to blame. Don't get me wrong. I found the images of Somali youth rejoicing over the battered and lifeless body of an American soldier as repulsive as anyone else. I grieved with the parents of that young man [...] And yet I felt I knew why Somalis had responded with unrestrained glee and merciless mockery. It was the celebration of the weak when the strong are brought down to size. They were rejoicing in the belittling of America's power, not in the murder of one of its sons. (Alagiah, 2001: 111)

Alagiah suggested that 'that, perhaps, is Somalia's true place in history'. As we have seen here, the evocative, empathy distance framing of the Somali crisis based on the 'us only' patriotic political interest journalism contributed to reducing the role of 'the CNN factor' and hence to the failure of the intervention. The US and the UN were ill prepared for dealing with local warlords, and after the killing of 23 Pakistani troops the US marines embarked on an ill-fated campaign against one of the main faction leaders, General Farah Aideed, which ended in a public humiliation and the ultimate withdrawal of the US forces (Shaw, 1996: 171). The controversial and humiliating manner in which the US/UN intervention ended generated a heated discussion about whether the US or the UN was to blame. While the US pointed the finger at the UN for turning the 'humanitarian mission' into a misconceived attempt at 'nation building' and 'peace enforcement' (Allard, 1995; Crocker, 2004), others see this claim simply as a US government attempt to shift the blame of its inglorious defeat in Somalia to the UN (Hammond, 2007b). Moreover, despite formerly handing over to the UN, the US still firmly remained in control, as all the main Security Council Resolutions were drafted by US officials and UNOSOM 11 was headed by retired American Admiral Jonathan Howe (Clarke and Herbst, 1996).

What is more, a look at the historical context of Somalia shows that the US involvement there during the Cold War period was largely implicated in the country's political crisis. Western aid seriously weakened the

Somali economy, as excess food produced by US farmers was dumped there in the name of PL480, as part of the USAID scheme. An economy largely dependent on foreign aid was created as Said Barre's regime exaggerated the numbers of refugees and displaced persons fleeing the war with Ethiopia over the disputed Ogaden region in order to secure more food aid. This dependency worsened state corruption and clan divisions, leading to state collapse, which was accelerated by the US withdrawal of support for Somalia after the end of the Cold War, as the US felt it was no longer needed to counter the Soviet influence in the region.

Second, there was a strong political economy angle to the US-led intervention motivation. Herman and Chomsky (1988), as well as Hammond (2000), allude to the West's use of humanitarianism as a smokescreen for promoting their liberal free market policies. As Manokha puts it, 'when talking about human rights (meaning exclusively political and civil rights) and their protection', Warren Christopher, US Secretary of State under the Clinton presidency, 'equated respect for these rights not only with freedom but also with free markets' (Manokha, 2008: 186). To be free in the dominant western discourse means respect for political and civil rights associated with neoliberal capitalism. Yet, putting the Somalia crisis in context in his book, Alagiah warned that the question that should be raised is not the obvious one 'about why the famine happened, but whether it could have been avoided altogether. People went hungry because the failure of the rains in successive years was compounded by the effects of civil war' – and, above all, 'the war itself might have been avoided if foreign-policy strategists in Washington, London and Paris had been as concerned about the effects of the post-Cold War transition in Africa as they were about its repercussions in Europe'. A great deal of money, some of it originally billed for Africa, was poured into central and Eastern Europe to facilitate the totalitarian passage to quasi-democracy rule (Alagiah, 2001: 112). What difference would it have made, had Alagiah brought this context into his dispatches from Somalia? Instead, permeating the mainstream media discourse were dominant empathy/distance frames such as 'emaciated', 'starving', 'slaughter', 'ancient warriors', 'self-destruction', 'complicated' and more – all of which only helped to reinforce the utilitarian logic of non-intervention and, in this case, of dramatic withdrawal. Yet a survey carried out by the Refugee Policy Group, an independent Washington-based Non-Governmental Organisation (NGO), on behalf the US government concluded that between 202,000 and 238,000 had died from famine in Somalia, while between 100,000 and 125,000 lives were lost as a result of 'delays in undertaking decisive action' in 1992, before the humanitarian intervention (Meredith, 2005: 477). In fact, according to UN figures, mortality rates had begun to drop well before the Americans set foot on Somali soil; Paul Mitchell, a spokesman for the World Ford Programme, said: 'What you have now are just pockets of famine.' This suggests that not only delayed intervention was at fault, but also getting the priorities wrong by focusing only on efforts to distribute relief food instead of stopping the mass killings, rape, torture and other human rights abuses.

Finally, cultural subjectivity frames[2] also contributed to the failure of the US intervention. Media researchers allude to specific historical or cultural frames to explain the failure of journalists in mainstream western media to offer 'adequately informed and nuanced accounts of African crises' (Carruthers, 2004: 163). Broadly speaking, Carruthers identified two diametrically opposed cultural frames of African crises: Africanism and ethnocentrism. In particular, she notes, 'many Africanists take issue with Western media's unthinking elevation of "tribalism" to explanatory primacy in accounting for warlordism in Somalia and genocide in Rwanda'. She argues that 'not only does this ethnocentrism (or indeed racism) omit the West's own implication in the roots of African state failure, economic collapse, and societal disintegration but it also has profound consequences for what types of action – or inaction – become thinkable in response' (Carruthers, 2004: 163). Pointing to ethnocentrism, Carruthers suggested that Peterson's account of Somalis' bloodlust as a function of these 'ancient nomadic warriors' having been catapulted 'by default into a new era' could have been lifted directly from accounts of Kenya's Mau Mau 'emergency' in the 1950s, which similarly explained Kikuyu 'atavism' as a crisis of modernisation, as backward tribes struggled with, and against, the disruptive impact of 'progress', holding on to ossified traditions and irrational beliefs (Peterson, 2000: 6; see also Carruthers, 1995: 128–93). Alagiah also alluded to some of the problematic evocative empathy distance frames that contributed to the failure of the intervention from the word go:

American planners were never really able to look beyond the apparently shambolic vision of men with rubber sandals and sarongs wielding worn-out weapons. Racial stereotyping may well have played its part in America's ultimately fatal underestimation of the task at hand. They saw poverty but mistook it for weakness. Because they could not see any uniforms, they assumed there was no discipline. Because Somali gun men did not salute, they believed there was no command and control. They were wrong every time. They failed to realise that even in these, the worst of all times, Somalis cherished a sense of national pride. After all, regardless of their clan affiliations, they speak the same language and worship the same God. (Alagiah, 2001: 105)

These historical frames were central to making the so-called 'Operation Restore Hope' short-lived. Even though the apparent 'CNN effect' may have provided a supportive role to the operation, it clearly failed to generate sustained support for what suddenly turned out to be a prolonged and costly intervention. TV images of bloated corpses of US soldiers being dragged through the dusty streets of Mogadishu, and, even more shocking... of a soldier with a rope tied around his ankles and his arms, splayed in the sign of the crucifix, dramatically generated an immediate announcement of the US troop withdrawal (Carruthers, 2004: 158). Mohamed Sahnoun, Special UN representative in Somalia at the time of the crisis, warned that a preventive approach would have had a fair chance of success without great expense, and without the need for a large military presence, had it been used in the three specific cases in Somalia: the uprising in the North in 1988; the manifesto group in 1990; and the national conference in 1991. The international community, led by the UN, abandoned Somalia to the warlords, as the three opportunities were missed (Sahnoun, 1994). The failure of the intervention was set to haunt the US for some time to come, for, as Alagiah notes, Somalia did to the collective US psyche in the 1990s what Vietnam had done in the 1970s, making Americans vow to stay clear from this 'ungrateful and complicated world'. Thus, when the whispers of the Rwandan Genocide reached the American diplomats at the UN two years later, 'they literally turned the other way' (Alagiah, 2001: 112–3).

7.3   The Rwandan Genocide

The Rwandan Genocide offers yet another classical case of the role of the media in the failure of western intervention to save hundreds of thousands of lives. The implication of this human wrongs journalism was a total neglect, by the international community, of a country that was desperately in need of outside help. The timing was not in Rwanda's favour, because that was a period when the rest of the big powers were turning their back on Africa after the end of the Cold War, in the early 1990s. Rwanda, in fact, stands out as the most egregious example of this post-Cold War neglect: its political moderates and the rest of the Tutsi population were left at the mercy of their killers (Melvern, 2000). The neglect of Africa had become so serious by the mid-1990s that the International Institute for Strategic Studies concluded: 'If there is a common thread running throughout Africa, it is fading international attention. The outstanding feature of Western policy in Africa is its absence.'[3]

The death in a plane crash of Rwandan President Juvenal Habyarimana on 6 April 1994 ostensibly sparked the mass killings of the minority Tutsis by Interahamwe militia and by civilians mobilised by the ruling party. Within the space of three months, about 800,000 Tutsis had been killed, mostly by machetes (Onana, 2001). The speed of the killings meant that any international response, to be effective, would have had to have been rapid. Four hundred Belgian troops were stationed in Rwanda, but these were used only to rescue European civilians; they then withdrew, leaving the local population to its fate (Shaw, 1996: 171). Discussion of the Rwandan Genocide has largely hovered around whether it was indeed genocide or mere 'tribal violence' between the Hutus and the Tutsis. Yet, while there is general agreement in the literature (Beattie et al., 1999; Livingston and Eachus, 2000; Melvern, 2000; Osabu-Kle, 2000; Alagiah, 2001; Carruthers, 2000, 2004; Hammond, 2007b) that the killings should be accepted as genocide, many critics have provided evidence to suggest that explanations of 'tribalism' were preferred in media reporting.

Hammond (2007b) argues that the 'tribalism' framework could be misleading: the difference between Hutu and Tutsi cannot be simply understood in 'ethnic' or 'tribal' terms, since both groups live in the same country and share a common language, customs and religious traditions. Mamdani (2001: 42) observes instead that western discussion of the distinction in the specialist literature has been influenced by colonial or anti-colonial attitudes, where some writers emphasised differences, others parallels. Under the 'divide and rule' strategy of the Belgians during the colonial rule of Rwanda under King Leopold, the Europeans saw the Tutsis as a non-indigenous and superior race; they were perceived to have a civilising influence on the backward Hutus. The Europeans thus considered that Tutsi privileges were worthy of protection for the maintainance of law and order; this is largely considered as the historical fact that set the stage for the hatred that developed between these two ethnic groups and eventually led to the genocide (Hammond, 2007b). As Philo et al. (1999: 221) suggest, however, media coverage of the genocide failed to take cognisance of this historical context in explaining the genocide, preferring instead the 'tribal' explanation; and the authors blame this approach on the media's over-reliance on elite official western sources, which were 'unlikely to dwell on the misdeeds of the former colonial powers'.

The role of the western media in making the world understand what was going on in Rwanda was critical; but unfortunately little or nothing was done. Only a few locally based reporters were able to supply images with graphic accounts of the early phases of the genocide for the western television. However, by the time the mainstream journalists went in, the genocide, which lasted about 100 days, had already ended, and so these journalists were only able to provide images of the aftermath of the killings and to relay accounts from interviews with refugees in Goma and Tanzania, most of whom were indeed the perpetrators of the genocide. For what has largely been attributed to political, economic and cultural factors, pretty much like the case of the failed 'Operation Restore Hope' in Somalia, most of the western media journalists who covered the Rwandan crisis in the wake of the genocide in 1994 simply lost the political angle of the story and concentrated instead on the refugee crisis in Goma, in Zaire (present day D.R. Congo). Here the journalists quickly opted for the 'empathy framed coverage', which tends to focus on the suffering of individuals, identifying them as victims in need of outside help. By hyping the cholera outbreak in Goma and neglecting the genocide in Rwanda, the journalists ostensibly became victims of a 'distance framing' of the genocide in Rwanda, which tended to minimise the pressure for an intervention designed to stop the killings and end the crisis (Shaw, 2007). I will now look at the political, economic and cultural factors that drove the empathy distance frames in the mainstream news media discourse and contributed to the abandoning of Rwanda by the international community at the hour of need.

First, the political and geo-strategic interests of the great powers – the US, Britain and France; and especially the latter, as part of the fall-out of the post-Cold War era – constituted a major factor. The US and Britain, which had earlier advocated a tough line on the compliance of the warring parties with the Arusha peace agreement, suddenly made a quick U-turn and threatened to call for a withdrawal of the UN force if the Belgians went ahead with their threat to withdraw their contingent from the UN Assistance Mission in Rwanda (UNAMIR) (Melvern, 2000). The Czech Republic ambassador at the UN, Karel Kovanda, said in an interview: 'No one was sure what, if anything needed to be done. Into this absolutely bizarre situation came the big powers [...] who said they could do nothing' (Melvern, 2000: 152). At least the British Ambassador to the UN, David Hannay, was on record to have helped to frame the

UN resolution on Rwanda so as to avoid any use of the word 'genocide', even when the mass killings were well underway (Melvern, 2001). Investigative journalist and author Linda Melvern said at a round table in London:

> The crucial period was the first five weeks when General Delerre of the UN peacekeepers produced an estimate that 5,000 troops might be able to stop the killing. I obtained a document that recalled what was said during the secret and informal meetings while the genocide was taking place and Delerre's estimate wasn't even discussed in the first five weeks [...] while the British press was reporting anarchy and chaos, organised slaughter was taking place – nowhere near civil war and I still don't think this story has been adequately covered. It is a scandal of huge proportions. (Melvern, 2001)

The empathy distance frames used by the mainstream media contained serious misinformation. While the estimated death toll in organised mass killing had reached 500,000 by 9 May, the House of Commons was told that 200,000 may have died in combat. The House waited until May 24 to debate the issue – when Labour MP Tony Worthington remarked that, if 500,000 white people had died, the crisis would have been extensively debated (Melvern, 2001). The Americans, too, shied away from calling the mass killings genocide.

There is a school of thought that holds that the genocide was unplanned, and therefore ultimately uncontrollable (Onana, 2001). However, as Alagiah argues, if you accept the principal role of the military and the armed militias, then you must also accept that there was a chain of command and control. Alagiah points to a UN commander in Kigali, who was told by an informant of a weapons cache held by extremists, and there was talk of an unusually large import of machetes in the months preceding the genocide (Alagiah, 2001: 127). Controversy, for example, abounds over the 'humanitarian credentials of the French intervention in Rwanda with some arguing it was motivated more by French geo-strategic goals in Africa than humanitarian concern' (Robinson, 2002b: 9). This came when the French under the Mitterrand presidency were desperately seeking to exact their neo-colonial influence in the central African region in the immediate post-Cold War era, following the withdrawal of the Belgians under King Leopold in the 1960s.

Scott Peterson wrote that the French were supplying munitions to Rwanda in May and June 1994 – well after the beginning of the genocide

(Peterson, 2000). Yet, while all this was going on, diplomats at the UN shied away from calling it genocide – if for nothing else, to avoid being called upon to intervene on moral grounds. Thus, as far as Rwanda was concerned, the Genocide Convention of 1946, signed in the aftermath of the Jewish Holocaust, which imposed the moral responsibility on member states to prevent genocide wherever it threatened to occur, was proved to signify nothing. When, in an apparent face-saving move, the French moved in with 2,500 troops in Operation Turquoise, which was endorsed by the UN Security Council, it was more to save what remained of their ally Kigali regime from advancing Rwandan Patriotic Front (RPF) rebels, and in a way to provide cover for the *génocidaires* to complete their work, than to stop the genocide. Osabu-Kle (2000: 243–4) notes that the Security Council resolution that followed the massacres was also suspect; it only went to confirm that the international diplomats shut their eyes to the genocide and diverted attention in the direction of the civil war between the government army and the RPF rebels. Furthermore, it made no provision whatsoever for the confiscation of arms, hence reducing the UN peacekeepers to mere spectators of the unfolding massacres. The media too had its own share of the blame. Although the genocide began before the South African elections in which Nelson Mandela was to win, the media were preoccupied with the latter.

Second, there was evidence to suggest a very strong economic motivation for the preference of empathy distance frames by the mainstream media. Peter Uvin's celebrated 1998 book *Aiding Violence: The Development Enterprise in Rwanda* freely talks about the political economy of the Rwandan Genocide, which the mainstream media relegated to the backwater to explain the genocide itself, preferring instead the simple use of empathy distance frames (Uvin, 1998). The book was premised on the fact that Rwanda was, until close to the 1994 genocide, considered by the World Bank 'a model developing country, doing well on the variables we cared about: decent macroeconomic growth, the presence of a great number of NGOs and peasants' associations, high vaccinations rates, and the like [...] Yet, with a few months, it would fall apart in a spasm of violence and destruction [...]' (Uvin, 2004). What went wrong?

Osabu-Kle argues that the case of Rwanda glaringly demonstrates that development is more complicated than simply getting the price of goods laid down correctly through market forces, implementing government policies that encourage growth in agricultural production, avoiding urban bias and so on. It confirms that having an 'enabling environment' in the liberal capitalist sense alone is not enough; this must be complemented by due regard to culture and historical forces. Worse still, Osabu-Kle adds, Rwanda, like most developing countries in sub-Saharan Africa, was a mono-crop country depending solely on coffee, and with fluctuations in the world market price of this commodity things were bound not to improve (2000: 212). Peter Uvin shared similar sentiments in his book *Aiding Violence*, where he talked a lot about the prevalence of *structural violence* – defined as a combination of high inequality, social exclusion, and humiliation – and the way it creates a fertile breeding ground for ethnic rhetoric and communal violence; it demonstrated in detail how most development aid, unintentionally and often unknowingly, strengthens the dynamics of structural violence rather than weakening them. The book also discussed the dynamics of social polarization, rising human rights violations, and militarisation of society that preceded the genocide, and criticised the way the development community's 'voluntary blindness' to these factors allowed it to continue 'business as usual' almost up to the last day (Uvin, 2004: 2–3).

The massive arms sale to Rwanda, which was supplied largely by France to the government and which the mainstream media glossed over, also contributed largely to the escalation of hostilities and hence to the genocide. According to the Human Rights Watch Arms Project Report published in January 1994, four months before the genocide started, military supplies by France to the Rwandan government included mortars, artillery, armoured cars and helicopters. The report confirms that these sales were not disputed by France. Profits accrued from these arms sales, including those from the sale of arms from funds donated by Rwandan exiles in North America and Europe, benefited the economies of the arms supplying countries in the developed world, while Rwanda remained impoverished. US military sales to Rwanda totalled 2.3 million between 1981 and 1992, according to the report. Yet, in its 1992 annual report to Congress justifying military aid programmes, the Bush government stated that 'relations with the US are excellent', and that 'there is no evidence of any systematic human rights abuses by the military or any other element of the Government of Rwanda'.[4] The massive arms imports to Rwanda seriously impacted on the country's economy, to the extent that President Habyarimana said in an official radio broadcast:

Our economy was already ailing in 1990, and of course the war has not resolved anything. We signed agreements with the IMF and the World Bank, which we have of course been unable to honour, because we have had to purchase weapons and supplies. Now we want to improve our macroeconomic outlook but we have a serious shortage of currency.

–Foreign Broadcast Information Service, FBIS-AFR-93-193,
7 October 1993, p. 2, cited in HRW Arms project report

This partly explains the sudden U-turn of Rwanda, from being a model of neoliberal development, as recognised by the World Bank in 1989, to being a country that was basically teetering on the edge. Instead of using cases like this to explain the worsening security situation in the country to the point where it led to genocide, the mainstream media focused their energy on the empathy distance images that reinforced the hopelessness of the situation and hence justified inaction. If the media had instead practised human rights journalism, calling a spade a spade and blaming the western powers for helping to create the crisis in the first place, this would have brought pressure on the West to act much earlier and to prevent the genocide.

Finally, cultural empathy distance frames contributed in a very big way to the abandonment of the real Rwandan story. Evoking the tribal or ethnic factor to explain African conflicts is more or less an empathy/distance frame that widens the gap between the concern of the audience (in this case, the western public) and the plight of the victims of the humanitarian crisis, thus making the case for non-intervention. Moreover, by foregrounding the cholera outbreak in the refugee camp in Goma in Eastern Congo and by neglecting the genocide in Rwanda, western journalists ostensibly became perpetrators of a 'distance framing' of the genocide, which in turn tended to minimise the pressure for intervention to end it (Shaw, 2007: 368, endnotes 18 and 19). Carruthers argues that, if Somalia represents 'exhibit A' in the debate regarding the CNN myth of manufacturing consent, then Rwanda provides a more pressing point of concern for Africanists anxious to deconstruct the shortcomings of the western media's coverage of 'small' wars. She contends that Rwanda represents by far the best example of western media resorting to the 'ancient ethnic hatreds' thesis to explain the country's crisis (Carruthers, 2004: 164) – what Preston (1996) described as 'distance framing'. The genocide was reduced to a simple tale of the 'bad Hutu' slaughtering their 'good Tutsi neighbours, a kind of repeat performance of an ongoing cycle of bloodletting since time immemorial' (Carruthers, 2004: 164, cites McNulty, 1999; de Waal, 1994). This became the prevailing narrative: Tutsi victims versus Hutu perpetrators. Paradoxically, however, Carruthers explains that, in their desperate bid to maintain these categories and to affirm the purity of refugee victimhood, many journalists reporting the post-genocide exodus into Tanzania and Zaire glossed over the fact that those who filled the camps around Rwanda's borders were in fact among the several thousands who had carried out the genocide – not, as reporting often implied, an indistinguishable mass of 'innocents' fleeing in fright (de Waal, 1994; F. Keane 1996: 186).

In an attempt to strike a balance between the evocative reporting of the humanitarian crisis unfolding in Goma and giving the political context of the genocide in Rwanda, BBC's Alagiah said that he quickly produced dispatches that framed the Hutu refugees as a humanitarian problem, but also – essentially – as a politically destabilising event: 'Today's defeated soldiers may well turn out to be tomorrow's rebels', Alagiah said in one of his dispatches, 'foreshadowing much of the unrest that is still shaking the region' (Alagiah, 2001).

He recognised that many of those who were now victims had themselves inflicted great suffering on the others by taking part in the genocide. However, he admitted to have lost the political plot when the UN refugee agency called a press conference to announce the outbreak of cholera among the refugees:

> The genocide was forgotten, and cholera became the story. That was all the newsroom wanted to know about. How were they treating it? How did it spread? What could Britain do to help? Could we follow a case from diagnosis to recovery – or death? I played my part. I fed the machine and, in the process, made my contribution to the idea back home that these people were primarily victims. (Alagiah, 2001: 122)

When things really came to a head, 'the few UN soldiers who were left in the Rwandan capital organised convoys of cars and trucks full, mainly, of white people, which drove through streets littered with corpses of black people. Every mutilated body, every gaping wound was a rebuke, a reminder of the cost of betrayal' (Alagiah, 2001: 130). The over-emphasis on the empathy/distance frames over the empathy/critical frames on the part of the mainstream western media was even more evident in Rwanda. As some western media journalists, including BBC's George Alagiah, were to admit, albeit with hindsight, the international community, after having largely ignored the genocide, now rushed to assist the mass of Hutu 'refugees' crammed into disease-ridden camps in the eastern Zairian city of Goma; they were prompted of course by television pictures of the Hutu exodus and of the outbreak of cholera in the camps. This media frenzy resonated well among policymakers in the West, as

US Air Force planes mounted an air drop of supplies while some 150 aid agencies descended on the scene. President Clinton described the 'refugee' camps as the worst humanitarian crisis in a generation. In a rather outrageous twist of irony, the UN, 'unable to mount an operation to prevent genocide, now found no difficulty in raising $1million a day to spend on a refugee crisis organised by *génocidaires* for their own purposes' (Meredith, 2005: 523). The new RPF rebel government was also accused of killing 3,000 Hutu refugees in a camp inside Rwanda in April 1995. The UN, having turned its back on the earlier genocide, now decided to take a strong line with the RPF government (Shaw, 1996: 173).

In conclusion, in the case of Kosovo, the media coverage was helpful, placing a good deal of emphasis on the empathy/critical frames over those of empathy/distance frames to call for a sustained military intervention by NATO forces to prevent the ethnic cleansing of the Albanian Muslims by the Orthodox Serbian Christians, and thus preventing genocide (Robinson, 2002b), as they had done for the Kurds earlier; but they failed to do the same in the case of Rwanda and Somalia, or in that of Sierra Leone, discussed in the previous chapter. Yet critics of the NATO intervention in Kosovo have blamed it for escalating rather than halting the violence: not only did the increasing Serbian attacks on Kosovars follow the start of the NATO air strikes on the Serbs, but the refugee crisis intensified too, with large numbers of ethnic Albanians and Serbs fleeing (Hammond, 2007b). The mainstream media were accused of ostensibly acting as mere propagandists for the NATO air strikes. Recounting his experience after the conflict, Robert Fisk of *The Independent* accused his fellow reporters of behaving either as 'sheep', who passively accepted official claims, or as 'frothers', who strongly identified with the proclaimed morality of the bombing (Fisk, *Independent*, 29 1999). Still, not all media analysts agree with this criticism. In his survey of the British television news coverage of the Kosovo intervention for example, McLaughlin (2002b: 122) argues that 'there was a real media counterweight to the NATO spin [...] in the news rooms back in London'.

Martin Shaw admits that 'the Rwandan situation was resolved not by media-driven UN action but by the military success of the opposition Rwandan Patriotic Front, which had quickly conquered most of the country' (Shaw, 1996: 172), albeit after the genocide had ended. However, while Shaw blames the mainstream media for reducing the genocide of 1994 perpetrated by the Hutu government and that of 1995 perpetrated by the rebel government to 'simple humanitarian disasters', his claim that 'the limitations of media coverage were hardly the reason for the UN's failure to intervene effectively to save hundreds of thousands of lives' (p. 173) is contradictory to say the least. So is his blaming of the international community's non-intervention on what he calls a lack of 'strongly perceived western strategic interests' in Rwanda. As this chapter shows, there is a problem with this assertion, considering the plethora of evidence discussed that points to the presence of strategic interests of the US and France in the case studies of both Somalia and Rwanda. The fact of the matter – which Martin Shaw apparently glossed over – is the failure of the mainstream media to fully discuss this political context, as they did in the case of Kosovo and Kurdistan: that would have generated empathy critical frames, public sympathy and pressure for action instead of an empathy distance framing of the political, economic and cultural factors – a framing aimed at discouraging action to do something early enough to avert the crises in Somalia and Rwanda.

8
The Politics of Humanitarian Intervention and Human Wrongs Journalism: The Case of Kosovo versus Sierra Leone

While political theorists such as Walzer (1992) have in the recent past been exploring why states intervene militarily to protect and promote human rights in countries where the state apparatus fails to do so, or even violates them, little has been done to explore why countries intervene or support humanitarian intervention in some countries but not in others in the context of the politics of humanitarian intervention. Simon Caney, Chris Brown and Martin Shaw are among the very few who have explored the political realism and cosmopolitan binary context of the humanitarian intervention debate. Even more limited, if present at all, is the role of the media in the equation, as I stressed in the introductory chapter. This chapter seeks to address this gap by exploring the role of human wrongs journalism in ensuring humanitarian intervention in Kosovo, but not in Sierra Leone, when the crises in the two countries peaked at the same time in 1999. While in the case of Kosovo the media usefully placed a great deal of emphasis on empathy/critical frames over empathy/distance frames to call for a sustained military intervention by North Atlantic Treaty Organisation (NATO) forces and to prevent the ethnic cleansing of the Albanian Muslims by the Orthodox Serbian Christians and, by extension, the genocide, they failed to do the same in the case of Somalia, Rwanda and Sierra Leone – to name just a few cases.

Robinson warns that, if 'the CNN effect' on Somalia was a myth, then that on Bosnia was for real, since,

by emphasising the failure of the West and empathising with the expelled population of Srebrenica, news media coverage was of a critical 'do something' nature [...] The theoretical insight provided by the policy-media interaction model is that under these conditions media coverage is likely to have influenced the policy process, causing a strong CNN effect to occur and helping to produce a decision to intervene in order to defend Gorazde. (Robinson, 2002b: 82)

The question is then raised as to why the CNN effect turned out to be real in the case of Kosovo and not in that of Somalia, Rwanda, or even Sierra Leone. Following Virgil Hawkins (2002), I argue that, while the CNN factor might have helped to bring pressure to bear on the international community to act in Kosovo, it might equally have helped the same community to turn away its attention from relatively distant crises such as in Sierra Leone, particularly when the two peaked at almost the same time. Drawing on my analysis of the media representation of Kosovo and Sierra Leone, I aim in this chapter to problematise political realism as human wrongs journalism and to suggest the existence of a nexus between cosmopolitanism and human rights journalism. This chapter will therefore open with a brief discussion of the cosmopolitan theory of human rights journalism, to determine how political realism undermines the cosmopolitan concept of global justice and how, in a similar way, human wrongs journalism, grounded in political realism, undermines human rights journalism. From here the chapter will examine how the CNN factor contributed to NATO's intervention in Kosovo and how the 'other side of the CNN factor' contributed to the abandonment of Sierra Leone by the international community at its hour of need.

8.1 A cosmopolitan theory of human rights journalism

Cosmopolitans believe that human rights imply some form of moral order, which must be in turn linked to some form of moral community. Political realists, on the other hand, pretty much like cultural relativists, believe that there are 'particular' and not 'universal' moral communities, based on diverse histories and cultures. As a way of striking a balance between political realism and cosmopolitanism, therefore, cosmopolitans propose the idea of a global or cosmopolitan community that has particular and limited communities as component parts. The concept of a 'cosmopolis' or world city originated from the ancient Stoic idea of a human community based upon the worth of reason in each and every human being (Anderson-Gold, 2001). This is a society where every human being or every life is important, and hence worth protecting in the cosmopolitan context of global justice. In short, we are dealing here with human rights without borders. A journalism that is based on selective rather than distributive justice cannot therefore be said to be human rights journalism. As this chapter seeks to show, the dominant western liberal journalism practice as we know it today is overly selective, not only in the types of human rights violations that make the news but also, and perhaps more importantly, in the culturally skewed way they are covered – if at all. Yet, as Kok-Chor Tan (2004) suggested, 'liberalism is committed to a cosmopolitan understanding of distributive justice'. In other words, liberals should apply distributive principles to all individuals of the world equally, regardless of their nationality or ethnic background. Thus this close affinity between liberalism and cosmopolitanism should ideally make the dominant western liberal journalism distributive more than selective. Unfortunately, there is more evidence, as this chapter demonstrates, to support the contrary.

This liberalism–cosmopolitanism nexus has been called into question by most liberals, who argue that the theory of nationalism is by implication liberal. The emergence of nationalist movements in different parts of the world following the end of the Second World War in 1945 and the renewed challenges of multiculturalism and migration in western liberal democratic countries has generated interest, among liberal theorists, in the idea of nationalism. The key fall-out of this new post-war nationalism is the growing consensus, among contemporary liberal theorists, that liberalism and nationalism, far from being contradictory ideals as once commonly thought, are not only compatible but indeed mutually reinforcing ideals (Kok-Chor Tan (2004). Putting the liberalism–cosmopolitanism nexus in the context of the Westphalia norm of state sovereignty versus humanitarian intervention, Chris Brown argues that the post-Westphalia norm introduced in 1945 had contradictory characteristics: first, it instituted a set of new human rights and, second, it introduced at the same time a strict norm of non-intervention. But 'both human rights and non-intervention are substantially new ideas, and it is a mistake to regard one as representing an old order displaced by the other' (Brown, 2002). Realists believe that states are rationally egoist entities that seek to promote their materialist interests in foreign policy (Morgenthau, 1967). Political realism assumes that state leaders have a primary ethical responsibility to protect the national community and that, while this does not preclude moral action in foreign policy, it is commitment to this ethical responsibility that takes precedence. Wheeler sees realism as predicated on a particular conception of the relationship between citizens and strangers that privileges what Robert H. Jackson calls an ethic of 'national responsibility' (Dunne and Wheeler, 1999). Realists believe that a country's vital strategic interests must be put above any action designed to save the lives of fellow humans; this runs contrary to what cosmopolitans stand for.

Chris Brown notes that humanitarian intervention is generally seen as a non-realist, even anti-realist principle, but he disagrees with the idea that intervention to protect human rights can be deemed not to be 'humanitarian' because there is an implicit materialist motive driving it. He argues that it is the positive effects of the intervention, and not the motives of its agent, that should count. Brown pointed out that his position is not based merely on abstract reasoning, because, looking at the history of the Westphalia doctrine, 'less unambiguous humanitarian effects' have often resulted from actions driven by 'very un-humanitarian concerns'. More still, even where humanitarian motives existed, they have often been punctuated with 'ethnocentric, racist assumptions' (Brown, 2002: 154–5). Brown therefore argues that, even if the Kosovo war was not fought as part of some US grand master plan to control the Euroasian continent, it certainly was fought partly in order to preserve NATO's credibility. Despite this political motive, the NATO intervention is said to have halted the ethnic cleansing of the Albanians by the Serbs in Kosovo. Little wonder that the official justifications employed to support the intervention ostensibly implied a right to intervene even when there was no explicit UN authorisation. Hence the intervention was deemed not legal but legitimate. Wheeler conceptualises legal and legitimate interventions as pluralist and solidarist respectively. In the case of pluralism, enforcement action is only justified if it upholds international order and is sanctioned by the Security Council, while solidarism maintains that humanitarian intervention is valid as an end in itself, and hence permissible even in the absence of UN authorisation (Wheeler, 1999: 175). It is this spirit of international humanitarian legitimacy or solidarism that Kant and others conceptualise as cosmopolitanism.

Although Martha Nussbaum (1997: 33) does not see that the global community is a world-state and that a world citizen is compatible with local identifications and affiliations, she argues that 'their (world citizen) attitude is strategically valuable in social life', since, by supporting a sense of commonality even with our political foes, it helps us to move beyond factions and to find reasoned solutions to our common problems. This resonates, somewhat glaringly, with the solution oriented-approach of human rights and peace journalism, as opposed to the problem-oriented approach of war and human wrongs journalism. The doctrine of Stoicism is predicated on the idea that a person's first allegiance is to the moral community of humankind. Cicero was an Academic Platonist who was deeply influenced by Stoicism because that was the philosophical koine of the first century BC. Cicero saw stoicism as entailing 'duties of hospitality to the foreigner, limitations on the conduct of war and the humane treatment of the vanquished' (Anderson-Gold, 2001: 11). Following Donnolly's idea of 'international human rights' (Donnelly, 1989), but specifically alluding to the cosmopolitan philosophy of Immanuel Kant (1963), Anderson-Gold observes that humanity is, by itself, a practical ideal that can only be fully realised by the human community as a whole, which makes human rights require a cosmopolitan condition. From this standpoint, human rights are important not because we are human but, as Ken Booth put it, 'to make us human' (Booth, 1999).

Kant believed in both peace and human rights and saw a clear overlap between the two notions. He, for instance, linked the moral development of any particular political community to 'the development of international law and a pacific federation of states' (Kant, 1963: 18) and argued that war, or even the preparation for it, brings into play attitudes and behaviours hostile to the realisation of human rights. Kant advocated a lawful form of international association, based on the cosmopolitan condition of interdependence. In an ideal cosmopolitan world, therefore, human rights are believed to be held equally by each person and, if that is the case, cosmopolitans argue that there can be common interest in the promotion and protection of such rights. 'A cosmopolitan community comes into being when a violation of human rights is felt to be of concern to the whole international community regardless of where it occurs' (Anderson-Gold, 2001: 21). The rhetoric is indeed fine, but unfortunately it is far removed from what we are seeing in reality. The case of why the international community acted to avert mass killings in Kosovo but not so in the case of Somalia, Rwanda and Sierra Leone (to name but a few African crises) is indeed one such critical example of what is so far a 'rhetorical cosmopolitanism'. All this is despite what Martin Shaw referred to in the immediate post-Cold War period as the beginning of the emergence of a *'global civil society* in which members of global society' are beginning to make the state system responsible in the same way in which national civil societies had hitherto called for the accountability of the sovereign states (Martin Shaw, 1994: 132, see also Chris Brown, 2002). For most of the 1980s, the doctrine of non-intervention reigned supreme, while the 1990s saw the dramatic re-emergence of the occasional willingness of the international community to intervene on 'humanitarian' grounds. At the centre of the development of global civil society is what Shaw called the concept of *global responsibility*, citing the cases of western intervention to protect the Kurds and in the intervention in Bosnia–Herzegovina on purely humanitarian grounds (Shaw, 1994).

Shaw's (1994) call for global responsibility in the promotion and protection of human rights, Frank's ethics and logic of justpeace (2007), and Kant's philosophical framework of the peace and human rights nexus (1963) largely resonate with Schirch's (2002) 'human rights paradigm' of justpeace as opposed to the 'realist paradigm', especially in the important cosmopolitan justice-based values of equality and interdependence. Below are two tables reflecting these two paradigms, which are also included in Schirch's justpeace map (2002). See Tables 8.1 (Realist Paradigm) and 8.2 (Human Rights Paradigm) below:

Table 8.1 Realist Paradigm

Realist Paradigm
Focus on meeting human needs and rights of self at expense of other
• Human relationships are structured hierarchically, where some people dominate over others in an effort to meet their own needs and obtain their own rights • Humans are independent of each other so that one person's gain can be another's loss. • Violence is often the only way of pursuing one's human needs and rights

Table 8.2 Human Rights Paradigm

Human Rights Paradigm
Focus on meeting human needs and rights of both self and other
• Many human relationships are structured in an egalitarian, partnership model, where people cooperate with each other to meet their needs. • Humans are interdependent, so that unmet human needs or rights of any individual or group ripple outwards towards the whole humanity • Nonviolent methods of ensuring human needs and rights are essential so that the very struggle to obtain rights does not violate the rights of an opposing group and reinforce the cycle of violence that will inevitably return to the perpetrators of violence

Apparently going with the realists, Shaw is, however, sceptical that, given the currency of the Westphalia principle of state sovereignty and non-intervention, there is little or nothing to suggest that states, especially in the West, are in a hurry to relinquish their sovereignty in a large way, let alone entirely, to the principles of *global responsibility* (1994). What we have seen instead in recent years is the constant conflict between the instincts of statesmen to maintain the principles of state sovereignty and non-intervention, and the pressure from the global civil society to overcome them. Shaw points to the instincts of US President Bush (senior) and British Prime Minister John Major to abstain, in practical terms, from the civil conflicts in Iraq after they had morally and politically incited rebellion against Saddam Hussein (Shaw, 1994).

While the Westphalia norm of non-intervention did not hold sway for too long in the case of the Kurds and of former Yugoslavia – culminating in the latter in NATO's military intervention to stop the ethnic cleansing of the minority Muslim Albanians of Kosovo against the onslaught of the Serbian regime of Slobodan Milosevic – it won the day, sadly enough, when it came down to Somalia, Rwanda and Sierra Leone. Moreover, the 'virtually unprecedented proposal for Kurdish safe havens' was made possible by the evocative and often highly critical media coverage of Kurdish refugees fleeing from Saddam Hussein's forces (Shaw, 1996: 88). Robinson referred to these 'modes of reporting as *empathy* and *critical* framing because the coverage encourages viewers to associate themselves with the suffering of people and criticises government inaction' (Robinson, 2002b: 29). Thus, while international political and media pressure was used to force world leaders to do something in the case of the Kurds and Kosovars, this was hardly the case in the African countries. How can we therefore explain the role of the media in the failure of the international community to avert total disaster in distant countries such as those in Africa? The following section attempts an answer to this question in the context of the CNN factor in Kosovo but not in Sierra Leone.

8.2   The CNN factor in Kosovo but not in Sierra Leone in 1999

The 1990s saw the notion of humanitarian intervention facing somewhat inexplicable challenges, especially in Africa and the former Yugoslavia. Why do states intervene to address human rights violations in some countries and not in others? What is considered just war/intervention or unjust war/non-intervention? Why intervene in Yugoslavia and not in Africa? Or, to be more specific, why intervene in Kosovo and not in Sierra Leone, when the conflicts in the two countries peaked at almost the same time in 1999? In fact, this largely explains why I elected to juxtapose the two case studies in this chapter, although in terms of numbers of casualties the situation was more desperate in Somalia and Rwanda five or six years earlier. Yet all three exceptions to the Westphalia norm advanced by John Stuart Mill in his famous 1859 treatise of liberty – first, containing two or more political communities that are fighting each other for control of a disputed border territory; second, counter-intervention against a hostile nation trying to bully another nation; and, third, the existence of gross human rights violations that the host nation cannot prevent or protect its people against (Walzer, 1992) – as well as most of the justifications for humanitarian intervention were as present in the conflict in Sierra Leone as in the conflicts of other parts of the world, including Kosovo (Shaw, 2007: 355). Moreover, all of Michael Walzer's five just war principles that justify intervention – just cause, proportionality, least awful option, legitimate authority and low costs – were as present in these distant countries as they were in Kosovo.[1] That Sierra Leone therefore ticks all the boxes from the point of view of humanitarian military intervention begs the question as to why it failed to benefit from the CNN factor and, by extension, from international attention and action.

Some political realists would argue that Sierra Leone did not serve any geo-strategic interest to make Britain and the rest of the international community risk the lives of their soldiers in the name of humanitarian solidarism. Yet, in addition to the fact that Sierra Leone indeed served such geo-strategic interest, as I will show later in this chapter, it also passed as a case of 'supreme humanitarian emergency' – to borrow the words of Wheeler and Walzer – which provides justification for lives to be risked (Walzer, 1992). A supreme humanitarian emergency is said to exist 'when the danger is so imminent, the character of the threat so horrifying, and when there is no other option available to assure the survival of a particular moral community than violating the rule against targeting civilians' (Wheeler,1999: 173). When human beings face genocide, mass murder or ethnic cleansing; when they are in an imminent danger of losing their life or they face appalling hardship; and when the only chance of surviving is military intervention, these conditions are believed to constitute a supreme humanitarian emergency. However, as Wheeler argues, what passes as supreme humanitarian emergency may be open to political manipulation by the intervening parties (Walzer, 1992; Wheeler,1999). Sometimes a state's decision to intervene or not is determined by which of the aggressors they are supporting for some strategic interests, while on other occasions the decision is determined by which of the aggressors are perpetrating most of the human rights violations and hence justify a situation of supreme humanitarian emergency. Sometimes the perpetrators of human rights violations – for example mass killings – come from the government side, and sometimes from the side of the insurgents or invaders. For example, British Foreign Secretary Robin Cook distinguished between cases like Sierra Leone, where rebel fighters perpetrate abuses and the government would like to fight back and stop them but is unable to do so, and cases like Kosovo, where the government itself is the source of the violations (cited in Wheeler, 1999: 173).[2] However, there is a problem with this distinction as far as the reference to Sierra Leone is concerned, as militias or troops loyal to the government were accused by human rights organisations such as Human Rights Watch of having also carried out human rights violations, albeit on a relatively minor scale (Human Rights Watch World Report 2005 – Sierra Leone).

For intervention to be effective, it has to involve the act of power, which sometimes involves taking sides, choosing which of the factions to support and imposing one's will by force (Brown, 2002). However, the problem is not so much the taking of sides in humanitarian intervention, be it by force or by peaceful means; rather it is more to do with siding with perpetrators of human rights abuses because of some geo-strategic interests. Sometimes inaction, or rather lukewarm action to stop or prevent human rights violations, can be caused by the support that the violators may be enjoying from some big powers whose geo-strategic interests are covered in the equation. Thus, despite its success in averting genocide or mass killings in Kosovo, the NATO-led military intervention was criticised not only for the imprecision bombings that caused many civilian casualties, including among the Kosovars whom NATO went in to protect (McLaughlin, 2002b: 257–66) but also, and perhaps more importantly, for serving the geo-strategic interests of the US in Euroasia, and above all the preservation of NATO's credibility in the region (Brown, 2002). However, it must be recognised that, although NATO's intervention in Kosovo failed to tick all the boxes of a truly cosmopolitan humanitarian intervention, it did succeed in halting the ethnic cleansing of the ethnic Muslim Albanians of Kosovo, and so it can arguably be classified as cosmopolitan. This explains why, despite lacking UN authorisation (and hence being deemed illegal in international law), the NATO-led intervention was celebrated as legitimate – indeed as a fine example of international solidarism. Little wonder that Jürgen Habermas (1999; cited in Brown, 2002: 166), a very influential voice in political communication theory, went as far as to say that one could 'see the action as just possibly serving as a precursor to the emergence of a more Kantian international system, a Pacific Union of liberal–democratic states'.

The role of the mainstream media in making this Kosovo intervention happen is very critical here; it consists in what Virgil Hawkins (2002) and Piers Robinson (2002b) call the CNN factor. Hawkins defines it as a concentrated media coverage of a selected conflict that evokes emotions from a people in a particular country – a people that then puts pressure on its leaders to do something (Hawkins, 2002: 225). I will go further to describe such media coverage as not only concentrated but critical – hence using the critical empathy frame – a coverage capable of mobilising public support for action and thus qualifying as a more holistic CNN factor. Although the extent of the impact of media coverage on foreign policy in the matter of addressing international conflicts is still the subject of a huge debate, it is agreed to a very large extent that in some cases this kind of impact and influence is palpable. Shaw, for example, points to the success of the CNN factor in influencing US and British action to protect refugees in Kurdistan (Shaw, 1996), while Robinson alludes to its success in Kosovo (Robinson, 2002b) but criticises its role in 'Operation Restore Hope' in Somalia as exaggerated. Sceptics, however, believe that television images contributed to initial action and inaction in Somalia (Mermin, 1997). Agreeing with this argument, Peter Jacobsen observes that the focus on the extent of the direct influence of the media on intervention decisions obscures an aspect of media coverage that has a far greater effect on conflict management (or lack thereof) (Peter Jakobsen, 2000: 132 cited in Hawkins, 2002). This effect stems from the failure of the media to cover most of the world's conflicts. As Hawkins argues, following Jacobson,

> if we accept that media coverage can play a role in forming or altering government policy relating to foreign conflict, it follows that lack of media coverage can also be a factor in the lack of policy. If the media play a role in policy agenda setting, then the media blackout of most of the world's major conflicts can also be linked to the absence of those conflicts from the agendas of foreign countries (Hawkins, 2002: 225–26).

This, Hawkins points out, can have the knock-on effect of providing little incentive for unaffected countries to get involved in any form of conflict management, relief effort or the worst case scenario of military intervention (Hawkins, 2002). Hawkins therefore suggests that there is a close relationship between lack of media coverage and lack of foreign policy – which he referred to as the 'other side of the CNN factor', where there is a relationship between media coverage and foreign policy, as we saw in the case of the Kurds and Kosovars. Hence, while the CNN factor was true in the case of the Kurds and the Kosovars, it is 'the other side of the CNN factor' that was true in the case of Somalia, Rwanda and Sierra Leone.

I will now focus in the rest of this chapter on answering the question why 'the CNN factor' worked in the case of Kosovo but failed to do so in the case of Sierra Leone, when the conflicts in the two countries peaked at around the same time in 1999. However, first I want to briefly discuss some of the factors that influence the selection and handling, in the form of 'news', of issues such as conflicts over other issues that could be newsworthy. Virgil Hawkins identifies four such factors: competition in the media industry on breaking news; advances in technology, especially TV news; accessibility to the place where the conflict is happening; and the influence of the government – or the 'reverse CNN factor'.[3] For the purposes of this chapter, I am particularly interested in the last factor, in which the government sets the agenda for the media; as I discussed in Chapter 3, this is made easier by the over-reliance of the media on government agencies and officials as 'credible' sources of information. In this way the government's national and geo-strategic interests take centre stage on the news agenda. Thus, while recognising the importance of the professional agenda-setting factors, I should say that it is those political, economic and cultural factors that make 'the CNN factor' real with respect to prompting action to avert human rights violations in some conflicts and not others, that are of particular interest in this chapter. In the case of 'Kosovo but not Sierra Leone', the political factors that made 'the CNN factor' real take two main forms: national interest/cultural proximity and fall-out of Cold War politics; and geo-strategic interests in terms of regional solidarism, security and spread of western democratic values in a 'good neighbourhood'.

First, going by Galtung and Ruge's (1973: 62–72) fourth news value criterion F4-meaningfulness, and in particular, F4.1-cultural proximity, we will see that Kosovo, located in Europe, was of greater national interest value to Britain, and indeed to the rest of the international community, dominated as it is by the western developed countries. The civil war in Sierra Leone started on 23 March 1991, when a small group of rebels of the Revolutionary United Front of Foday Sankoh captured the eastern border town of Beudu from their base in Liberia. It quickly joined the growing list of Africa's forgotten wars. Sierra Leone was colonised and governed by Britain between 1808 and 1961. Yet Sierra Leone's former colonial master shied away from getting involved on humanitarian grounds until ten years later, after tens of thousands of lives and property had been wasted. A modest estimate put the death toll at 120,000, with tens of thousands mutilated and over 2 million displaced and forced into exile by the time the war officially ended in 2001 (Agence France Presse, 14 January 2010). Evocative, empathy distance framed reporting by the mainstream media largely contributed to creating 'the other side of the CNN factor' and hence to the abandonment or banalisation of the Sierra Leone story.

The coverage of the joint Revolutionary United Front (RUF) and Armed Forces Revolutionary Council (AFRC)junta invasion of Freetown on 6 January 1999, by far the most deadly attack of the civil war, claiming an estimated 30,000 lives at one fell swoop, is instructive here. The reporting was focused on providing relief aid for the wounded and displaced civilians caught up in the fighting (evocative) rather than on 'doing something' to halt the fighting and human rights abuses (diagnostic), as is evident in this report by Alex Duval Smith of *The Independent*:

> The £200,000 worth of aid, as well as two ambulances and surgical supplies is intended to treat thousands of people who yesterday continued to flock into the centre of the capital, fleeing fighting in the Eastend, Kissy and Wellington areas [...] The aid – the first large-scale international effort since fighting began on 6 January – arrived yesterday at Lungi airport, north of Freetown. Seven Royal Marines and crew from HMS Norfolk, moored off Freetown for the past 10 days, were due to oversee its distribution.
>
> —'Sierra Leone aid may be wasted', *The Independent*
> (25 January 1999)

There were only very few cases of diagnostic, critical, empathy framed reporting of the Sierra Leone crisis, and most of it in fact came long after the damage had been done and hence can be seen more or less as 'the other side of the CNN factor' rather than 'the CNN factor'. BBC West African correspondent Mark Doyle's report on BBC online is very illustrative of this. Doyle reported UN Human Rights Commissioner Mary Robinson as saying, during her visit to Sierra Leone, over six months after that deadly rebel invasion of 6 January, that 'there had been more loss of life in Sierra Leone than in Kosovo. More suffering, more mutilations and more basic violations of human rights'. Yet Doyle describes Mrs Robinson's comparison of Sierra Leone with Kosovo as 'shocking':

> Here was the former President of Ireland, a highly respected European figure, saying that the human rights situation in Sierra Leone was worse than that in (the) Yugoslav province. It may be that a debate about which situation is worse is fruitless, like somehow comparing Hades with Hell.

West Stands by
> But the UN human rights commissioner's comments do raise several questions. If the situation in Sierra Leone is so bad, how come there are 50,000 NATO troops in Kosovo and just a few dozen unarmed UN observers in Sierra Leone? If the needs are so huge in Sierra Leone, how come independent aid agencies there, such as Oxfam, say that their funds are being cut to help finance projects in Kosovo? And, if it is objectively true, as no less a person than the UN Human Rights Commissioner says, how come journalists who report these things are sometimes accused of exaggerating? I don't mind being accused of exaggerating. Back in 1994, before the extent of the genocide in Rwanda was widely accepted, lots of people said we journalists were over-dramatising the situation. We were not. And now, perhaps it's not an exaggeration to suggest, just tentatively, that the international reaction to Sierra Leone might have been very different if all those people with their limbs chopped off had been white.
> —Sierra Leone: Worse than Kosovo? 03 July 1999 16: 49
> (BBC online, accessed 17 November 2003)

Here, we can see that Doyle did justice to the diagnosis but, as in the reporting of the genocide in Rwanda, this only came with hindsight, after the mass human rights violations had occurred. Thus, though the diagnosis may help to prevent future Sierra Leones and Rwandas, it did not help to promote human rights journalism. Moreover, the cultural proximity criterion – Kosovo being culturally closer to countries of the West than Sierra Leone – was rendered problematic by Mary Robinson's comparison between Sierra Leone and Kosovo, as this makes Sierra Leone score higher than Kosovo in the news value criterion F2 (threshold) on the basis of the size of the damage caused (Galtung and Ruge, 1973 cited in Fowler 2001: 13–14). An article by Richard Norton-Taylor and Chris McGreal (*The Guardian*, 08 May 2000), which covered the mass evacuations of British nationals from Sierra Leone to British ships on the Atlantic Ocean at the height of the conflict in 1997 and 1999, also goes to demonstrate how issues of national interest, rather than any genuine concern to end the civil war, were at play. Moreover, the British rescue mission by paratroopers to free six British military hostages and one Sierra Leonean held by rebels in September 2000 was unfortunately dramatised and celebrated in the British media as a successful British military humanitarian intervention (Kampfner, 2004). Nothing could be further removed from the truth: not only did it happen in 2000, after Sierra Leoneans had already endured the worst human rights violations since the start of the civil war in 1991, but, when it did come, the mission was in reality intended to rescue British military hostages rather than inspired by any genuine concern for the suffering of human rights violations by the local population. Added to the evocative national interest/cultural proximity frame was the post-Cold War fall-out frame, which apparently increased the isolation of geo-strategically distant African countries such as Sierra Leone, Rwanda, Somalia and the DR Congo (among others).

Second, efforts by the mainstream media to promote the geo-strategic interests of the NATO member countries in terms of regional solidarity and security in Europe, and also to promote the spread of western liberal democracy in good European neighbours, contributed to making the CNN factor more real in the case of Kosovo than in the case of Sierra Leone. Here the 'reverse CNN factor' featured prominently, because the NATO secretariat in Brussels and western governments set the agenda for the media in their framing of Serbia as the problem in Kosovo. A case in point is the reporting from the NATO briefings in Brussels. Sharing his experience as Sky News correspondent, then based in Brussels, Jake Lynch said:

> journalists were prepared to accept the fundamental framing of the conflict which NATO was conveying, namely that this was all the fault of Slobodan Milosevic for being unreasonable [...] and that therefore the only way of resolving it was to coerce the Serbs into backing down. That [...] was internalised, unexamined, by journalists despite the unease, criticism and anger on the part of many of them at the texture of the NATO contact with us. (Lynch, in an interview with McGlauglin, 2002: 258)

However, while former Liberian president Charles Taylor[4] was framed by some sections of the mainstream media as the problem of fanning the civil war in Sierra Leone, coverage of this framing was less concentrated and saturated compared to what we saw in the case of the problematising of Milosevic in the Kosovo crisis. In fact this 'other side of the CNN factor' largely accounted for why the British government did not show interest in ending the conflict in Sierra Leone until it became apparent in mid-1999 that the French were using their surrogate, Taylor, in the West African region, to spread their influence in diamond-rich Sierra Leone through the RUF rebels of Foday Sankoh. Thus the Sierra Leone war quickly turned out to be a pawn in the historic Franco-British rivalry, dating back to 'Fashoda' in Egypt in the nineteenth century. This explains the strong British and French media interest in the historic meeting between British Foreign Minister Robin Cook and his French counterpart Hubert Vedrine in the Ghanaian capital Accra, with the main aim of reconciling their strategic or geopolitical interests in Africa (Leridon, AFP-11 March 1999). This came on the heels of the 'Saint Malo Declaration' by British Prime Minister Tony Blair and French President Jacques Chirac in December 1998, where the two agreed to share information about the situation in Africa and in a way put an end to their rivalry in that part of the world (Leridon, AFP-10 March 1999). However, while the Accra meeting on Sierra Leone took place to pick up the pieces after the worst human rights violations had happened, NATOs meeting in Ramboilliet in France, largely initiated by French President Chirac, came just before the military intervention to rescue Kosovo from Serbia.

Therefore, although the NATO bombing caused many casualties among the Serbs as well as among the Kosovars, it did play a vital, though indecisive role in producing a political settlement. The refusal by Russia to come to the rescue of Milosevic when the bombing started and NATO's 'plan B' for a land invasion of Kosovo contributed equally towards pressuring Milosevic to accept the entry of the NATO-led intervention force in the province of Kosovo. This made it possible for Albanaian Kosovar refugees to return home and enjoy a substantial measure of political autonomy, which they would have been denied in the absence of NATO intervention (Wheeler, 2003: 191). A NATO/UN protectorate was set up under the administration of French Philanthropist and politician Bernard Kouchner following the Kosovo war, and although this protectorate met with limited success in post-war reconstruction efforts, it laid the foundations for the spread of western-style democracy in the former Yugoslavia and the rest of Eastern Europe.

The economic interests of Western European powers, as well as of the US, in supporting their overseas businesses and in promoting the expansion of their markets and neoliberal capitalism in 'good European neighbours', also contributed to making the CNN factor real in the case of Kosovo but not that of Sierra Leone. The use of private military companies and the sale of arms to distant, war-torn countries for purely economic gains, as in the case of Sandline in Sierra Leone, are very illustrative here. Questions were for instance asked when the British authorities allegedly assisted the British mercenary company Sandline to break the arms embargo imposed on Sierra Leone by the UN by supplying the arms that were used by pro-government troops, including mercenaries, to remove the AFRC junta and restore the elected Government of Tejan Kabbah. What emerged was that the majority of the sympathy of the western media lay more with Sandline and the British government than with the local population and the elected government that was eventually restored to power. Sam Kiley of the *Times*, for example, tried to reduce the impact of the damage caused by this scandal by arguing that at least the arms were used to flush out the rebels, the 'bad' guys, in favour of the government, the 'good' guys (Kiley, 11 May 1998). This economic frame was reinforced by the fact that Sandline was, as part of the deal, promised mining concessions in the country's huge diamond industry. Thus, while the international community was prepared to risk the lives of NATO troops to avert mass killings in Kosovo, countries such as Sierra Leone were forced to resort to the hiring of private military companies, at huge costs that can only be met by the granting of mining concessions. This resulted in further loss of national resources and caused more instability for the future.

Blood diamonds also constituted an important economic frame in the news discourse. A dominant discourse in the news suggested that diamonds were used by the rebels to fuel the war. However, while diamonds were serving the interests of the rebels, the real beneficiaries turned out to be the overseas and local companies engaged in this illegal trade. At least the *Washington Post*'s Steve Coll admitted in an interview to have met an American businessman working for the RUF, which, he said, facilitated his visit to the rebel territory[5]. George Alagiah also alluded to the conflict diamonds frame, or the frame about diamonds that cause conflict, in his BBC documentary on 'war for wealth'. Moreover, writing for the *Washington Post*, Douglas Farah peppered the 'blood diamond' factor of the war with a terrorism angle (Farah, 02 November 2001). Quoting CIA sources, Farah revealed that some diamond dealers working directly for Bin Laden's network had been, for three years running, engaged in buying gems cheaply from the RUF and in reselling them in Europe and elsewhere, netting huge profits that they used in their terrorist operations. However, yet again, while conveniently picking on

Libya, Liberia and Burkina Faso in this lucrative trade, Farah failed to see the role of the big western powers in the broader picture.

There is a conspiracy theory that accuses the West of not showing much interest in ending conflicts in developing countries because these conflicts serve their economic interests of obtaining otherwise very expensive mineral resources very cheaply. As Buzan Barry notes, 'economics and politics are different analytical sectors of a single reality; views of reality through different analytical lenses, and like all lenses, each brings some things into clearer focus while pushing others into the background' (Barry, 1994: 89). One key interplay between the two sectors is the 'linking of anarchic political structures and capitalist economic ones' (Barry, 1994: 90). Thus the political economy of humanitarian intervention, as we saw in the case of distant African conflicts, can be conceptualised as the centre-periphery thesis – that is, of the possibility of integration or fragmentation in the centre, and of intervention at the periphery. Capitalism – the maximisation of profits – is more likely to take place when there is no evident central authority.

The booming parallel humanitarian economy represented yet another important economic frame in the context of 'the other side of the CNN factor' in Sierra Leone. There was, for instance, an overriding dominance of the evocative frame in the reporting, simply aimed at sensitising public opinion towards the humanitarian crisis of the war, with the ultimate aim of boosting the relief donations and little or no regard for the diagnostic approach, which will instead favour the ending or prevention of this crisis situation, and hence will render appeals for relief donations unnecessary. In what she referred to as her best dispatch for the Agence France Presse (AFP) in terms of market value,[6] Léridon (30 September 1998 – 12: 56 Paris time) portrayed the amputees waiting on the Netland hospital corridor for their turn of the 'krukenberg operation',[7] more or less as a people without any hope, a frame often reserved for victims of African wars. Thus, while the evocative frames (for example distance empathy, humanitarian, economic, relief donations) inform 'the other side of the CNN factor' in the case of Sierra Leone, it is the diagnostic frames (for example, critical empathy, geostrategic, economic neoliberal trade and so on) that inform 'the CNN factor' in the case of Kosovo.

The 'historical baggage' of the West about Africa being a place where the only thing that is real is violence stood out as a major cultural frame that contributed to the other side of the CNN factor in the case of Sierra Leone. This was especially true for special correspondents, who were literally parachutted in at short notice by UN or Economic Community of West African States Military Group (ECOMOG) choppers. Some people may want to attribute this 'other side of the CNN factor' to the professional constraint of access to zones of conflict by the international media, but the cultural subjectivity factor explains it better. Apart from the risks involved, there has been a growing tendency among war correspondents to associate glamour with their work. Wherever they go to report conflicts, they have a tendency to cling together, sharing the same hotel, sometimes using the same fixers and translators, and above all visiting the same pubs and other leisure places. The Sierra Leone war no doubt provided a typical example of this tendency, with the Mammy Yoko and later the Cape Sierra hotel and Paddy's beach bar serving among the most popular attractions.

However, there are some obvious ups and downs in this frontline journalistic fraternity. On the upside, its members can complement each other by sharing sources of information, but not leads, as Sam Kiley (*The Times*) and Mark Doyle (*BBC*) admitted,[8] and they can forge relationships, as we saw Francois Picard (RFI and *Le Monde*) and Alyson James (freelance) tying the wedding knot in Sierra Leone, a country they said they quickly fell in love with.[9] On the down side, they easily end up working as a pack, pursuing more or less a mainstream or a pack mentality approach in their reporting, even when this results in producing distorted stories. Any deviation from this approach is often taken to mean deviation from normal reporting. In this case reporting becomes more of a routine dictated largely by cultural subjectivity and not an intellectual exercise dictated by reason and political context. When Steve Coll (Washington Post) stood out of the pack to venture into rebel territory before coming to the government controlled metropolitan areas, bringing something fresh (the angle of the rebels – 'the devils') into the western news discourse, he was targeted for arrest at the airport on his way out but had a narrow escape.[10]

The historical baggage factor also represents an important cultural framing of the war. We saw this in Alex Duval Smith's (*The Independent*) spinning of the tribal factor – or better 'ancient ethnic hatred', as Preston (1996) described it – to explain the war, a view she borrowed from Graham Greene's *Heart of the Matter* (Smith, 30 May 2000). This view, like that expressed by Kaplan's barbarism thesis discussed in detail in Chapter 6, helped to reinforce the 'distance framing', which turned out to have a far-reaching influence on the 'do nothing' attitude of the international community in the case of Sierra Leone and other distant African countries.

8.3   Conclusion

In conclusion, I have tried throughout this chapter to show how the 'I don't care' attitude of the British government in Sierra Leone was informed more by political, economic and cultural empathy/distance frames than by empathy/critical frames in the mainstream western media news discourse, and above all how this framing contributed to the other side of the CNN factor in Sierra Leone, as opposed to the CNN factor in the case of Kosovo. We also saw how the 'reverse CNN factor', as demonstrated by the calling of the shots for the media by NATO, was more evident in the case of Kosovo than in that of Sierra Leone. Hence, by preventing or delaying humanitarian intervention, the 'other side of the CNN factor' or the 'lack of CNN factor' is problematised as 'reactive' and typical of human wrongs journalism rather than 'proactive' and typical of human rights journalism. No wonder Caney warns that humanitarian intervention so far remains largely 'a "reactive" policy that is adopted after people's needs and rights have been harmed' (Caney, 2000: 131). I argue elsewhere that this largely explains the high failure rate of humanitarian interventions, especially to avert distant crises. Shaw's solution is to agree with Caney's strong case for tackling the roots of these problems and seeking to prevent them from occurring rather than responding to them once they have arisen (Shaw, 2007). Hence, it is this preventive or pro-active humanitarian intervention that makes the intervention itself attain the holistic human rights principle of cosmopolitanism, or global justice. Humanitarian intervention can only be seen to be right when it is done pro-actively – if one intervenes when the crisis erupts, rather than waiting until things become worse – or when the political or economic stakes are high. It is in this context that this chapter sees the British 'intervention' in Sierra Leone in 2000 as nothing near humanitarian intervention, despite wild claims to the contrary made by some sections of the British media.

Part III

Human Rights Journalism and the Representing of Structural and Cultural Violence

Having examined the role of the media in the reporting of direct political or physical violence such as genocide, civil war and ethnic cleansing, where we saw a dominance of human wrongs journalism over human rights journalism in Part II, we now turn to that of the reporting of indirect structural violence such as poverty, famine, forced migration and unfair trade to determine the extent of human wrongs journalism or human rights journalism. The argument is made that journalists who want to practise human rights journalism should focus on deconstructing the underlying structural causes of political violence such as poverty, famine, exclusion of minorities, youth marginalisation, human trafficking and forced labour rather than merely covering direct and uncensored violence that only benefits the political elites of society. In short, I make the case for a more robust, pro-active (preventive) rather than dramatic, reactive (prescriptive) role of the media in humanitarian intervention. Unfortunately, however, as I have demonstrated in the preceding parts of the book, which I hope to build on in this part, it is the latter role of the global media that appears to be the more evident. As Caney (2000: 131) puts it, humanitarian intervention so far essentially remains 'a "reactive" policy that is adopted after people's needs or rights have been harmed'. I argue that this largely explains the high failure rate of humanitarian interventions, especially to avert distant crises. To overcome this problem, I therefore go with Caney's 'strong case for tackling the roots of these problems' (Ibid.: 131) that make it necessary for military humanitarian intervention in the first place.

Within the context of human rights journalism, media practitioners are encouraged not only to report the news as it is, but to do so in a pro-active, agency way, by not only giving a voice to both the dominant and vulnerable participants of the direct physical violence but – perhaps more importantly – by giving its political context by way of illuminating its root political, economic and cultural causes, and in this way allow more proactive responses to resolving or even preventing, it from happening or going out of control. In fact, in line with Kant's pacifist cosmopolitanism, I argue that the practice of human rights journalism is central to cosmopolitan-based human rights approaches to tackling issues of global governance, conflict resolution, migration, poverty and global inequality. This practice is premised on the notion that the ideal cosmopolitan society is where peace and human rights co-exist, where the one cannot go without the other without creating an imbalance.

In this final part I build on my central argument in this book – that, if indirect and somewhat invisible forms of cultural and structural violence are managed pro-actively by human rights journalism, the direct forms of physical violence would be minimised or prevented all together. Hence, having dealt with the first part of the Galtung ABC conflict triangle – *Behaviour*, which represents visible and direct violence – I now focus in this final part on the other two: *Attitude* – representing invisible and indirect cultural violence – and *Contradictions* – representing invisible and indirect structural violence (Lynch and McGoldrick, 2005). This part covers three chapters: the politics of development and global poverty eradication; the EU–Africa Summit in Lisbon; and the reporting of asylum seekers and refugees in the UK.

9
The Politics of Development and Global Poverty Eradication

In this chapter I examine the corruption, racist and economic injustice forms of structural violence, such as extreme global poverty, within the context of the politics of the rights-based approach to development. My main aim here is to analyse the implications of the politics of the right to development (RTD) and of human wrongs journalism on the eradication of extreme global poverty, which is arguably the key among the eight Millennium Development Goals (MDGs) in the context of human development and global justice. In September 2000, world leaders met at the UN headquarters in New York and agreed on the groundbreaking 8 MDGs, including the key one of global poverty eradication, for which the set term is 2015. The question is often asked as to whether global poverty can be eradicated without the realisation of the RTD. I argue in this chapter that, for a solution to be found for the eradication of global poverty, the obstacles or controversies standing in the way of the realisation of the right to development as finally adopted in Vienna in 1993 must be resolved or removed. It is these obstacles or controversies that I problematise in this chapter as the politics of the right to development. I also argue that, for these controversies or obstacles standing in the way of the right to development to be addressed, one needs to adopt the human rights journalism approach. This chapter has the following structure: the right to development; global poverty and human rights-based development; and human rights journalism and social movements: the case of Indymedia in Seattle.

9.1 The right to development

The RTD is enshrined in the Universal Declaration of Human Rights through the determination to 'promote social progress and better standards of life in larger freedom' (Shah, 2005). The increasing interest in the links between human rights and development inspired scholarly work into developing the dimensions, scope and content of a distinct RTD, culminating in the UN Declaration of the Right to Development (DRD) in 1986 (Shah, 2005). The DRD defines development as a 'comprehensive economic, social, cultural and political process, which aims at the constant improvement of the well-being of the entire population and of all individuals on the basis of their active, free and meaningful participation in development and in the fair distribution' of its benefits' (Shah, 2005:...). It makes five crucial contributions to the content of the RTD: it specifies the right to self-determination; it specifies the RTD for all individuals and peoples; it calls for a departure from the narrow definition of development as something based on economic growth to one that values a human being as an active participant and beneficiary of RTD; it emphasises the importance of both first- and second-generation rights; and, finally, it recognises both state and global society as duty bearers in the realisation of the RTD.

Yet, from the outset, the RTD was a politically divisive issue. There are those who support the first-generation rights (civil and political) in the liberal western discourse of the developed countries of the North and those who support the second-generation rights (economic, social and cultural) in the Third World discourse of the developing countries of the South. These first- and second-generation rights were enshrined in the 1966 twin covenants of the Universal Declaration of Human Rights. The RTD has its roots in the political economy of the 1970s and 1980s, when developing countries called for the New International Economic Order (NIEO), urging the developed countries of the Global North to facilitate the growth and development in the Global South through aid, trade and investment. Controversies between the two divides continue not only to undermine the realisation of human rights for a life of freedom and dignity but also to challenge the growing support among cosmopolitans for the idea that global poverty is an affront to human rights. The controversies span the South accusing the North for refusing to recognise its role as duty bearer and that of the South as beneficiary; the South blaming the North for globalisation while the latter blames the former for corruption; the South blaming the North for imposing western values (universalism) while the latter blames the former for hiding behind its culture (cultural relativism) to violate people's rights; the South blaming the North for having misplaced priorities as it focuses more on service delivery than on institutional development while the latter blames the former for not doing enough in capacity building. These controversies largely fuelled the development debate, bringing into question the neoliberal capitalist model based on the Washington Consensus grounded on the deregulation of the markets, which emphasises economic growth over economic development.

Mainstream economists have generally seen economic development as the whole gamut of economic growth, accompanied by changes in output distribution and economic structure. These changes, according to Nafziger (2006), may include a fundamental improvement in the material well-being of the poorer half of the population; a fall in agriculture's share of gross national product (GNP) and a corresponding rise in the GNP share of manufacturing, finance, construction, and government administration; an increase in the education and skills of the labour force; and visible technical advances initiated within the country in question. However, economic development has often been confused with economic growth. Thus, to address this puzzle, Marxist economists or economists of the dependency school have come to view the concept of economic development differently. For them, the argument of mainstream economists that development can be measured by a country's growth per GNP is a far cry from the reality, as the two concepts are not identical. The shifting development paradigm posits that growth may be necessary but not sufficient for development. While mainstream economists see development in the light of economic growth, which refers to increases in a country's production or income per capita, often measured in the country's GNP, economists of the dependency school argue that strategies that rely on raising productivity in developing countries are inadequate without programmes that directly focus on meeting the basic needs of the poorest section of the population – the basic needs approach.

This shift in paradigm came on the heels of the end of the United Nations' first development decade, which had often stressed economic growth in developing countries. Since the benefits of growth woefully failed to trickle down to the poorer half of the population, which in most cases formed in the majority, disenchantment with the decade's 'progress' was widespread. Africa, which stands out as the region worst hit by this development dilemma, unfortunately inherited the modernisation theory of development from its former colonial masters in the West. As Bourghault puts it, since independence, economists (among others) have invited Africa to partake in the prosperity of the industrialised world by adopting a course of "development" based on the neoliberal capitalist system. Development implied industrialisation, a process which was seen as the cornerstone of the Western world's astonishing ascent to prominence in world affairs and its unparalleled ability to provide its citizens with material well-being. (Bourghault, 1995)

9.2   Global poverty and human rights-based development

It is ironic that, for all the growing global average income, billions of people are still wallowing in life-threatening poverty, facing low life expectancy, social exclusion, ill health, illiteracy, dependency and effective enslavement. Eighteen million people die every year from poverty-related causes, while a little over 2.7 billion live below $2 a day and consume only 1.3 per cent of the global product. With the rich world's average per capita income, which is 180 times greater than that of the world poor (at market exchange rates), 'we could eradicate severe poverty worldwide if we chose to try – in fact we could have eradicated it decades ago' (Pogge, 2005). It is often argued that development and poverty eradication are very much linked, as a lack of development leads to poverty. Poverty refers to a situation in which a people are unable to provide enough to sustain their livelihood. Poverty, however, varies from place to place, depending on what is designated as the poverty line below which one is declared poor. Poverty is closely linked to the concept of equality: 'for a given mean income, the more unequal the income distribution, the larger the percentage of the population living in the income-poverty' (PovertyNet, World Bank, 9 February 2000).

Various viewpoints have been advanced to explain the origins or causes of world poverty. One theory holds that world poverty is the result of too many people and too few goods – a view based on the Malthusian theory of 'population explosion' (Kaplan, 1994). For those who hold this view, one basic strategy is to reduce the growth of population and to increase the supply of goods. Some conspiracy theorists of the dependency school have even pointed the finger at the developed countries of the North for desperately using the acquired immune deficiency syndrome (AIDS) debate to control the growing population in the Third World. The anti-AIDS drive has been supported by the increasing sale of condoms and expensive drugs to stem its spread. Others, of the neoliberal economic school, have blamed world poverty on hopes that the laws of supply and demand will establish optimal equilibrium in the national and international markets. For them, the only way to avoid world poverty under these circumstances is by not interfering with the 'operation of these laws' (Elliot, 1975: 1–2). Some economists from the dependency school have, however, argued that the 'fundamental cause of world poverty is the ability of the privileged to protect and extend their privileges'. For them, world poverty can only be eradicated when the rich take a closer look at the structure of their 'own society as a necessary precondition'.

Robert Chambers (1995) is considered to be the father of the rapid, participatory rural appraisal approach to development for his celebrated work in the 1990s on synthesizing decades of work with local communities throughout the world. From the point of view of the poor, he argued that there is more to deprivation than just lack of income: 'Deprivation is characterised by social inferiority, isolation, physical weakness, vulnerability, seasonal deprivation, powerlessness, and humiliation' (cited in Uvin, 2004: 207). When the margins of poverty are stretched to the extent of reaching deprivation, then we say that the situation is really desperate; in fact, it can be likened to a situation of ringing alarm bells for famine, or with famine itself. World Bank research based on the interviews of thousands of poor people in the world found poverty to be a multidimensional problem: going beyond low income, it also involves lack of access to health and education, as well as vulnerability, voicelessness and powerlessness (World Bank, 2000, cited in Peter Uvin (2004: 207)). Uvin therefore argues that, for effective poverty alleviation to take place, each of these problems would need to be addressed (Uvin, 2004).

Amartrya Sen's capability approach has been advanced as an effective human rights-based route to overcoming deprivation. In his book *Development as Freedom* (1999), Sen defines development as the expansion of capabilities or substantive human freedoms (Sen, 1999). The central argument of Sen's human rights-based development thesis is rooted in the idea that development would only be said to have taken place for a person if he or she has the capacity to lead the kind of life he or she 'has reason to value' (Sen, 1999: 87). Sen calls for the elimination of all obstacles that prevent or limit the enjoyment of this fundamental freedom – obstacles such as 'poverty as well as tyranny, poor economic opportunities as well as systematic social deprivation, neglect of public facilities as well as intolerance or over-activity of repressive states' (Sen, 1999: 1). Uvin argues that, although Sen did state and reaffirm, clearly, important and well-argued conceptual insights, he did not talk about their implementation (Uvin, 2004: 125). Yet, despite Sen's seminal contribution to this new people-centred paradigm of development in the late 1990s, the North-South development debate continues to rage, the fall-out of an ever-widening gap between economic growth (centred on wealth creation) and economic development (centred on people development) being largely evident in the widening gap between the rich on the one hand and the poor on the other hand. Moreover, most of these developing countries that registered economic growth can hardly be said to have attained economic development, since the windfall of this 'growth' all too often failed to trickle down to the poor – the majority of the population. This is what Samir Amin called 'growth without development' (Amin, 1990).The policies of what came to be known as the 'old order' failed to match expectations for most of the world's poor countries. The few countries like China, India, Vietnam and Uganda, which did make some progress, did so for the most part because they did not necessarily follow the Washington Consensus agenda (Held and McGrew, 2007: 220).

In his groundbreaking book *The End of Poverty* (2005), Geffrey Sachs, who is of the neoliberal economics school, identifies eight key factors that tend to make economies stagnate. These are poverty – because there is no income to invest in the future; physical geography – which means that some countries need to make extra investments; a fiscal trap – as some governments lack money for infrastructural investments; governments failing to provide suitable conditions for investment, notably peace and security; cultural barriers – notably concerning women's rights; geopolitics – in the form of trade barriers that can cause stagnation; a lack of innovation – especially away from coastal locations; and also the demographic trap – whereby the poorest of the poor still have very high fertility rates (ibid., pp. 56–66). In the case of Africa, Sachs identifies four more problems that need to be overcome if the continent is to make any headway: malaria; the concentration of populations in the rural areas; reliance of Africa's food production on rain-fed agriculture; and the high rates of nutrient depletion of most of its soils (Sachs, 2005).

Tim Unwin, a leading dependency school theorist, in his article 'No End to Poverty' (2007), recognises the role of Sach's work in pushing forward the case for the Millennium Development Goals, which prioritise the eradication of poverty. However, he criticises Sachs for seeing the world simply through the lens of 'economics' instead of 'morality'. Unwin problematises Sach's central argument about how economic growth can reduce poverty, on the grounds that Sachs does not consider 'why we should seek to do this' (Unwin, 2007: 939). Much of this emphasis on economic growth as a solution to poverty came from experiences gained by economic advisers, including Sachs, in Latin America during the 1970s and 1980s (Unwin, 2007). Central to Unwin's counterargument to Sach's hegemonic economic growth model as a panacea for global poverty is his scepticism about the possibility of ending poverty going by the route advocated by that model. Unwin therefore calls for an alternative model, which he offers by calling for a move from the 'maximising of profits' (that is, economic growth), to the 'minimising of inequality' (development) (Unwin, 2007: 949).

'For too long, rhetoric and practice have been dominated by economic growth. If we forget the principle of equality, it will only be a matter of time before the oppressed and exploited of the world rise up in violent opposition' (p. 941). Unwin calls on those entrusted with promoting development to listen more closely to the 'voices of the poor, to their dreams and aspirations', and to encourage them to deliver them. He also calls on those cosmopolitans in the West pushing for the morality of aid to focus their energy on campaigning for a change in the policies of multinational financial institutions such as the World Bank (WB), the International Monetary Fund (IMF), the World Trade Organisation (WTO), and the European Union (EU) to make the playing field more level (Unwin, 2007: 949).

The debate between Sachs and Unwin resonates very much with that earlier one between two cosmopolitans – Peter Singer, who believes in 'development as charity', and Andrew Kuper, who prefers the alternative 'institutional development' as the more sustainable approach (Kuper, 2002). Kuper admires Singer's commitment to social activism but criticises his approach to global poverty relief in his book *The Singer Solution to World Poverty* as 'irremediably lacking as a theoretical orientation for action' (Kuper, 2002). He dismisses this simple cosmopolitan philosophy of giving charity to the poor, advocated by Singer, as 'misleading and potentially dangerous because of its methodological individualism and limited scope – temporal and spatial. The last thing we can afford to be is ahistorical, acontextual, and noninstitutional in our approach to global poverty relief. We need a political philosophy' (ibid., pp. 114). Kuper proposes the 'political philosophy' approach based on a theoretical orientation for development and politics as an alternative. He identifies three contributions of this political philosophy approach:

a *political economy* that charts the causal dynamics of the global economy and indicates the extent to which these could be controlled; a *theory of justice* that supplies a metric for evaluating goals and derives a set of principles with which to approach the problems of development; and a *political sociology* that encompasses and distinguishes the respective roles of individuals and various institutions in advancing these moral ends. (Kuper, 2002:114)

While Singer and Kuper are cosmopolitans in their own rights as far as the conceptual underpinning of distributive justice is concerned, their approaches are fundamentally different in the sense that, while the former's focus is on 'relief now or death', the latter's focus is on 'relief now and tomorrow'.

In line with Kuper's argument, Krinjer (1987) sees the contrast between poverty and wealth as an integral aspect of the prevailing mode of capitalist production. He argues that the reason why a peasant works with poor material is entirely that he is poor. He sees the peasant as a victim of a political system – he is being exploited as he receives too little payment for his labour. Krinjer adds:

> Here the same thing happens as it occurs in unequal exchanges in international commerce [...] Exploitation can assume such virulent forms that the peasant decides to produce nothing for the market any more. He withdraws into self-sufficiency. This is what I found in Peru, and the Iranian revolutionary, Bizhan Jazani, reported the same reaction in Iran during the pre-Sha era. (Krinjer, 1987: 74–75)

However, a more down-to-earth and recent perspective in support of Kuper's political philosophy approach is that provided by Thomas Pogge in his celebrated symposium 'World Poverty and Human Rights', where he called upon the affluent Global North not only to pay for the 'harm' their forefathers have inflicted on the Global South through slave trade and colonialism, but to stop inflicting this 'harm' in its present form, of neo-colonialism (Pogge, 2005). Pogge warns:

> We are *harming* the global poor if and insofar as we collaborate in imposing an *unjust* global institutional order upon them. And this institutional order is definitely unjust if and insofar as it foreseeably perpetuates large-scale human rights deficits that would be reasonably avoidable through feasible institutional modifications [...] Global institutional arrangements are causally implicated in the reproduction of massive severe poverty. Governments of our affluent countries bear primary responsibility for these global institutional arrangements and can foresee their detrimental effects. And many citizens of these affluent countries bear responsibility for the global institutional arrangements their governments have negotiated in their names. (Pogge, 2005: 4–5)

Pogge has a very pro-active view on humanitarian intervention to alleviate or end global poverty, basing it on what I call the Kantian pacifist cosmopolitan thinking of 'do no harm' or refrain from conducting actions that would violate the rights of people to live in peace and dignity. He argues that, while we are bound by moral duty to 'rescue people from life-threatening poverty, it can be misleading to focus just on that when more stringent negative duties are also in play: duties not to expose people to life-threatening poverty and duties to shield them from harm for which we would be actively responsible' (Pogge, 2005: 5). The mainstream media, rather than coming to play an agency role in ending global poverty, following the prescriptions set by cosmopolitans such as Kuper and Pogge, have unfortunately been enlisted to serve as vehicles in spreading the message of the free market neoliberal economic model. At least it is documented that the media have done badly in allowing any debate on free trade issues. Herman writes authoritatively about media apathy and apparent double standards. He accuses the media of being largely reluctant to take issue with 'labour bargaining power and inequality', and 'often explicitly or implicitly denying that there were any losers', albeit 'occasionally accepting that there were losers as well as winners' (Herman, 2002: 72). Herman argues that mainstream media often used the friendly phrase 'free trade' to describe arrangements that were in the first place 'about investor rights, not trade, and failed even to mention those investor rights' (ibid.). Herman adds:

> They have also persistently ignored the fact that intellectual property rights, like patents, are monopoly rights that interfere with the freedom of trade, and in urging the benefits of free trade to developing countries, the media have failed to acknowledge that all the great industrialised countries – including Germany, Japan, the United Kingdom, and United States – and the Asian Tigers used protectionism for extended periods to help them compete globally before taking off into sustained growth. (Herman, 2002: 72)

It is, however, unfortunate that, despite the failure of this model to break ice in Africa and other parts of the developing world, a development that ushered in the paradigmatic shift in development thinking in favour of the basic needs approach, coverage of Africa by the western media continues to be not only distorted, but largely skewed towards fanning rather than putting off the many crises that have threatened the survival of the continent.

It is recognised that the three dominant variables of poverty, democracy and conflict, which are central to crises in Africa, Latin America, the Middle East, the Gulf and South East Asia, are largely interdependent, as they constantly flow into each other as cause and effect variables, depending on how one sees each of them individually or collectively. Poverty, for instance, leads to conflicts, and vice versa, while lack of democratisation often leads to conflicts, and perhaps vice versa. However, while some attempts have been made by some media and political economy scholars to explore these overlaps, very little, if anything at all, has been done by the mainstream media to contextually engage them in a way that would help the campaign of some leading cosmopolitans in the fight against global poverty (Herman and Chomsky, 1988; Edward Herman, 2002).

It is often argued that poverty and democracy are not as dramatic as conflict, especially violent conflict, and so do not often make the international news. Thus, international reporting is all too often about 'mega-disasters' (Herbert 2001: 2). Yet, as Herbert argues, 'international reporting of the life of countries and people should be about more than disasters and wars. It should give outsiders an understanding of the people of a country to others, elsewhere' (Herbert 2001: 3). As this book shows, this largely remains a normative, if not rhetorical, idea. Instead of merely coming in to capture gory images of famine or violence, global or international journalists have an ethical obligation, within the context of human rights journalism, to let others not only know how, but – perhaps more importantly – why poor people everywhere (be it within or without borders) have to live with problems such as social exclusion and deprivation. People in the developed countries of the North would only take action to push for a more pro-active humanitarian intervention to end extreme global poverty, such as the one advocated by cosmopolitans like Pogge, if they were to get a better understanding of the political context of the problem itself. However, if the mainstream media that have an obligation to create this understanding and mobilise the public into action fail to do so, their effectiveness in using cosmopolitan-based humanitarian intervention to end global poverty is in question. In the next section of this chapter, I will explore how social movements and their alternative media have tried to fill in the void left by the mainstream media's failure to practise human rights journalism by briefly looking at the case of Indymedia and the Seattle demonstrations against the WTO in 1999.

9.3   Human rights journalism and social movements: The case of Indymedia in Seattle

The 1960s witnessed the emergence of new social movements (hereafter NSMs) that had tremendous impact on the local and global social initiatives adopted in the struggles to promote and protect human rights. Societal imbalances, which Neil Stammers (2009) problematises as 'human wrongs', were behind the rise of these NSMs. Human rights were therefore needed to right these 'human wrongs'. In explaining such societal imbalances, Stammers (2009: 148) identified sites of power across cultural, political and economic domains 'organised around sex and gender, ethnicity and the control of information and knowledge'. NSMs such as feminist and anti-racist movements saw the close link between information, knowledge and power, made popular in academia through Foucault's work on power/knowledge (Foucault, 1980, 1982, cited in Stammers, 2009). Stammers, however, argues that these NSMs were re-identifying sites of power that date back thousands of years and predate modern structures of political and economic power; therefore they did not necessarily identify new ones.

Melucci (1989: 76) argues that one of the systemic effects of NSMs was 'rendering power visible', which Stammers (2009: 149) extends 'to social movement activism in general'. In political theory, Held and McGrew (2007) has identified seven sites of power in *Democracy and the Global Order*, which he then extends to a series of rights. He, however, uses a cognitive 'thought experiment' process rather than making any link to the history of the struggles of social movements around human rights. Finally, Mann (1986: 29) identifies four sources of social power from historical sociology in his ideological, economic, military and political (IEMP) model – sources that, he argues, have trans-historical and trans-cultural value. Stammers (2009: 149) argues that, if we can identify trans-historical and trans-cultural 'sites of power', then the implication is that 'we can also identify trans-historical and trans-cultural forms of "power over" – forms of oppression (old human wrongs) – emanating from these sites'. This, notes Stammers, raises the question as to whether the history of the struggles of social movements for human rights has, in the context of socio-historical praxis, identified a corresponding set of 'old wrongs'. Stammers recognises that in-depth interrogation of this issue in the human rights literature is lacking, but he notes that few studies have at least referred to it.

In her groundbreaking book *The Human Rights Reader*, Micheline Ishay (1997: xiii) states: '[at] every stage of history, voices of protest against oppression have been heard; in every age, visions of human liberation have also been eclipsed'. Leading postcolonial theorist Gayatri Chakravorty Spivak, argues that 'Human Rights' is not only about having or claiming a right or set of rights; it is also about righting wrongs' (Spivak, 2004: 523). Alan Dershowitz (2004) goes even further, to propose a secular theory of human rights in his *Rights from Wrongs*. He argues that 'rights are those fundamental preferences that experience or history – especially of great injustices – have taught are so essential that the citizenry should be persuaded to entrench them and not make them subject to easy change by shifting majorities' (Dershowitz 2004: 81). He cites great wrongs such as 'the Crusades, the Inquisition, slavery, the Stalinist starvation and purges, the Holocaust, the Cambodian slaughter' and other easily recognisable abuses. Spivak's notion of righting wrongs and that of Dershowitz regarding delivering human rights from human wrongs resonate with Pogge's idea of the need not only to address 'global poverty' as a 'human wrong' but to stop perpetuating it. Dershowitz's thesis of rights from wrongs, however, tends to focus only on negative rights (civil and political) against the violation of which people should be protected – as most, if not all, of his examples of serious human wrongs suggest. Moreover, as Stammers puts it, Dershowitz's account lacks theoretical and historical context to make it credible; '[t]here is no history, no conflict and no struggle in his account of the wrongs that generated human rights' (Dershowitz 2004: 81).

Ken Booth, in contrast, seeks to provide context by arguing that a universalist understanding of human rights 'can be based on the secure but sad fact of universal human wrongs' (1999: 46). He argues that human wrongs are everywhere (hence are universal), in ways in which human rights are not. He says it is universally accepted as bad for someone to be tortured or starved, humiliated or hurt. He argues that a universalist perspective that supports the bottom-up perspective of human wrongs 'has the crucial effect of humanising the powerless' and 'allows the victim to assert and define his or her humanity, with the help of solidarist groups elsewhere' (ibid., p. 63). Booth's argument is premised on the idea that the existence of human wrongs (problems) demands that there should be human rights (emancipation from these problems).

Most of these discussions of the human rights/human wrongs binary, albeit lacking in depth, have identified a series of 'old wrongs' – 'forms of oppression, domination, exclusion and silencing' – which Stammers 'associated with the five sites of power identified and challenged by a range of historical social movements' (Stammers, 2009: 151). Stammers, however, hesitates to accept Booth's suggestion of 'universal' rather than 'old' wrongs, partly because, as he puts it, the term 'universal' tends to drag us away from the analysis of social praxis, but also because the 'timeliness' associated with 'universal' implies that these wrongs will always be with us (ibid., p. 151).

If the 1960s, 1970s and 1980s saw the emergence of NSMs, the late 1990s saw the resurgence of 'critical social movements' (Walker, 1988) around the world. These movements were variously described as anti-globalisation, anti-capitalist and as a movement of movements. Questions have been asked as to whether these latest movements are natural continuations of the earlier NSMs. There is evidence to suggest that most of the international non-governmental organisations (NGOs) that arose from these NSMs are involved in processes such as the World Social Forum and participated in protests against the G8, the G20 and the WTO. However, these contemporary critical social movements are different in that their focus is on addressing issues of global, economic and political imbalances of society rather than imbalances related to identity and lifestyle (for example, ethnicity and sexual orientation), which are typical of some of the earlier NSMs (Stammers, 2009). Nonetheless, strong links, suggesting continuity, still exist between these radical movements and the earlier NSMs. 'A critique of existing forms of institutional power – not just economic power – is strong throughout the new movements' (Brecher et al., 2000; Fisher and Ponniah, 2003; Mertes, 2004; Sen et al., 2004; Stammers, 2009). William's (2005) anthropological study of contemporary anti-capitalist activism in France provides further evidence of this continuity with NSM-type struggles, especially those of the 1970s and 1980s. Moreover, the study identifies a 'strong positive orientation towards human rights and an understanding of anti-capitalism as being, above all, a critic of power' (William, 2005, cited in Stammers, 2009: 157).

Within the context of socio-historical practices, Stammers (2009: 158) argues, 'we can see struggles for human rights as struggles against "old wrongs" emanating from all these five sites of power' – namely economy, politics, sex and gender, ethnicity, and the control of information and knowledge. Stammers notes that the discussion of the sites of power shows how crucial the integration of non-legal and pre-legal dimensions of human rights is for achieving a holistic understanding of the doctrine. He, however, notes the very limited literature available in the human rights field to address this lack of a corresponding set of 'old wrongs' and human rights. In order to address this gap, I will end this chapter by exploring how human wrongs journalism, typical of Stammers' notion of 'old wrongs' (2009), was evident in silencing and excluding the concerns and voices of protesters against trade ministers attending the November 1999 WTO summit in Seattle. This contributed to the emergence of critical social movements, including movements of movements such as the World Social Forum, and more radical alternative media such as the Independent Media Channel (Indymedia).

What quickly came to be known as the 'battle of Seattle' began when thousands of ordinary citizens took to the streets of the city to protest against what they considered to be the negative impact of the global, economic regime of free trade on global poverty. 'Free trade, in the opinion of many, was not fair trade, especially where the interests of developing countries were concerned' (Allan, 2006: 123). Days ahead of the WTO summit – the main target of the protesters – the Internet provided the rallying point for discussions among social activists about the best strategies in co-ordinating the demonstrations. Descending on Seattle for the day were people from all walks of life, including anti-poverty activists, Greenpeace groups, trade unions, women's groups, Third World advocacy groups, fair trade activists, farmers and lobbyists from NGOs. The protesters surrounded the main Paramount Theatre, where the opening ceremonies were scheduled to take place, and seriously disrupted the proceedings of trade ministers representing 135 WTO member countries. To their greatest shock, the protesters met stiff resistance from heavily armoured riot police firing CS spray and pepper gas at close range. Despite this, the demonstrators were unmoved; in fact a vast majority of them remained peaceful while others were chanting, 'The whole world is watching' in front of TV cameras. A small number lit bonfires in the streets and smashed what was perceived to be iconic symbols of US corporate culture, including shops such as Starbucks, Nike, Gap and branches of the Bank of America (ibid., p. 123).

The city mayor declared a state of emergency and invoked a night-time curfew around the conference venue. Reinforcements from National Guardsman and Washington State Patrol troopers arrived to help to impose a 50-block 'no protest zone' across the city. The conference delegates were frustrated because by the end of the meeting they realised that they had not achieved anything of substance. What is more, they ended up postponing the new round of talks (Allan, 2006: 124). Lori Wallach of the Public Citizen's Global Trade Watch declared: 'History has been made in Seattle as the allegedly irresistible forces of corporate economic globalisation were stopped in their tracks by the immovable object of grassroots democracy' (cited in Weissman, 1999).

The Seattle protests quickly dominated the headlines around the world. However, much of the mainstream media, unsurprisingly, only narrowly focused on the flashpoints of confrontation between police and protesters, offering little context for the issues at stake. What was even worse was that some local news organisations refused to cover protests that were not officially sanctioned by the City of Seattle, thereby dramatically reducing the scope of their reporting. Thus, not only were the voices of the protesters and the context of the stakes not articulated in the mainstream media reporting of the demonstrations, but the reporting itself was either non-existent or too limited in scope to make any impact. The very right to communicate what was going on was itself under threat. With this massive deficit in human rights journalism, various activist-led media organisations tried to provide their own news coverage of the protests in order to give a true picture of what was really happening, as a counter-hegemonic discourse to what the mainstream media were reporting. The Internet quickly came to the rescue with the Independent Media Centre (IMC), which played the role of a clearing house for all the activist media. Volunteer journalists and activists, including video makers, radio producers and web techies, deployed all across Seattle to bear witness to their own protests (Allan, 2006). With the 'open source' reporting becoming ever popular as the protests intensified, the buzz words 'Don't hate the media; be the media' quickly became the rallying cry for the hurriedly assembled Seattle IMC, which had about 400 volunteers and registered 1.5 million hits during the protests, more than what CNN had during the same period. The Seattle example of the IMC saw the emergence of many more like it: first in Boston, then in Washington, London, Canada, Mexico City, Prague, Belgium, France and Italy (this continues today).

The emergence of the Seattle IMC, which I represent here as human rights journalism, from the democratic deficit of exclusion and silence of the mainstream media of the voices of the protesters, which I problematise here as human wrongs journalism (old wrongs), provides a fine example of the juxtaposition of the economic and political control of information and knowledge sites of power on the one hand, and old wrongs, or forms of oppression, on the other hand. Human rights journalism, by way of the Seattle IMC, therefore provided a counter-balance or counter-hegemonic discourse to the oppressive old wrongs by way of excluding and silencing the mainstream media. The lesson we can learn from the Seattle IMC is that there can be a problem in narrowing the theorising of journalism, or even peace journalism, to what Keeble refers to as 'an aspiration-focusing too much on the journalist as professional producer' (2010: 56). Keeble calls for the need to follow John Hartley in his proposal to radically transform journalism theory. 'We need to move away from the concept of the audience as a passive consumer of a professional product to seeing the audience as producers of their own (written or visual) media' (Keeble, 2010: 56). Hartley draws on Article 19 of the Universal Declaration of Human Rights, which radically stipulates that everyone has the right not only to seek and receive but to 'impart' (which means communicate) information and ideas (Hartley, 2008: 42, cited in Keeble, 2009: 56). With alternative citizen media, where people narrate stories of their own activities, journalism has moved from a modern expert system to contemporary open innovation – from 'one-to-many' to 'many-to-many' (Hartley, 2008: 42), as we saw in the case of the Seattle IMC.

To conclude, poverty eradication has been identified by the United Nations as the largest challenge facing international society in the search for a global society based on cosmopolitan justice. This chapter discussed the two approaches of poverty eradication at two binary levels: economic growth versus economic development, which is advocated by the neoliberal and dependency schools of economics and championed by Sachs and Unwin respectively, and 'development as a charity' versus 'institutional development', which is advocated by the 'now' cosmopolitans such as Singer and the 'now and tomorrow' cosmopolitans such as Kuper and Pogge, respectively. I made a case for the more pragmatic and pro-active economic development/institutional development model, as the human rights-based one, instead of the more normative and reactive economic growth/development model, like the charity one, in discussing the best approach to eradicate extreme global poverty. I argue that the practice of human rights journalism based on media activism can provide tremendous support to critical social movements in exposing and challenging, through non-violent channels such as peaceful protests and industrial action (like the battle for Seattle described in the second section of this chapter), the structures of economic injustice that perpetuate global economic inequalities and extreme poverty. Human rights journalism can promote the pro-active economic/institutional development and hence avert the physical violence and famine that we saw in Ethiopia in 1984. In the next chapter, I will examine human wrongs journalism in the British media reporting of the EU–Africa Lisbon summit in 2007, which undermined efforts at promoting the Global Partnership for Africa – which is the eighth and by far the most important of the Millennium Development Goals.

10
The EU–Africa Lisbon Summit and 'the Global Partnership for Africa'

At the time of writing this book, the UN Secretary General Ban Ki-moon was calling world leaders to a summit in September 2010 to mark the tenth anniversary of the Millennium Development Goals (MDGs) and to boost progress towards their achievement, with only five years left for the 2015 deadline. Ki-moon said that, while a good deal had been achieved in reaching some of the ambitious goals, 'variously targeting core sources of global poverty and obstacles to development – from maternal health and education to managing infectious disease, progress in other critical areas lags badly' (Ki-Moon, 2010). A report published in 2009 by the MDGs Gap Task Force, which was set up by the secretary general to track progress on the development partnership created to realise the goals, warned that, although development assistance rose to record levels in 2008, donors are falling short by $35 billion per year on the 2005 pledge on annual aid flows made by the Group of Eight in Gleneagles, and by $20 billion a year on aid to Africa. Moreover, with the exception of two Nordic countries, Norway and Sweden, developed countries are still far behind in reaching the agreed target of donating 0.7 of their Gross Domestic Product (GDP) in aid to poor countries by 2015 (MDG Task Force Report, 2009).

What is more, major challenges still remain unattended, despite the adoption of a global action plan to achieve the eight anti-poverty goals by their 2015 target, despite renewed commitments to women's and children's health, and despite the introduction of major new initiatives in the global battle against poverty, hunger and disease at the major UN conference on 20–22 September 2010 in New York, which was intended to review progress to date. For example, although development aid for the achievement of the MDGs from developed countries has seen a slight surge over recent years, it has been revealed that more than

181

half of it has gone towards the relief of debt owed by poor countries. Moreover, it has emerged that the remaining aid money goes towards natural disaster relief and military aid, which do not necessarily advance the countries' development goals (Wikipedia, accessed online 24 October 2010). According to the United Nations Department of Economic and Social Affairs (2006), the 50 least developed countries (LDCs) only receive about one-third of all the aid that flows in from developed countries, a state of affairs raising the issue of aid not moving from rich to poor depending on their development needs, but rather from rich to their closest allies (Singer, 2008).

It is, however, unfortunate that, with almost a third of the 15-year target remaining, the world is still more oriented towards the 'development as charity' approach advocated by the likes of Peter Singer, instead of the more pragmatic cosmopolitan approach of the 'institutional development' advocated by Andrew Kuper and Thomas Pogge (see Chapter 9). In fact, for Noam Chomsky, another scholar of the 'institutional development' school, the 2000 New York meeting of world leaders to adopt the MDGs is a déjà vu. He drew attention, for instance, to significant lacunae in the text by comparing and contrasting the showpiece event in New York with an earlier conclave, in Havana: the South Summit of the G77, which met in 1964 for the first United Nations Conference on Trade and Development (UNCTAD), bringing together leaders of the 77 developing countries. The South Summit communiqué made extensive reference to the need, if human rights were to be meaningfully attained by the majority of humanity, for positive measures to extend security and opportunity in the economic and social spheres: 'Our highest priority is to overcome underdevelopment, which implies the eradication of hunger, illiteracy, disease and poverty.' The G77 leaders went on to 'urge the international community to adopt urgent and resolute actions, with a comprehensive and multidimensional approach, to assist in overcoming these scourges, and to establish international economic relations based on justice and equity', deploring '[a]symmetries and imbalances that have intensified international economic relations' to the detriment of the South and calling for a reform of 'international economic governance' and of the 'international financial architecture' to make them 'more democratic, more transparent and better attuned to solving the problems of development'.

The difference lay, in other words, in the acknowledgement, built into the G77 Declaration but omitted or glossed over in the equivalent document from the UN meeting, that unjust political economic structures, put and kept in place for the benefit or interest of the powerful in the rich world, have the effect of preventing people in most of the world from realising the rights recognised for them in the well-known international instruments.

The mainstream of minority-world journalism is generally on the same side of this distinction as the official rhetoric and the policy stance of the governments of the countries in which this journalism is itself produced. Where human rights violations make the news, they are usually reported as the actions of individual perpetrators, not as the product of a system and of structures that construct and sustain long-term relations in conflict (Shaw, 2011).

Now returning to the New York Summit, it is worth noting all the MDGs (see Table 10.1):

Table 10.1 Eight Millennium Development Goals

Goal 1	Eradicate extreme poverty and hunger
Goal 2	Achieve universal primary education
Goal 3	Promote gender equality and empower women
Goal 4	Reduce child mortality
Goal 5	Improve maternal health
Goal 6	Combat HIV/AIDS, malaria and other diseases
Goal 7	Ensure environmental sustainability
Goal 8	Develop a global partnership for development

It is the eighth goal that comes much closer ... to the human rights-based 'institutional development' model – especially its target 2, which calls for fair trade, for example through the removal of all discriminatory trade barriers. Other targets of the 'global partnership for development' include a commitment to good governance; debt relief; decent and productive jobs for the young; access to affordable essential drugs and new technologies such as cell phones and the Internet. While improvements have been observed in some of these targets, only slow progress has been made in hitting target 2 of the eighth MDG: developing further 'an open, rule-based, predictable, non-discriminatory trading and financial system and providing tariff- and quota-free access for exports' from the LDCs.

Building on my arguments for a human rights approach to development in Chapter 9, which focused on the structural violence of global poverty as an economic injustice and on the non-reporting or misreporting of it, I will now focus in this chapter on the non-reporting or misreporting of the global partnership for development; first, as it relates to poverty, slave trade, colonialism and unfair trade in Africa in general, and, second, as it relates to the Africa–EU Lisbon Summit of 8–9 December, 2007 in particular.

10.1   Poverty, the slave trade, colonialism and unfair trade

It is argued that it is not possible to sincerely talk about extreme poverty and how to overcome it through a global partnership for development approach without talking about how it is inextricably linked to the slave trade, the colonial period and the immediate postcolonial one. Central to Africa's poverty syndrome is the burning issue of the trade imbalance, which was caused by the neoliberal 'free trade theory', handed down to the newly emerging post colonial states as the roadmap of their development. Goldsmith traces this trade imbalance to the colonial and the immediate post colonial periods, when the strong and affluent colonial powers bullied their colonies and former colonies by making sure that their development activities served the interests of the metropoles better than their own. In short, Goldsmith (1996) identifies the phenomenon of 'development as colonialism'. He goes along with Francois Partant, who puts it this way: 'The developed nations have discovered for themselves a new mission – to help the Third World advance along the road to development [...] which is nothing more than the road on which the West has guided the rest of humanity for several centuries' (Partant, 1982). Development is thus likened to what Marxists called 'imperialism', although most prefer to call it by its more familiar and loaded name 'colonialism'. However, the pan-Africanist Kwame Nkrumah developed the idea further and termed the continuum between colonialism and development 'neo-colonialism', which he describes as the 'last phase of imperialism'.

It is not difficult to see the clear but disturbing continuity between the colonial era and the era of development in Third World countries. This explains why the governments of these newly independent countries have never been in a hurry to re-draw their frontiers or to return to the pre-colonial ways of doing things in their own cultures. In fact, even on the hot political issue of land, the pattern left behind by the colonialists has been maintained (Goldsmith, 1996). Randall Baker describes the story as one of continuity (Baker, 1984). As Jacoby puts it, peasants who linked their struggle for national independence with the fight to regain their land never recovered it (Jacoby, 1983). Goldsmith therefore argues that the dramatic shift by the western powers from colonialism to independence was informed more by national and economic interests than by any genuine human rights concerns:

> The massive efforts to develop the Third World in the years since World War 2 were not motivated by purely philanthropic considerations but by the need to bring the Third World into the orbit of the Western trading system in order to create an ever-expanding market for their goods and services and a source of cheap labour and raw materials for the industries of the Western metropoles. This has also been the goal of colonialism especially during its last phase, which started in the 1870s. For that reason, there is a striking continuity between the colonial era and the era of development, both in the methods used to achieve their common goal and in the social and ecological consequences of applying them. (Goldsmith, 1996)

The links between colonialism and development are aptly illustrated by English businessman and colonialist Cecil Rhodes, who named present-day Zimbabwe 'Rhodesia', after himself. Rhodes frankly declared that 'we must find new lands from which we can easily obtain raw materials and at the same time exploit the cheap, slave labour that is available from the natives of the colonies. The colonies would also provide a dumping ground for the surplus goods produced in our factories' (cited in Goldsmith, 1996: 254). Lord Frederick Lugard, the British governor of colonial Nigeria, and the former French President Jules Ferry expressed similar sentiments. However, as Africa was seen as the soft touch for colonialism, and later neo-colonialism, the continuum between colonialism and development was more evident there than elsewhere – say, in Asia, South Asia or Latin America. In fact many countries in Asia and elsewhere were simply not ready and willing to give western powers free access to their markets, or to the cheap labour and raw materials required of them (Goldsmith, 1996). Hence this colonialism–development continuum, which from the beginning was based on the human and material exploitation of the weak and vulnerable (colonies/former colonies) by the strong and dominant (colonial metropoles), has been extended to this very day, in the form of an unequal global development partnership, with unfair and unjust trade as one of its most obvious manifestations.

Global inequality and poverty are enduring features of the capitalist world economy (Held and McGraw, 2007). Pogge (2005) ranks poverty as the greatest source of human misery today. Gilpin sees it in the light of the centre–periphery thesis, whereby the poor, the LDCs, are marginalised through the concentration of global economic activity in the regional cores of the Organisation of Economic Cooperation and Development (OECD) countries. Powerful states channel global economic forces favourable to their national interests. Moreover, as the global capitalist system is made up of dominant and subordinate states, it is not likely to achieve a democratic egalitarian order (Gilpin, 2001). Yet we hardly find, represented in the mainstream media discourse, the political context of what we know today as the growing global inequality and extreme poverty. There are, however, a few exceptions. As admitted by the *Economist*, albeit in a banal way, Africa would earn an honest living if it were allowed fair trade with the rest of the developed world:

> The World Bank reckons that, if North America, Europe and Japan were to eliminate all barriers to imports from sub-Saharan Africa, the region's exports would rise by 14%, an annual increase worth about $25 billion. Another calculation shows that developed countries' farm subsidies amount to over $360 billion a year, some $30 billion more than Africa's GDP. And while the prices of rich countries' exports have been rising, those of Africa's primary products have, on average, been falling (by 25% in 1997–99) [...] Meanwhile the aid that helped to assuage western consciences has often been tied to western exports. (*Economist*, 24 February 2001: 17)

It is not difficult to deduce from the above that Africa is poor today because it has been involved in an unfair deal in the world market, largely controlled by the developed economies, which have also not been doing enough to cushion the adverse effects of these unfavourable terms of trade by way of untied aid. This explains why Africa is pressing hard for reparations from Europe and North America for their lead role in the trans-Atlantic slave trade, which has been described as the worst crime against humanity. It has been argued that the developed world's unfair trade with Africa began with the slave trade, where human beings were cheaply bought for wine, rum and other manufactured products and made to work in the plantations of the New World. It is believed that massive untied aid from the North, like the Marshall Plan fund given to Western Europe to cushion the effects of the Second World War, is needed to bail Africa out of poverty.

Some nations in the North, while recognising their role in this crime against humanity, have steadfastly refused to heed calls for reparation. In a cover story on slavery, for instance, Paul Michaud wrote in the

New African: 'At long last, the French are admitting their role in slavery. A law to declare slavery a "crime against humanity" is making its way through the French parliament, but paying reparations for that despicable crime is proving too difficult for the French to accept' (*New African*, July/August 2001: 23). Enlisted to forcefully drive the latter point home are the western media, especially the British media. I refer here to one such comment article, in the British centre-left daily *The Independent*, authored by the Africa editor of the *Economist*, Richard Dowden, with the clear headline: 'Don't compensate Africa for Slavery'. Dowden wrote:

> There are many bogus fund-raising wheezes coming out of Africa these days... An even larger-scale wheeze is the demand for reparations for slavery, and Mary Robinson, the outgoing United Nations High Commissioner for Human Rights, has fallen for it [...] The attempt to beg money by playing on guilt over slavery and imperialism argues that between the 15th and 19th centuries Europeans enslaved millions of Africans and carried them off to America. That was a crime against humanity. Africa demands compensation for that and for colonial rule. Don't fall for this argument [...]/. (Dowden, 28 March 2001: 5)

Dowden also went on to dismiss as false the image of white people roaming through West Africa capturing and dragging Africans in chains to the coast. He added that slaves were 'either captured in raids and war or forced into slavery through poverty' (ibid.). However, Dowden admitted that the slave trade started when

> surplus slaves were sold to European traders in return for textiles, iron bars, booze and beads and taken to the New World to work the sugar plantations and farms [...] The European trade hugely increased the demand for slaves. No longer a by-product of war or poverty, slaves became the cause of war and banditry. (Dowden, 2001: 5)

After reading Dowden's article, I quickly distilled a number of inadequacies, distortions, contradictions and provocative expressions. In an interview with him on Friday 28 September 2001, I challenged him on the obvious shortcomings of this piece. When I asked why he tended to see reparation only in financial terms and not in terms of injustice and immorality, Dowden said:

> Yes a terrible injustice was committed, a crime against humanity possibly – this I don't doubt. But to somehow say that the successor

states, one successor state of the states that existed in Europe, for instance Britain, Holland, France and Portugal should be compensating for what their traders did 200 to 300 years ago, I think is crazy because then everybody in the world would be wanting some reparations for something, and maybe I've to sue Italy because the Roman Empire invaded Britain and my ancestors were forced into slavery. I think the connection is just too tenuous. (Dowden, 28 September 2001)

However, Dowden's reply, like some of his assumptions in his original article, is fraught with inadequacies and contradictions. For instance, he admitted that he is in no doubt that the slave trade was a crime against humanity, but he rejected compensation by comparing that trade with others, such as the one committed against the British by the Roman Empire, when his ancestors were forced into slavery. Worse still, he deliberately closed his eyes to the fact that the slavery into which his ancestors were forced during the time of the Roman Empire cannot be compared to the Atlantic slave trade and thus does not qualify it as a crime against humanity. What he also refused to mention in his reply is that the slave trade largely contributed in impoverishing Africa by letting its human resources be exploited to build the economy of the New World (North America and the rest of the global economy). While I agreed with Dowden that slavery took place in Africa too, albeit on a small scale, and that some Africans were indeed involved in the capturing and selling of slaves, I, however, asked how he can reconcile those claims with his other claim in the article, 'that slaves were either captured in raids and war or were forced into slavery through poverty', and I asked him what he can say about those who provided the arms and other manufactured items that fuelled the African wars. Dowden, visibly shaking, replied:

In fact, in West Africa, most societies seemed to own slaves and they found when the European traders came, this immensely boosted their power; not only did they become wealthy by selling their slaves or whatever but also the Europeans then fed them with better weaponry and so they were able to go out and capture more slaves for the market. I absolutely accept in my article I was being naïve, really I was being provocative but of course like journalists should be. But I totally accept that historically the market for those slaves – the extra market – was created by the European slave trade to the Americas. Yes in that sense they created the market. But I think [...] the Africans on shore [...] were controlling it and they controlled the price and they were in a better position than the European slave traders. (Ibid.)

Though it is gratifying that Dowden was able to admit his guilt of being 'naïve and provocative' in his article, he was glaringly economical with the truth when he declared that the African offshore traders, and not the Europeans, dictated the terms of trade. One should only look at an article in the *New African* by Baffour Ankomah, to see how weak Dowden's declaration is. Baffour writes:

> We must learn lessons from how our ancestors allowed themselves to be taken advantage of – how on earth they thought they were 'selling' (as we are now told) whole human beings sometimes for two bottles of rum each, or as happened in Benin in 1500, five African human being 'sold' for a horse offered by a Portuguese slaver. Today [...] Africa and its people are still being taken advantage of–through all sorts of [...] sustainable development, liberalisation, structural adjustment programmes, privatisation, globalisation [...] The richest natural-resources-endowed continent in the world is yet the poorest! And yet our resources power the world! (Ankomah, 2001a: 21)

Here Ankomah was bringing out a curtain raiser to the UN World Conference against racism in Durban, South Africa, in 2001 – for which he said that a multinational corporation, Mercedes Benz, refused to give advertisement to his magazine. If one were to put his analysis side by side with Dowden's declaration, one can safely argue that, since the beginning of the slave trade era, unfair trade has been central to how the developed North has been reinforcing Africa's poverty. Even Dowden could not help but admit, in the conclusion of his controversial article in *The Independent*, that fair trade would help to bail Africa out of poverty:

> The rich countries that subsidise their own farmers are the same ones that insist African governments cut subsidies on food and force their farmers to pay the full costs of fuel, fertiliser and transport. If we want to help Africa, a little bit of well-targeted aid will be helpful, but it is far more important to give Africa the chance to earn its living in a fair market place. (Dowden, 2001: 5)

This is a very reasonable conclusion. I also see that the sentiments expressed in this conclusion are similar to those in the *Economist* lead comment cited earlier in this chapter, which is titled 'Africa's Elusive Dawn'. Yet, like in that article, these sentiments were played down. If Dowden had used this argument as the central concern of what turned out to be a controversial piece, it could certainly have changed the tone. Still, the conclusion, sound as it is, appears to contradict the rest of his arguments about how Africa does not deserve reparation.

If Africa has suffered unfair trade during the slave trade era up to the present, it is reasonable that it is compensated one way or the other. The compensation I am talking about here can take the form of debt relief: increased aid with no neoliberal capitalist strings attached and, above all, the creation of an enabling environment through fair trade such as the one advocated by Kuper and Pogge – and not necessarily the charity type of ad hoc support advocated by Singer. I argue that the Kuper–Pogge roadmap of 'institutional development' in addressing global poverty and tackling the widening gap between the rich and the poor nations of the world can only take place through a constructive partnership for development, as set out in the eighth MDG target. As we have seen from the perspectives offered by Dowden and Ankomah in the first part of this chapter, journalists indeed have a great role in putting this cosmopolitan-based development approach on the news agenda and, ultimately, on the public agenda in the context of human rights journalism. Sadly, however, as we witness in the second part of this chapter, issues of national interest and pretentious human rights framed the British news media discourse of the historic Africa–EU Lisbon Summit of 7–9 December 2007 more than concerns for a global partnership for development did – although such a partnership was, in fact, the main theme of the event.

10.2   The Africa–EU Summit in Lisbon: A missed opportunity for human rights journalism in Britain

> The unimaginable has happened, to the displeasure of arrogant Europe. Africa, thought to be so good that it would agree to anything, has said no in rebellious pride. No to the straightjacket of the Economic Partnership Agreements (EPAs), no to the complete liberalisation of trade, no to the latest manifestations of the colonial pact. (Ramonet, 13 January 2008).

This is how the South African *Mail and The Guardian* online reported the second EU–Africa Summit in Lisbon, 7–9 December 2007. While this was the chorus in most of the African media, the reporting was hardly the same for the European media, especially the British, which almost exclusively focused its coverage on the controversy over the presence of Zimbabwe's President Robert Mugabe and the absence of British

Prime Minister Gordon Brown. Having covered in the first section of this chapter the non-reporting or misreporting of the global partnership for development as it relates to the problem of the lack of fair trade in general in Africa, I now turn in this section to how it (lack of fair trade) relates to this Africa–EU Lisbon Summit.

The Lisbon Summit was the second one to take place between heads of state and government from the EU and Africa (the first was held in Cairo in 2000). It was hosted by Portugal, then holder of the EU's rotating presidency. Although the 'Joint EU–Africa Strategy', the 'Action Plan' and the Lisbon Declaration were adopted by the delegates, the summit was judged a qualified failure, as there were fundamental disagreements regarding the economic partnership agreements (EPAs) put together by the EU to replace the existing preferential trade agreements that existed between the EU and African Caribbean and Pacific (ACP) countries – agreements that were perceived to be incompatible with the rules of free trade set by the World Trade Organisation (WTO) and were to expire by December 2007. The African delegations rejected the EPAs outright, as soon as they were presented (Bugge, 12 September 2007). This constituted a major crack in the new global partnership for development forged between the western countries in Europe and North America and Africa, and it was seen as a serious setback to one of the objectives of the Doha Round of trade negotiations initiated in 2001 to address the needs of developing countries according to a 'Development Agenda'. The issue of global partnership for Africa was meant to be an important subject of discussion in the mainstream media as far as human rights journalism is concerned, as it is at the centre of the fair trade debate. But this subject was relegated to the backwater of news media reporting of the Lisbon Summit. What took centre stage instead was the controversy surrounding the presence at the summit of Zimbabwe's President Robert Mugabe. This was especially true in the case of the British media.

Apparently, largely due to the British media framing of Mugabe as a human rights violator on account of his presiding over the eviction of white Zimbabwean farmers of British origin, British Prime Minister Gordon Brown boycotted the summit but sent former development secretary, Baroness Amos, to represent him. Human rights campaigners such as Human Rights Watch (HRW) and Amnesty International (AI) called for the human rights violations in Zimbabwe and Darfur to be put on the agenda of the summit. Although these were discussed in passing at the summit, they never constituted an agenda item; besides, the EU President Manuel Barossa, himself a Portuguese, defied all opposition and invited Mugabe to attend the summit. He defended his action

by saying: 'If international leaders decided not to go to those conferences involving countries which do not have reasonable human rights
records, I'm afraid we would not be attending many conferences at all'
(Barrosso, 2007). Barrosso's defiant action was criticised by human rights
activists as undermining the 'political conditionality' – which , as Uvin
puts it, emphasises strong links between human rights and development
(Uvin, 2004). This involves donors putting human rights promotion and
protection as one of the principal conditionalities in deciding who the
recipients of their aid will be, and it calls for the blacklisting of countries that are in violation of the aid of human rights. But the maze of
available evidence to the effect that, until recently, countries that were
heavy human rights abusers received significantly more aid than others,
in particular Ethiopia, Uganda and Rwanda, suggests that the issue of
human rights is often only used as a cover in dealing with countries that
fail to conform to the national and geo-strategic interests of the affluent countries. The case of the former Soviet republics of Tajikistan and
Turkmenistan, both of them having 'terrible human rights records and
a history of suppressing the media' and yet being supported by western
countries such as the US – ostensibly for being part of the alliance on
the war on terror – is also illustrative here (Dadge, 2004: 194). Speaking
at a Reporting the World Round Table in London, *Sunday Times* diplomatic correspondent Tom Walker was very critical of this type of western
double standards:

> In Uganda we allow Museveni to get away with ruling very autocrat-
> ically but we don't allow Mugabe to do that. I think there's an awful
> lot of hypocrisy, not only in the media coverage but also in Western
> foreign policy which also dictates to a certain extent the way we look
> at the problems. (Walker, 2001)

Here Tom Walker confirms the 'reverse CNN factor', where the agenda
is set by the public authorities. From the previous analysis we can therefore infer that human rights are merely used as a front cover by the
authorities and, by extension, by the media, to push their national
interests. The implication is the banalisation of the real political context of the Lisbon Summit itself: global partnership for development
(or lack of it). This type of journalism passes as the 'other side of the
CNN factor' (human wrongs journalism) rather than the much favoured
cosmopolitan 'CNN factor' (human rights journalism).

Drawing largely on a quantitative content analysis of seven British
national newspapers and, to some extent, on the qualitative discourse

analysis of some selected aspects of their coverage, juxtaposed with coverage from some African papers, this section seeks to demonstrate how the British media coverage was framed more by issues of national interest and human rights excuses than by concerns of 'global partnership for development' – by far the most important Millennium Development Goal. By juxtaposing this problematic media framing of the second Euro-Africa Summit with that of some African and other media, this chapter seeks to provide scholarly criticism of the role of the mainstream media in efforts to achieve the Millennium Development Goals by 2015 within the cosmopolitan context of global justice. I will attempt to answer two fundamental questions in the rest of this chapter: first, to what extent does Gilpin's centre–periphery argument inform the western media coverage of the problematic 'European global partnership' with Africa? Second, why did the British media fail to promote global partnership for development in their coverage of the Lisbon Africa-Euro Summit?

In order to answer the first question I used quantitative content analysis of seven selected British newspapers: *Financial Times, The Times, The Guardian, Daily Telegraph, Daily Mirror, Sunday Mirror* and *The Independent*. I chose these papers for this content analysis because they are mostly quality papers (except the *Mirror*, which is a tabloid) read widely by the elite middle class in the UK and other parts of Europe and North America, and, above all, because of their extensive coverage of foreign or international news. However, first of all I will problematise Gilpin's centre–periphery thesis – the marginalisation of the weak by the strong – as 'the other side of the CNN factor' (or empathy distance frame, as I called it in this book), and hence as human wrongs journalism. I draw on De Bonville's (2000) model of content analysis on the basis of the quantitative statistical measurement of the aggregate data from all the articles of the seven selected British national newspapers, coded with a view to observing how they framed the following three issues: 'British national interest' (BNI); 'human rights excuse' (HRE); and 'global partnership for development' (GPD). I attempt the statistical measurement of the above three issues on the basis of their presence or absence in the articles analysed. I use Entman's definition of framing, which is based on the idea that the more an issue is framed in the media, the more it is likely to remain on their agenda – which has the knock-on effect of setting the agenda for the public as well (Entman, 1993). Using the media content search engine lexis–nexis, I collapsed the total number of 64 articles published by these seven newspapers between mid-September 2007 and mid-March 2008 using the search words 'EU–Africa Summit'. I chose this long period, although the summit itself lasted a matter of days, because the issue was discussed in the media long before and after the summit itself. The content analysis of the seven selected British newspaper is reflected in Tables 10.2–10.7 below:

Table 10.2   Financial   Times   (London   and   USA editions), 7 articles

Issue Framed	Number of times
BNI	50
HRE	7
GPD	6
Total frames	63

Table 10.3   The Times (London), 16 articles

Issue Framed	Number of times
BNI	31
HRE	52
GPD	10
Total frames	93

Table 10.4   The Guardian, 10 articles

Issue Framed	Number of times
BNI	26
HRE	16
GPD	19
Total frames	61

Table 10.5   Daily Telegraph, 10 articles

Issue Framed	Number of times
BNI	17
HRE	12
GPD	5
Total frames	34

Table 10.6   Mirror and Sunday Mirror, 4 articles

Issue Framed	Number of times
BNI	3
HRE	4
GPD	2
Total frames	9

Table 10.7   The Independent, 17 articles

Issue Framed	Number of times
BNI	19
HRE	13
GPD	12
Total frames	44

10.2.1   Discussion

To start with, from the content analysis above we can see that the total number of times (304) that the three issues, BNI, HRE and GPD, were framed by the seven British newspapers in all 64 total articles examined was too limited to make any significant impact on the media agenda (and by extension on the public agenda), especially given the length of time of the coverage between mid-September 2007 and mid-March 2008. Moreover, the analysis shows that the BNI was framed many more times (146) by all seven papers than the HRE (104) and the GPD (44), suggesting that most of the mainstream British newspapers were more interested in their country's national interest and used the smokescreen of human rights rather than being interested in the global partnership for development – which is the eighth and most powerful MDG. Even the HRE featured far more than the GPD.

While the BNI and the HRE are presented as problematic issues as far as human rights promotion and protection are concerned, the GPD is presented as the alternative paradigm in efforts to address global poverty and inequality within the cosmopolitan context of global justice. However, The Guardian did relatively better than the other newspapers in the framing of the GPD, scoring 19 – better than HRE at 16, but slightly lower than BNI at 26 (see Table 10.4), while The Independent, next to it in order of performance, scored 12 for GPD and 13 for HRE (both are below the BNI scoring of 19). The worst performance in terms of the framing of the GPD comes from the Daily Telegraph and the Mirror, which scored 5 and 2 respectively, while doing far better in BNI and HRE (there the scores are 17, 12 and 3, 4 respectively). In fact the framing of the GPD becomes even more marginal when you combine the framing of HRE and BNI in all the seven newspapers, since the last two are more or less the same thing – if you go by the fact that in most of the cases human rights were just used as a front, to advance British national interests. Thus we can see from this analysis that, while BNI and HRE framed most of the coverage of the EU–Africa Summit by the seven newspapers studied, constituting the 'reverse CNN factor', the GPD was relegated to second or third place, constituting 'the other side of the CNN factor', and hence it is a fine example of 'human wrongs journalism' the antithesis of 'human rights journalism'. This marginalisation of the GPD in favour of the BNI and HRE therefore resonates with Gilpin's centre–periphery thesis based on the concentration of global economic activity in the regional cores of the developed Organisation of Economic Cooperation and Development (OECD) countries at the expense of the marginalisation of the LDCs (Gilpin, 2001).

In answering the second question of this section – why the British media failed in promoting the global partnership for development in their skewed coverage of the Lisbon Africa–Euro Summit where others in Africa succeeded – I will proceed by exploring how the over-framing of British national interest and the human rights excuse largely factored in the equation. I will underpin the discussion by juxtaposing the coverage of the seven British newspapers with that of others in Africa, France and the US.

The over-framing of the British national interest, sometimes used in the guise of human rights, contributed to the relegation of the global partnership for development to the margins. As the content analysis shows, almost all of the seven papers welcomed British Prime Minister Gordon Brown's boycott of the Lisbon Summit as heroic, because of the eminent presence of Zimbabwe's President Mugabe – although *The Guardian* was more cautious in its manner. While some of the newspapers openly endorsed Brown's decision, others did so by using the campaign for human rights as a front in order to do so. Writing a commentary in the *Daily Telegraph*, Simon Heffer heaped praises on Brown for his firm stance against the Zimbabwean president, whom he described as 'the insane and evil Marxist dictator "Butcher Bob" Mugabe. I thought Mr Brown was quite right not to attend the recent EU-Africa summit, because the EU was wrong to bend the rules to the let the tyrant into its airspace' (Heffer, 5 January 2008). Kate Hoey, Labour MP and Chair of the Parliamentary Committee on Zimbabwe, said it is more honourable to be denounced by Mugabe than praised by him, adding that Brown should be commended for his refusal to attend the summit (Hoey, 2007). *New Statesman* editor John Kampfner wrote that Brown made waves by staying away (Kampfner, 14 December 2007). On the 'human rights excuse' front, Ben Russell notes that Brown is boycotting the two-day summit after urging his European colleagues to turn Mugabe away because of 'human rights abuses and economic collapse' in Zimbabwe (Russell, 2007). However, a few of the papers, such as *The Guardian*, were slightly critical of the wisdom of Brown's boycott, describing it as 'self-defeating', which indirectly leans towards the politics of human rights. In a leading article on the summit, *The Guardian* writes:

> By staying away, Mr Brown is selflessly letting the summit get on with its serious business. This may go down well in an age when messages are dominated by pictures rather than words, but it is a weak and specious argument. Summits are shop windows. Very little that happens in them is spontaneous, and they are carefully choreographed. And even if the stage designers goofed and Mr Brown and Mr Mugabe met in the lift, or the loo, what would it matter? This is not the first time that dictators responsible for ruining their countries have attended international conferences [...]. (*The Guardian*, 8 December 2007)

The Guardian editorial warned that the idea of imposing bans on bad leaders from attending international conferences should be balanced against the 'politics of the greater good'. It added:

> Britain's principled stand is not absolute. Look at the blind eye Britain is turning towards the actions of the Ethiopian army in Mogadishu, because it fits comfortably into the narrative of the war on terror. But it was principle, not politics, which provided the moral backbone to the boycott of the apartheid regime.... (*Guardian*, Editorial, 2007)

There is no doubt that this is a critical editorial from *The Guardian*, but the subject of attack was basically the British hypocrisy and double standards in using human rights to mask the real national interests; it(the subject of attack) was not against the apparently problematic EPAs (Economic Partnership Agreements), which the African leaders rejected outright at the Lisbon Summit.

Nevertheless, the criticism of the fact that Brown boycotted the Lisbon Summit because he did not want to meet face to face with his sworn

Zimbabwean foe but failed to do the same with respect to other leaders, who had an equally bad record of violating human rights, is important: it helps to debunk the myth of any genuine intentions of protecting and promoting human rights in Zimbabwe that Brown and his government may appear to have entertained. Yet *The Guardian* editorial's call for a balancing act between human rights and 'the politics of the greater good' gives the impression that the editorial line was influenced more by concerns of national interest than by human rights. In other words, *The Guardian* editorial appears to be saying that the human rights-based global partnership for development can be traded off for the utilitarian 'greater good' of the British people. Moreover, the over-framing of the British national interest and its human rights front overshadowed the more human rights-based issue of global partnership for development, especially the aspects dealing with fair trade. This is a fine example of 'the other side of the CNN factor' or human wrongs journalism. This is also evident in Marcel Berlin's comment in *The Guardian*, where he accused Brown of being hypocritical with Mugabe while praising the French president for openly and bravely visiting Libya's Muammar Gaddafi – another 'bad' leader – and bagging a 10-billion euro trade deal for France (Berlin, 12 December 2007). Berlin writes:

> The prime minister did, it's true, demonstrate his human rights credentials with his easy, unnecessary, pointless and possibly counter-productive boycott of the EU-Africa summit last week, because Robert Mugabe was there. But then, Zimbabwe isn't buying billions of pounds' worth of British goods. (Berlin, 12 December 2007)

However, what *The Guardian* and other mainstream media failed to do here in their leading articles, they managed to do, albeit sparingly, in some of their few reports of the summit, which at least reflect some of the critical viewpoints of some African leaders, as the *Financial Times* illustrates: Senegal's president warned Europe that it was losing the trade and influence battle to China, adding that you can buy two Chinese cars for the price of one European car. He said it takes at least five years to complete a deal with the World Bank to construct a road, whereas with the Chinese this is just a matter of days (Bounds and Wallis, 10 December 2007).

Despite Wade's warning, the Portuguese foreign minister Luis Amado was upbeat about the prospects of a new dawn in the EU-Africa relations dubbed by the hopeful as the 'spirit of Lisbon'. Amado said: 'After long years we were able to break the ice and to stop talking in terms of – colonised and colonising – peoples.' But Amado's optimism did not deter African Union Chairman Alpha Oumar Konare to issue the most critical remark yet, touching on the very nerve of the global partnership for development debate: 'This is a point of departure but one very much informed by history. Africa is not poor. That is the paradox. This poverty is not fate. It is the result we have to admit of unequal relations. It is also the result of bad governance.' By going the extra mile in reflecting the dissenting views of the African leaders, the *Financial Times* showed that it could have very easily provided a political context of the EU–Africa disagreements over EPAs if it had wanted to do so. What was, however, lacking in this *Financial Times* report, like in those of many other British newspapers, was a clear-cut reference to the controversial EPAs – not to talk of critical perspectives regarding their implications for undermining the global partnership for development by the 2015 MDG target. However, while this political context was lacking in the British mainstream media, it featured prominently in some of the leading African and French media. A commentary by Ignacio Ramonet, published first in the *Le Monde Diplomatique* in France and then reproduced in the *South African Mail and The Guardian*, is instructive:

> It happened in December at the second EU-Africa summit in Lisbon, where the main objective was to force the African countries to sign new trade agreements by December 31 2007 in accordance with the Cotonou Convention of 2000 which wound up the 1975 Lome accords. Under these, goods from former colonies in Africa, the Caribbean and the Pacific are imported into the European Union more or less duty free, except for products such as sugar, meat and bananas, which are a problem for European producers.

Ramonet (2008) noted that the WTO has in fact called for the dismantling of these preferential arrangements or for their replacement by 'trade agreements based on reciprocity, claiming that this is the only way African countries can continue to enjoy different treatment'. Yet Ramonet argued that the 'EU opted for completely free trade in the guise of the EPAs' – which meant that African, Caribbean and Pacific countries should allow 'EU goods and services to enter their markets duty free' (Ramonet, 2008). Ramonet added:

> The president of Senegal, Abdoulaye Wade, denounced these strong-arm tactics, refused to sign and stormed out. South Africa's Thabo Mbeki immediately supported his stand and Namibia also decided not to sign (bravely, since an increase in EU customs duties would

make it impossible for Namibia to export or continue to produce beef). (Ramonet, 13 January 2008)

Here Ramonet provides enough political context to help to promote a
better understanding of the undercurrents of the controversy over the
EPAs and to make a case for a global partnership for development. This
style of diagnostic reporting within the context of human rights journalism can help to generate a CNN factor of the 'do something' type in
the UK and the rest of Europe if it is adopted and sustained by a large
section of the mainstream British media. Yet, as we have seen, the issue
of national interest and its human rights front meant that this did not
happen.

However, with all this opposition, 15 ACP countries, including 13
from Africa, signed initialled the interim EPAs with the EU to satisfy
WTO rules from January 2008, albeit negotiations were mostly concluded with individual countries and not at regional levels before the
end of the summit. AU Commission Chairman Konare warned EU
negotiators to 'avoid playing certain African regions off against each
other [...] A number of countries have signed up. If the partnerships
are based on the weakness of African Unity there will be a problem'
(Barnetson, 9 December 2007). Oxfam was also critical of the EPAs, urging the EU to 'review its approach'. Oxfam spokeswoman Amy Barry
said: 'The dissatisfaction and anger expressed by some African leaders about the trade negotiations should be a wake-up call to European
leaders and development-minded member states' (Barnetson, 9 December 2007). Zambian President Dr Mwanawasa urged 'EU countries to
relax non-tariff barriers and remove agricultural subsidies to enable agricultural produce from Africa to penetrate the European market' (*New
Times*, Kigali, 12 December 2007). The Director of HRW in the UK, Tom
Porteous, was even more categorical when he expressed scepticism as
to whether the EU would dislodge China in Africa; 'it is one of the
biggest donors, if not the biggest, in Africa'. He said that, because of
their increasing demand for commodities and energy, the Chinese do
not impose conditionality. He therefore warned that, if 'the EU claims
that it is competing with China for influence in Africa, the first thing
it should do is break down its protectionist trade barriers and then
speak up more forcefully for human rights, which is crucial for civil
society' (Dempsey, 14 December 2007). Here we can see that both the
humanitarian (Oxfam) and the human rights (HRW) organisations see
the need for a balanced global partnership for development between
the EU and Africa as crucial to the promotion and protection of human

rights. Oxfam therefore embraced institutional development here and hence departed significantly from its original focus on 'development as charity', as advocated in the Singer approach.

In conclusion, I have tried as best as possible in this chapter to demonstrate the continuum or link between development as advocated by the Washington consensus or neoliberal economics and the eras of the slave trade, colonialism and immediate postcolonialism, and how this (neoliberal model of development and exploitation), and its apparent fall-out – the issue of national interest – have combined to undermine efforts at achieving a global partnership for development (the eighth MDG), which is needed as a sustainable way of addressing the global poverty and inequality problem. I made the case that, as Africa has been the victim of unfair trade from the slave trade era up to the present, compensation one way or the other should not be seen to be asking for too much. The compensation I allude to here can take the form of debt relief; increased aid with no neoliberal capitalist strings attached; and, above all, the creation of an enabling environment through fair trade such as that advocated by Kuper and Pogge, and not necessarily the charity type ad hoc support advocated by Singer. I argue that the Kuper–Pogge roadmap of 'institutional development', in addressing global poverty and tackling the widening gap between the rich and poor nations of the world, can only take place through a constructive partnership for development as set out in the eighth MDG target. As we have seen from the perspectives offered by Dowden and Ankomah in the first part of this chapter, journalists have a great role in putting this cosmopolitan-based development approach on the news agenda and ultimately on the public agenda, in the context of human rights journalism. Sadly, however, as we witnessed in the second part of this chapter, the reverse remains the reality. The quantitative analysis of seven British newspapers, as well as the qualitative discourse analyses of some of the articles of these papers, juxtaposed with others from the African, French and US media, show that issues of national interest and pretentious human rights framed the British news media discourse of the historic Africa–EU Lisbon Summit of 7–9 December 2007 more than concerns of a global partnership for development, which should have been the main theme of the event. In the chapter to follow I will continue the study of the British media in the context of human rights journalism or human wrongs journalism, but this time looking at their representation of migrants in general, and refugees and asylum seekers in particular.

11
Reporting Asylum Seekers and Refugees in the UK: The Myths and the Facts

The aim of this chapter is to examine how the failure of the British media to practice human rights journalism has contributed to the failure to provide protection to asylum seekers and refugees within the context of the cosmopolitan-based human rights. This chapter draws on research I conducted as part of consultancy work commissioned by the Bristol City Council in the summer of 2009, in order to rewrite the 'Asylum Seekers and Refugees' myth-busting booklet aimed at addressing public hostility towards people seeking sanctuary in the UK. In the past decade the debate surrounding immigrants, and asylum seekers and refugees in particular, has climbed up the agenda. It has now become a perfect punch bag for politicians who use it to score political points. Small wonder that it can become a primary political issue whenever Britain holds elections. The asylum seeker and refugee debate is generally characterised by highly distorted stereotypical representations, which have implications for the promotion and protection of the rights of people seeking sanctuary.

I problematise the reporting, or misreporting, of asylum seekers and refugees in the UK as cultural violence, drawing on the Galtung ABC conflict triangle, I mean its first component- (attitude; representing invisible and indirect violence). The other two components of this triangle are *behaviour* (meaning direct physical violence) and *contradictions* (meaning indirect, or invicible, structural violence as discussed in detail in Chapter 1 of this book. Thus here asylum seekers and refugees are simply represented as the 'other', and therefore not worthy of being part of the mainstream or of 'chosen people'. The chapter is divided into two main sections: first I examine the binary notions of cosmopolitanism and nationalism in the context of the reporting of asylum seekers and refugees, and how focus on the latter in the British media has not been helpful for the realisation of human rights journalism; and, second, I explore some of the myths and facts in the reporting of asylum seekers and refugees in the UK.

11.1 Cosmopolitanism versus nationalism in the reporting of asylum seekers and refugees

Since cosmopolitan justice is rooted in the notion that the boundaries of morality transcend those of the nation-state, any journalism oriented towards selective justice and nationalism is an antithesis of human rights, and therefore has no place in human rights journalism. As I argued earlier in this book, for journalism to be based on human rights, it must cut across national borders: in other words, it must be based on the cosmopolitan perspective of human rights, which favours a global scope of justice, with a focus on the rights of the individual, be they asylum seekers or refugees. As cosmopolitans such as van den Anker and Waldrun argue, all individuals must be treated equally in the cosmopolitan global society (Van den Anker, 2005).

Asylum seekers and refugees, as part of the non-national minorities, suffer, however, from social, organisational and institutional barriers such as racism – being discriminated against on the basis of race or ethnic origin. Individuals and institutions that practise racism are essentially microcosms of the wider British society. Racism itself becomes institutionalised when policies and practices are inspired by social and political pressures. The implications include the exclusion and under-representation of ethnic minorities, of which refugees are the worst hit in the equation. Propelling the racist attitude is the 'othering' or arms-length approach, which emphasises the 'us' only. This 'us' and 'them' binary largely informs the blurring of the distinction between economic and forced migration in the UK. Most Britons can hardly tell the difference, for example, between a forced migrant (refugee) and an economic refugee (migrant worker). Moreover, the political elites' suspicion that asylum seeking has become a form of 'economic migration' contributes to the overt politicisation of the status of asylum seekers to the extent of reducing them to 'unwanted economic migrants'; hence the media stigmatise them as 'bogus' (Statham, 2003).

The exiled Iranian scholar Sharam Khosravi describes the notion of 'othering' in the context of borders of nation-states, which, he warns, have become not only 'simple edges of a state' but also an essential reference of national identity (Khorsravi, 2010: 2). Khosravi is particularly concerned about how borders, 'based on a capitalist-oriented and racial discriminating way of thinking, regulate movements of people'. He warns that in this age of global inequality freedom of movement for some people is only made possible through the systemic exclusion of others (Khosravi, 2008). The discursive construction of "illegal immigrants" as anti-citizens creates moral panic in society. This is what happens when "experts", mass media and authorities evoke statistics, diagnoses and prognoses to frame and proclaim a "danger to society" (Khosravi, 2010). My interest in this chapter is to explore the largely problematic media representation of asylum seekers and refugees and its implication for policy and practice in their reception and integration into British society.

In the past, especially in the aftermath of the First and the Second World War, there was more North–North migration; but in the recent past we have been seeing more South–North movement of people. Yet, as Vanessa Pupavac notes, up to the Cold War period, asylum seekers and refugees, including those in the South–North movement praxis, were celebrated as political heroes forced into exile because of their political beliefs and activities. They were portrayed in the media as 'political heroes and courageous defenders of freedom, not traumatised victims. The familiar image of the refugee was associated with the political dissident' (Pupavac, 2008: 270–92). Vanessa Pupavac also alludes to Joshua Rubenstein's *Soviet Dissidents: Their Struggle for Human Rights* (1981), which encapsulates how Cold War refugees from East Europe were presented as public intellectuals, moral thinkers, samizdat writers and artists standing up for freedom of artistic expression against political oppression. How can we therefore explain the representation of the Cold War archetypal refugee as a courageous political exile defying the totalitarian state, while the present-day archetypal refugee is simply portrayed as a traumatised victim, often as the 'scrounging bogus asylum seeker', and hence easily feeding into and reinforcing 'society's fears and political disenchantment' against the 'other'. As Jeff Huysmans put it, questions of national political identity defining who belongs to a political community reinforce the notion of 'othering':

> On the one hand, immigrants live and work in a country. They pay taxes and social security contributions. They consume. They rent or buy property etc. They are thus integrated into the social fabric of a country through a complex network of social and economic relations. Similarly, refugees are tied into national and international

fabrics of rights and duties that define limits and opportunities. On the other hand, immigrants and refugees remain strangers [...]. (Huysmans, 2006: 107)

Central to my aim in this chapter is to problematise this simplification of the asylum–migration nexus to the level of seeing asylum seekers and refugees only as victims of trauma, who are only there to be cared for and hence constitute a problem to society. More importantly, I aim to explore the role of the British media in the equation. In this respect, I go along with Pupavac's point of how refugee advocacy in Britain, rather than depicting refugees as especially talented, 'represents them as traumatised, depoliticised, feminised subjects' (Huysmans, 2006: 107). Thus my opinion here, like Pupavac's, is 'informed by the compelling analyses of the philosopher Hannah Arendt on refugees and the sociologist Talcott Parsons on the sick role' (Pupavac, 2008: 270–92). Arendt's views are predicated on the notion that the rights of refugees are more likely to be respected if they are regarded as belonging to a political community than if they are not (Arendt, 1985). In other words, the more the refugees are treated as the 'other', the more their rights are likely to be violated. For Arendt, the notion of borders or nationalism must not take precedence over that of the cosmopolitan society, where all individuals must enjoy their human rights. On the other level, while compassion drives the present-day representation of refugees as victims of trauma, this 'sick role' framing can have the implication of representing them as hopeless, more or less as patients who admit to having an impaired capacity and surrender their welfare to others. 'Their interests risk becoming determined for them – and to their detriment' (Parsons, 1965, cited in Pupavac, 2008;272). It is therefore easy to see how racist, or somewhat nationalist assumptions have helped to undermine the rights of asylum seekers and refugees. Yet at the same time it is difficult to understand how journalists and some advocates of refugee rights can compromise the civil freedoms refugees are supposed to enjoy, among them the right to seek asylum in dignity.

The notion of 'othering', caused by the widening chasm between cosmopolitanism and nationalism, largely contributed to the problem of a 'declining willingness on the part of states to admit and accommodate large numbers of refugees', leading the United Nations High Commissioner for Refugees (UNHCR), Mrs Sadako Ogata, to remark in 1995: 'The threat to asylum has taken on a global character' (Crisp, 2003). Domestic politics and, by extension, public opinion in most West European countries have largely favoured the legitimisation of anti-asylum policies.

Statham argues that 'publics and politicians who already see national identity and sovereignty under challenge from the combined forces of "Europeanization" and globalisation have found a convenient outlet for expressing these grievances in a populist reassertion of the national community, united against these "bogus" intruders' (Statham, 2003: 165). The fall-outs have been an increase in the focus of asylum conflicts on the ethnic differences between the local population and the 'others' and the increasing politicisation of the asylum system in most European countries, especially in the UK, France and the Netherlands (Statham, 2003). The asylum problem itself started, as I emphasised earlier, with the reduction of the value of seeking sanctuary heralded by the end of the Cold War in the early 1990s: the granting of asylum 'to the enemies of one's enemies' was no longer 'a relatively pure foreign policy issue' (Selm, 2003: 23).

While Article 19 of the Human Rights Charter provides for freedom of expression, it emphasises responsibility in the enjoyment of this freedom. Moreover, Article 20, paragraph 2 requires states to prohibit by law 'any advocacy of national, racial or religious hatred that constitutes incitement to discrimination, hostility or violence'. Considering the hateful vitriol to which refugees and asylum seekers are subjected in some countries, this article may put into use in a claim seeking state protection from such hate speech (Bayefsky et al., 2002). In the UK, where hate propaganda against people seeking sanctuary is even more nationalist, or rather racist, sentiments are more likely to be exaggerated. While in Canada a man's telephone line was cut off because he used it to disseminate derogatory messages about Jewish exiles (refugees) by invoking Article 20 (ibid.), in the UK we are yet to see anybody, including journalists, punished for the many derogatory remarks and sometimes hate propaganda against refugees and asylum seekers constantly permeating the British media.

The consistently negative portrayal of asylum seekers and refugees by the mainstream UK media has culminated into a legacy of public hostility against them and other immigrants. The implications of this hostility peaked in 1997, when local authorities became obliged to support destitute asylum seekers, then again in 2001, following the 9/11 terrorist attacks on the US, in the run-up to the general elections of May 2005 and of the July 2005 London terrorist attacks, and most recently in the June 2009 local and European elections and in the May 2010 general elections in the UK. As things stand now, there is nothing to suggest that they will improve. Sensational stories with eye-catching headlines have been rampant: for example, 'Swan Bake: Asylum Seekers Steal the Queen's Birds for Barbecues' (*The Sun*, 4 July 2003). In other circumstances such stories might be dismissed as outrageous;

> but the page one treatment they received ensured that they took on the role, at least for a time, of urban myths – to be repeated in queues and pubs, or to the next reporter with a note book or microphone who turns up in search of an opinion on asylum seekers. (Jones, 2005: 4).

People seeking sanctuary are on the receiving end. A young refugee, Al Hajji Kamara, suffered racist abuse and was punched and kicked to the ground in a violent attack (*South Wales Evening Post*, 27 December 2005), while the media and the authorities were blamed for the killing of a refugee in Wales (Wood, 23 September 2004).

Public hostility towards asylum seekers and refugees, encouraged by the media, is nothing new in the UK. Similar prejudices against would-be immigrants have been evident since the 1930s, together with overt support for the fascist movement found in the mainstream press at the time. Publications such as the *Daily Mail* and its sister papers, under their owner, the first Lord Rothermere, reinforced growing fears about the level of migrants coming into Britain. In the last decade, stories about asylum seekers and refugees have become a

> staple in the tabloid diet. In the last year alone [...] our tabloid newspapers have blamed asylum seekers for terrorism, TB, AIDS, SARS, failing schools and failing hospitals [...] They have been blamed for everything from road accidents to dwindling fish stocks. *The Sun* blamed them for declining numbers of swans. The *Daily Star* blamed them for missing donkeys. (Maisokwadzo, 2005: 59).

The need for dispelling these myths is becoming increasingly important. Research projects such as 'What's the story?', conducted by Article 19 in partnership with the Cardiff University School of Journalism in 2003, cast light on the depraved techniques employed by popular media sources when reporting on asylum issues. This research, which scrutinised media coverage of refugees and asylum seekers in the UK, calls attention to the common but inaccurate use of statistics when reporting on these issues. The report's 12-week print monitoring found that, of the 113 printed articles that made a reference to the numbers of asylum seekers and refugees, just over half (52 per cent) quoted numbers without attributing them to a source. In addition, the contextual analysis of the relevance and meaning of the statistics is never explained.

The research calls on the British media to report the issue 'fairly and accurately' and not to minimise or sanitise it: 'immigration policy is fertile ground for political mischief. If we cannot rely on our politicians to give a lead, we desperately need newspapers and broadcasters who put their duty to inform ahead of their duty to corner market share' (www.article19.org). Similarly, in 2004 the Greater London Authority (GLA) commissioned a report entitled Media Image, Community Impact, which was conducted by the Information Centre for Asylum Seekers and Refugees (ICAR). The report found 'evidence of negative, unbalanced and inaccurate reporting likely to promote fear and tension within communities across London. Significantly, the report found that there was most evidence of this in the national press rather than either the local or black and minority ethnic press.' Moreover, research conducted by the Institute of Public Policy Research found that these negative media reports made large portions of the public doubt whether many asylum seekers are 'genuine', further fuelling resentment and fear of their presence in the UK (Lewis, 2005).

A consequence of this negative and distorted portrayal of asylum issues is an increased feeling of victimisation amongst asylum seekers themselves. Not only do they have to contend with the reality of unfavourable government policies towards them, such as the restriction of access to the National Health Service (NHS) (Kelley and Stevenson, 2006), but they feel that the media has passed a collective judgement on them even before their cases have been heard. Many recent research efforts explored the link between media coverage of asylum and public attitudes. For example, studies by Finney (2003), ICAR (2004), Newman (2007) and Lewis (2006) argue that, although it is not always easy to determine the exact influence of the media, it is clear that they do play a role in shaping the way people behave and, in particular, in offering the (albeit inaccurate in most cases) evidence the public requires to justify existing prejudices.

It was in the context of these myths and of the need to address public hostility towards people seeking sanctuary that Bristol City Council commissioned the 'Asylum Seekers and Reffugees' myth-busting booklet, first in 2003, and again in 2009. However, rather than just presenting the myths, as was done in the first version, the recent one attempts, on the basis of the research presented in this chapter, to juxtapose myths and facts, by way of minimising the risk that the more gullible readers would take the myths for granted. In its work on social housing (commissioned by the Equality and Human Rights Commission: Rutter and Latorre, 2009) and on communicating asylum (Newman, 2007), the

Institute of Public Policy Research discovered that focusing on the myths alone runs the danger of reinforcing them, because the public is easily influenced by what is constantly churned out in the public domain. Thus, in order to challenge rather than reinforce them, these myths, drawn largely from the UK media, are placed side by side with the facts, which are drawn from accurate data and from the real stories and experiences of asylum seekers and refugees who participated in two separate focus groups in Bristol.

11.1.1 Research methodology

Articles since 2004, collapsed (selected) from lexis–nexis using the search words 'asylum seekers' and 'refugees', were content analysed: I looked especially at headlines in the context of the research questions – in this case, the seven frequently asked questions about asylum seekers and refugees (see below). Twenty asylum seekers and refugees from diverse geographical backgrounds participated in two separate focus groups in Bristol. These were randomly selected by using local migrant community networks with large percentages of refugee and asylum-seeking communities. These community networks were the Somali Resource Centre, the Amana Education Trust, Asylum Care and Housing, the Bristol Sudanese Association, the Darfur Association, the Zimbabwe Bristol Association and the Bristol Francophone Development Association. The focus groups, the first on 23 September 2009, at Amana Education Trust, and the second on 4 October 2009, at the Centre of Excellence for Enterprise Development (CEED), provided data for the personal testimonies of refugees and asylum seekers, some of which were used to counter some of the media myths analysed.

11.2 Seven frequently asked questions: The myths and the facts

The analysis of these myths and facts is carried out in the context of providing answers for the following seven frequently asked questions in the media and public domains about asylum seekers and refugees: Is Britain a 'soft touch' for asylum seekers and refugees? Do asylum seekers choose Britain because it is a 'soft touch'? Why do people leave their own country to seek refuge and sanctuary? Are asylum seekers illegal immigrants? Are asylum seekers economic migrants in disguise? Are asylum seekers bringing HIV AIDS and Tuberculosis (TB) to Britain? Are asylum seekers draining our public services and taking our jobs and houses?

11.2.1   Is Britain a 'soft touch' for asylum seekers and refugees?

MYTH:

We're soft on asylum. (*News of the World*, 30 December 2007)

FACT:

Britain has increasingly restrictive asylum policies. (UNHCR, 2005)

According to UNHCR statistics, the number of refugees fell globally to 8.7 million in 2005, the lowest level since 1980, but the refugee agency warned that there has not been a similar decrease in the numbers of internally displaced and stateless people. According to UNHCR's 2005 annual statistics, the total number of people of concern to UNHCR rose to 21 million from 19.5 million the previous year. This figure includes refugees, asylum seekers, returnees, stateless people and a portion of the world's internally displaced persons (IDPs). The increase was mainly due to the growing number of stateless persons identified by United Nations' High Commissioner for Refugees (UNHCR), in addition to a greater number of UNHCR protected/assisted IDPs (UNHCR report, 2005).

As Table 11.1 below shows,

Table 11.1   Asylum seekers – Number of new claims

	2003	2004	2005
France	59,800	58,500	49,700
USA	73,800	56,100	48,900
Thailand	4,000	2,500	47,700
Kenya	4,200	9,300	39,000
UK	60,000	40,600	30,800
Germany	50,600	35,600	28,900

(UNHCR report, 2005)

France received the highest number of asylum seekers in 2005, with 49,700 new applications lodged – a significant reduction from 2004. In other large industrialised countries (the USA, the UK, Germany), there was a similar decrease in applications. This reduction is linked to increasingly restrictive national asylum policies. The rise in the numbers of applications in Thailand and Kenya is mainly due to the arrival and screening of asylum seekers from Burma and Somalia respectively (UNHCR report, 2005). The statistics below show that the UK is fifth on the list of countries with the greatest number of asylum applications, behind France, USA, Thailand and Kenya. These statistics are important because they debunk the widely held myth that Britain is a 'soft touch' for people seeking sanctuary by comparison with other western countries.

According to Home Office asylum statistics released in August 2008, applications for asylum, excluding dependants, fell by 1 per cent in 2007, to 23,430. The nationalities accounting for the highest numbers of applicants were Afghan, Iranian, Chinese, Iraqi and Eritrean.

Including dependants, applications to countries in the rest of the EU increased by 13 per cent in 2007 compared with a minuscule fall for the UK.

Sixteen per cent of the initial decisions in 2007 were granted refugee status in the UK (compared to 10 per cent in 2006); 6,800 cases were awaiting an initial decision at the end of 2007.

In 2007, 14,935 asylum appeals were determined: 23 per cent were allowed and 72 per cent were dismissed. These figures go further to dispel the myth that Britain is a 'soft touch' for asylum seekers, as they highlight the fact that asylum applications have decreased in the last two years and almost three quarters of the applicants were dismissed (Home Office, 2008).

According to Home Office 2008 asylum statistics, initial decisions on asylum taken in Quarter (Q) 1 2008 were 26 per cent lower than those taken in Q1 2007. This shows how tough Britain is becoming on asylum decisions, despite the slight increase in the number of applications between the two periods; 4,435 initial decisions were made in Q1 2008, 26 per cent lower than Q1 2007 (6005).

Initial asylum decisions in Q1 2008 include the following:

- 21 per cent were granted;
- 11 per cent were granted humanitarian protection or discretionary leave;
- 68 per cent were refused; all this to be compared with:
- 15 per cent, 10 per cent and 75 per cent respectively in Q1 2007.

Moreover, 20,090 initial decisions were made in 2007/8, which is 3 per cent lower than in 2006/7 (20,690).

Among initial asylum decisions in 2007/8

- 18 per cent were granted;
- 10 per cent were granted humanitarian protection or discretionary leave;

- 72 per cent were refused; all this to be compared with:
- 12 per cent, 10 per cent and 78 per cent respectively in 2006/07 (Home Office, 2008).

These figures show that Britain is becoming tougher, and not softer on the issue of asylum.

11.2.2   Do asylum seekers choose Britain because it is a 'soft touch'?

MYTH 1:
Why were illegal migrants taken 2000 miles to the UK? (*Daily Mail*, 23 August 2006)

FACT:
'I did not choose Britain; I found myself in Britain' – Refugee female, 30, from Cameroon. (Focus Group, 4 October 2009)

Asylum seekers and refugees come to the UK in search of refuge from persecution. In 2007, 23,430 asylum applications were lodged in the UK, among which only 16 per cent were granted refugee status; another 11 per cent were granted humanitarian protection or discretionary leave to remain. This means that some 73 per cent were refused and only 23 per cent of those who appealed were successful. The fact that the majority of applications were refused goes to challenge the theory widely trumpeted by the media that Britain is a 'soft touch' for asylum seekers.

A study by the Home Office concluded that most people chose to come to the UK because of its historical or colonial ties with their countries of origin – presence of family and friends – or because English is a global language, and not because they know about the UK asylum or benefit system. An asylum seeker from Zimbabwe (male, 36) who participated in the focus group on 4 October 2009 said: 'I chose the UK because the British government appeared sympathetic to Zimbabweans as South African Development Cooperation (SADC) countries rallied behind the Mugabe government and because I felt I would be safe here.'

MYTH: 2:
asylum cheats are still flocking in quicker than we can boot them out. (*The Sun*, 22 August 2007)

FACT:
The number of asylum seekers to the UK has dropped dramatically in the last few years. (Donna Covey, Chief Executive of Refugee Council, 30 July 2009)

A series of new laws followed the Immigration and Asylum Act 1999, which removed asylum seekers from the welfare benefits system. The National Asylum Support Service (NASS) provides support to destitute asylum applicants. NASS support is very basic indeed, and yet the government announced in July 2009 that it is considering cutting financial provision for destitute asylum seekers over the age of 25 and waiting for a decision from £42.16 to £35.15 per week from October 2009, leaving asylum seekers with only £5 per day to live on.

This is despite the fact that the 'consumer price index' estimated a 'real term' rate of inflation of 5.2 in 2009. This means that destitute single asylum seekers aged 25 or over will be more than £9 per week worse off (Refugee Council, 30 July 2009). Donna Covey, Chief Executive of the Refugee Council said:

> We are appalled that the government has moved to cut support to asylum seekers, who are some of the most vulnerable people in our society. Of course, these are hard times for everybody and no-one should receive preferential treatment. But asylum seekers who are destitute only receive 70 per cent of income support as it is, and are not allowed to work. These changes mean they will receive a little over half of what the government says is the minimum people need to live on.

11.2.3 Why do people leave their own country to seek refuge and sanctuary? How is the term "refugee" misused?

The term "refugee" has slipped into common usage, albeit erroneously in most cases, to cover a range of people, including those displaced by natural disaster or environmental change. In some other cases, refugees are confused with migrants and with asylum seekers whose status has not yet been determined. In international law, the term has a specific meaning.

What do you mean by the term "refugee"?

Under international law (the 1951 Convention relating to the Status of Refugees or the 'Geneva Convention'), the word 'refugee' has a very precise meaning. According to the UNHCR, the most important parts of the refugee definition are: refugees have to be outside their country of origin; the reason for their flight has to be a fear of persecution; the fear of persecution has to be well-founded, in other words they have to have experienced persecution or be likely to experience it if they return; the persecution has to result from one or more of the five grounds listed in the definition; and refugees have to be unwilling or unable to seek the protection of their country.

International law defines a 'refugee' as a person who has fled from, and cannot return to, his/her country due to a well-founded fear of persecution, including war or civil conflict. The Refugee Council defines a refugee as 'someone whose asylum application has been successful and who is allowed to stay in another country having proved they would face persecution back home'.

What do you mean by the term "asylum seeker"?

The Refugee Council defines an asylum seeker as 'someone who has fled persecution in their homeland, has arrived in another country, made themselves known to the authorities and exercised the legal right to apply for asylum' (www.refugeecouncil.org.uk, accessed 12/07/09). A handbook published by Refugee Action in 2006 warns the media and the public not to confuse asylum seekers with illegal immigrants, defining the latter 'as someone who decides to leave their native country and goes to another to live – but does it without telling the authorities.' This situation is different from that of asylum seekers, who have made themselves known to the authorities and are legally allowed to stay until their case is assessed.

What do you mean by the term "economic refugee"?

This phrase is not correct. The accurate description of people who leave their country or place of residence because they want to seek a better life is 'economic migrant'.

What do you mean by the term "economic migrant"?

Migrants make a conscious choice to leave their country of origin and can return there without a problem. If things do not work out as they had hoped or if they get homesick, it is safe for them to return home. The *Bristol Evening Post* (19 April 2006) describes economic migrants as 'those seeking a better life abroad, such as the high number of Brits who emigrate to Australia'.

11.2.4   Are asylum seekers illegal immigrants? Should asylum seekers be detained?

MYTH:

90 per cent of Illegals Stay in the UK. (*The Sun*, 23 January 2009)

FACT:
In 2007/08, 64,930 persons were removed from the UK, a figure that is 3 per cent higher than in 2006/07 (63,200). (Home Office Asylum statistics, 2008)

The Universal Declaration of Human Rights (UDHR, 1948) claims that 'everyone has the right to seek and to enjoy in other countries asylum from persecution'. One of UNHCR's primary responsibilities is to ensure that refugees have access to protection. This includes promoting a state's full adherence to the principle of non-refoulement, which prohibits returning asylum seekers or refugees to places where their life or liberty would be at risk, or denying them access to safe territory. It also includes promoting a state's full adherence to implementing activities to prevent unwarranted arrests and the detention of asylum seekers and refugees.

Preventing refoulement and arbitrary detention are among the core protection priorities of UNHCR. Most asylum seekers arriving in Britain are fleeing nations gripped by civil war, the persecution of minorities and brutal dictatorships. The fact that an asylum seeker may have entered the country illegally does not mean that their case lacks credibility. It is almost impossible for people fleeing persecution to reach Britain without resorting to the use of false documents. In recognition of this fact, Article 31 of the 1951 Convention on Refugees prohibits governments from penalising refugees who use false documents.

The number of initial decisions to refuse or grant asylum was up 3 per cent, with 4,720 decisions being made in the last quarter of 2008, compared to 4,570 made over the same period in 2007; and such refusals often have nothing to do with the substance or credibility of a claim. In the UK, the Home Office's poor standards of decision-making have been well documented by Asylum Aid. A large number of asylum seekers have their applications refused on purely procedural grounds. For example, many are unable to complete the Statement of Evidence Form, in which they have to outline, in English, their reasons for seeking asylum, within the required ten-day deadline (www.asylumaid.org.uk). Between October and December 2008 16,525 people were removed or departed voluntarily from the United Kingdom. This includes 2,570 failed asylum seekers and their dependants and 13,950 non-asylum cases. This is a 2 per cent fall from the same period the previous year.

A yearly comparison shows that, overall, removals and voluntary departures are up by 5 per cent – increasing from 63,365 in 2007 to 66,275 in 2008. There was a fall of 15 per cent to 11,640 for those leaving who had claimed asylum (including dependants), but an increase of 10 per cent to 54,635 for non-asylum cases in 2008.[1]

Going by these figures, it is clear that the majority of failed asylum seekers have been voluntarily or involuntarily removed from the UK despite the myth quoted above, that 90 per cent of 'illegals' are able to stay in Britain.

11.2.5   Are asylum seekers economic migrants in disguise? Why do they come to the UK?

MYTH:

Government bungles means bogus refugees allowed to stay. (*Daily Mail*, 18 August 2006)

FACT:

... refugees are those who have been granted asylum.... (*Bristol Evening Post*, 19 April 2006)

According to the 1951 UN Geneva Convention, a refugee is an asylum seeker who has been granted legal status to live in his/her country of sanctuary, and so it is wrong to classify any officially recognised refugee as 'bogus'. When the number of asylum applications is compared with that of the total population of the state in which the applications are made (applications per 1,000 inhabitants), the UK does not rank high. From 1989 until 2002, asylum migration increased in the UK. However, asylum numbers have decreased since then, as reported under FAQ 1. In fact most people seek asylum in their immediate neighbouring countries. Some of the poorest countries in the world support the largest numbers of refugees.

Most asylum seekers do not choose their country of asylum: where they end up depends mostly on how quickly they flee and by what means. Of those who are able to choose, important factors are existing communities, colonial bonds and knowledge of language. Only a few are influenced by economic factors, and most have little previous knowledge of regulations about work or welfare support in the UK. Lack of context in the mainstream media coverage of asylum and refugees is not helpful in promoting better understanding of their plight and thereby encouraging public empathy for them.

One of the key findings of the IPPR research 'Communicating Asylum' (2007) is that providing context in media coverage is vital in helping people to engage with the subject of asylum. For example, of all the facts about asylum seekers that the IPPR presented to poll respondents, the one that encouraged most people to have a more favourable attitude towards them was that 'many asylum seekers would return to their home country if the political situation there allowed'. Fifty-nine per cent of those polled said that this made their attitude to asylum seekers more favourable (Newman, 2007, Lewis, 2006).

Personal testimonies of asylum seekers and refugees

An asylum seeker from Zimbabwe (male, 36) explains:

> I was a trained and qualified tobacco buyer who supported the opposition MDC party. I was afraid for my life as all my in-laws had been beaten and some thrown in prison while the others had taken refuge in my home.

Another asylum seeker from Zimbabwe (female, 32):

> I endured persecution because I did not support the ruling party; I was beaten by young thugs who were the law. I was living in hell. And yet I am not feeling welcome in the UK because I am still waiting for a decision on my asylum case and being told to wait in the queue till 2011, with no right to study or work. If things get settled in Zimbabwe, I would definitely go back as I still love my country.

An asylum seeker from Eritrea (male, 28):

> My family is held hostage by the government and I ran away to look for somewhere safe. My friends were raped and others sent to jail. I was put in prison for three months for expressing my political views. I pray that things change for the better so that I can go back and help my people

A refugee from Iraq (male, 27):

> I was a police officer. I left my country because my life was in danger. I was shot in the stomach and had to undergo a major operation to remove the bullet. I was also in a car when a bomb exploded; I was terribly injured and I am lucky to be alive today. I was beaten, tortured and locked away.

A refugee from Somalia (male, 48):

> I was a doctor in the radiology department in Mogadishu hospital when the war broke out. I was living a good life with my family and never dreamt of leaving to settle in another country. Unfortunately, with the start of the civil war I had to find somewhere safe to live.

An asylum seeker from Somalia (female, 22):

> I was a little girl living with my family, and was happy until our house was burned in the civil war. I left my country because my life was at risk. I used to hide from one place to another to save my life. My two elder sisters were raped while my brother was killed as he tried to save us from the soldiers. They kidnapped and raped me, and locked me for three months giving me only water and bread. I am still having nightmare of this experience. On arrival the UK immigration welcomed me well but now I am feeling unwelcome because I have been waiting for over six years for my status and I feel I am wasting with no right to study and work, and I am living a destitute life.

A refugee from Somalia (male, 34):

> I am here because I ran away from being killed in the civil war. If my country becomes safe again I will return because I prefer it there and I would have the opportunity to continue my business, which was good.

A refugee from Cameroon (female, 30):

> I had my business and was doing a degree in rural sociology. I left my country for fear of political persecution. I did not choose Britain, I found myself in Britain. I was a member of the Southern Cameroon National Council (SCNC). This is a pressure group mostly run by the English Cameroon in order to gain their independence from French Cameroon. When my political problem is over, I would return to my country and continue my work.

A refugee from Sudan (Darfur) (male, 33):

> I was working in El-Fasher University in Darfur as a manager in the Human Resources Department. I was targeted by the authorities and their militias because of my role as leader of the Student Union. I was put in prison because of that. I did not choose the UK but when I came here I felt safe.

MYTH:
2000 Queue for Britain. (*The Sun*, 23 January 2009)

FACT:
There's no place like home. (*Bristol Evening Post*, 16 June 2005)

When we look at the facts outlined in the personal stories of asylum seekers and refugees above, it is clear that most people who come to the UK seeking sanctuary do so because they are fleeing political persecution or civil wars or are just looking for somewhere relatively safe to live.

In response to the publication of the first quarterly asylum statistics for 2009, Donna Covey, chief executive of the Refugee Council, said:

> These statistics are a clear reminder of why providing sanctuary in Britain is more important than ever. If we just take the top few countries of origin of asylum claimants: Zimbabwe, Eritrea, Afghanistan, Iran, Iraq – they are all countries where violence and human rights abuses are rife and well-documented.

11.2.6 Are asylum seekers bringing AIDS and TB to Britain?

MYTH:
Many asylum-seekers enter Britain penniless as 'health tourists' seeking costly HIV and AIDS treatment. (*The Sun*, 12 April 2008)

FACT:
There is no evidence to suggest that asylum seekers come to the UK to get free treatment for existing health problems. (Home Office Research, 2003)

The mainstream media is full of stereotypes and clichés portraying asylum seekers and refugees as carriers of all sorts of infectious diseases, ranging from TB and HIV AIDS to swine flu. Yet, according to research conducted by the Home Office (2003), there is no evidence to suggest that asylum seekers come to the UK to get free treatment for existing health problems. A government TB screening pilot in Dover tested around 5,000 asylum seekers over a six-month period in 2003 and found not a single case of symptomatic TB. What doctors did find, however, was evidence of maltreatment and torture – evidence of the reasons why these people had had to flee. As for HIV, doctors working with a small group of asylum seekers who are HIV positive say that most are unaware of their status until they are diagnosed (Home Office). In the UK, the British Medical Association found in a research in 2003 that asylum seekers are more likely to become ill once they have arrived in the UK, due to poor living conditions and lack of money for basic needs.

A joint study by Oxfam and the Refugee Council in 2004 showed that the asylum system, far from making the UK 'a land of milk and honey' for asylum seekers, institutionalises poverty. The report was produced on the basis of studying 40 organisations working with asylum seekers and refugees, which revealed that, of those with whom they have contact, 85 per cent experience hunger; 95 per cent cannot afford to buy clothes or shoes; and 80 per cent are not able to maintain good health. The report reveals that many asylum seekers do not receive the basic support they may be entitled to because the system is badly designed, extremely bureaucratic and poorly run (Oxfam and Refugee Council Report, 2004).

In 2006, Oxfam and the Refugee Council jointly commissioned a report by Kelly and Stevenson, entitled *First Do No Harm: Denying Healthcare to People Whose Asylum Claims Have Failed*, criticising the government's amended regulations in 2004, which slashed health care support for failed asylum seekers. The report found that refugees and asylum seekers 'have complex health needs, arising from trauma and deprivation in their countries of origin, compounded by trauma and deprivation in the UK. Meeting those care needs', the report argues, 'should be the sole focus of the NHS, not assessing immigration status and invoicing' (Kelley and Stevenson, 2006).

The campaigns and pressures appeared to have paid off, as a joint Department of Health (DOH) and Home Office review was launched in 2007 to examine the rules on charging non-UK residents for access to NHS services in England. The review report released in July 2009 concluded that there should not be any significant change for either primary or secondary care. A proposal agreed upon by government was that unaccompanied children, including those in local authority care, and asylum seekers whose claim has been refused but who are being supported because there are recognised barriers to their return home should be exempt from charges.[2] Health Minister Ann Keen said: 'These changes will support a clearer and fairer system of access to free NHS services that will maintain the confidence of the public and prevent inappropriate access while maintaining our commitment to human rights' (HOD web site accessed 7/8/09).[3]

The Refugee Council described the government review as 'a step forward for our campaign on healthcare – but not far enough', and Donna Covey, chief executive of the Refugee Council added:

only a few refused asylum seekers who are unable to return home qualify for 'Section 4' support, which means that the vast majority will remain unable to access free care. As a result, people with serious health problems such as kidney failure or cancer will still not be entitled to treatment until their condition becomes life-threatening. This is inhumane, and completely cost-ineffective – emergency treatment is extremely expensive [...] There is no evidence that asylum seekers come to the UK seeking healthcare, and indeed nothing to suggest they put pressure on hospital resources. (Ibid., p. 1)

Despite this progress, there remains a perception amongst popular media outlets that asylum seekers make huge or disproportionate demands on the British health service. *The Sun* criticised the government for allegedly accommodating 'foreigners settling here and even coming specifically to give birth' (*The Sun*, 2 February 2008). It even wrote that, according to a BBC investigation, 'ten years ago one baby in every eight was born to an immigrant mum'. It added that 'that figure is now one in two', without giving any source for this assertion. This is another example of an unsubstantiated claim in the popular press, and it should therefore be dismissed.

11.2.7 Are asylum seekers draining our public services and taking our jobs and houses?

MYTH:
'British jobs for British workers'[4]
Brown's slogan during the 2010 election campaigns. (*Yorkshire Post*, 12 November 2009)

FACT:
under EU rules, workers from EU nations are able to take jobs in this country, as much as any British person may choose to go and work in Germany, France, Poland or any other Eastern European nation.

A report by IPPR (Pillai, 2007) found a number of worrying trends influencing the reception of new migrants in the UK, as well as questioning the capacity of local authorities to promote integration amid increased diversity. At the centre of how migrants are received are misconceptions and misinformation within communities. The media play a key role in filling what is often a vacuum of accurate information on the dynamics of social change at the local level.

These "misperceptions" are largely forged along the fault lines of race, ethnicity and religion, with white migrants in England reporting a broadly more positive reception than non-white migrants. The reception of new migrants is also influenced by local labour markets, local housing pressures, local and regional demographics, and political leadership on migration' (Pillai, 2007). The report found that a number of research participants had hostile attitudes towards migrants. Most of the hostilities were closely linked to perceived economic threats – specifically, job displacement and wage deflation at the low-skilled end of the labour market.

The IPPR report findings also point to misconceptions about migrants' entitlements to welfare, housing and other public services. Much of the hostility stemmed from the perception that new migrant communities were given preferential treatment over established communities. Such negative sentiments, sometimes also coming from more established black and ethnic minority communities, and often fuelled by the mainstream media, were mostly directed against asylum seekers and refugees. However, migration did not feature as a major issue for any of the communities engaged in the research. This is consistent with recent CRE/Ipsos MORI research (2007), which found immigration to be seen as an important issue for the nation, but not as a priority issue for people personally. 'Instead, when research participants were asked what they thought were some of the negative aspects of their community or how they thought their community had changed for the worse, local issues such as transport and crime cropped up' (Pillai, 2007).

A research report by Rutter and Latorre (2009) commissioned by the Equality and Human Rights Commission (EHRC) found that the sale of social housing in many parts of the UK and its rental accommodation for migrants have fuelled misconceptions about the allocation of social housing in favour of immigrant communities. Findings of the research claim that 'perceptions that migrants displace UK-born may arise from the fact that some private rented housing, which is now home to migrants, is former social housing stock. Local residents may believe it is still "owned by the council" despite it now being in the private sector' (Rutter and Latorre, 2009: 10). The EHRC report found no evidence to suggest that 'social housing allocation systems favour one community over another, or to show that migrant populations are disproportionately committing tenancy fraud' (ibid.). It did, however, find that perceptions that 'migrants displace British social housing applicants persist'. The report concluded that more social housing and affordable private housing is needed in order to address the failure of the social housing supply to meet the demands of the population. This is the real issue at stake, and not the unfounded public perceptions of house queue-jumping by immigrants.

MYTH:
They think it's great, they love it, and they get off a lorry and are given everything [...] money, a house, payouts. (White male, Barking and Dagenham, cited in Pillar, 2007)

FACT:
Immigrant home lies. (*Evening Chronicle*, Newcastle, 7 July 2009)

Most people do not know that, since 2000, asylum seekers have not been able to claim welfare benefits. The new scheme for housing asylum seekers involves dispersing applicants away from London and the south-east to other regions of the UK. NASS is the Home Office department, which takes responsibility for supporting asylum seekers and allocating accommodation. Asylum seekers are no longer able to claim housing benefit or local authority housing. New applicants who need financial assistance must apply to NASS, which may grant support if the asylum seeker 'appears likely to become destitute within 14 days', but no actual amounts are given. The total number of asylum seekers in receipt of asylum support was 33,865 in Q1 2008 – 31 per cent lower than at the end of Q1 2007 (48,800), according to Home office 2009 statistics.

MYTH:
You Pay GBP 73m so Illegals Can stay;
They get free food and rent. (*Daily Star*, 22 June 2009)

FACTS:
They get flats no one wants. (*Bristol Evening Post*, 24 May 2003)

They [...] receive a little over half of what the government says is the minimum people need to live on. (Donna Covey, Chief executive of Refugee Council, 30 July 2009)

Refugees bring with them a wealth of skills and experience – even the Home Office has recognised this and made a commitment, through its Integration Unit, to put such skills to good use. The NHS relies heavily on foreign labour – according to the Greater London Authority, 23 per cent of doctors and 47 per cent of nurses working within the NHS were born outside the UK. According to an IPPR report on the economic profile of Britain's immigrants (IPPR Report, 2007), 'most immigrant groups do better in economic terms than the UK-born population'. Taking into account the relative size of the groups studied in the report, 'it would seem that the average immigrant has better economic characteristics than the average UK-born person'. Moreover, the IPPR report supported earlier research highlighting contributions that immigrants make, both fiscally (Sriskandarajah et al., 2007) and in wider economic terms (Glover et al., 2001), by confirming that

> many immigrant groups are making positive economic contributions, either through paying high levels of tax and national insurance contributions, staffing our public services, or working long hours in potentially undesirable jobs. Many of these groups also appear to put little pressure on the welfare state in terms of claiming benefits, which has been a key concern in public debates around migration. (IPPR 2007: 44).

MYTH:
Four out of five migrants 'take more from economy than they put back'. (*Daily Mail*, 29 August 2006)

FACT:
Many immigrant groups are making positive economic contributions, either through paying high levels of tax and national insurance contributions, staffing our public services, or working long hours in potentially undesirable jobs. (IPPR 2007 report: Economic profile of Britain's immigrants)

New research jointly undertaken by the Refugee Council and the Zimbabwe Association in July 2009 reveals the range of skills the UK is losing by denying the vast majority of asylum seekers entitlement to work. Although the focus of the research was on the Zimbabwean community, many of its findings also apply to people from other countries, who are keen to contribute their skills and experience to the UK. The survey of 292 Zimbabwean refugees showed the following results:

Sixty-four per cent are educated to General Certificate in Secondary Education (GCSE) level and beyond, and only three were unemployed and staying at home. The highest proportion (15 per cent) are qualified teachers or lecturers.

People from other occupations varied widely – from town planners, surveyors and transport managers to engineers, mechanics and IT specialists. Significantly, 63 per cent said they would like to return to Zimbabwe when it is safe to do so.

Donna Covey of the Refugee Council said: 'This study shows that denying those who want to work the opportunity to do so is an appalling waste of skills and indeed of money' (www.refugeecouncil.org.uk accessed 2/8/09).

Bristol City Council (BCC) has been supporting Refugee Week in recent years, in recognition of the positive contribution immigrants make to society. Lorraine Ayensu of the BCC said: 'Refugee Week is a unique time when we can all celebrate the contribution that refugees have made over the years to the UK – both culturally and economically' (*Bristol Evening Post*, 16 June 2005).

By way of conclusion, it is obvious from some of the key findings presented here that there has been a considerable improvement in the media representation of some of the contentious issues about asylum seekers and refugees since the last myth-busting report on them was published in 2003. This improvement was more evident in the local and regional papers analysed in this report, especially the *Bristol Evening Post* and the *South Wales Evening Post*. Such improvement could largely be attributed to the impact of awareness-raising projects by refugee rights campaigns and support organisations, for instance the Refugee Council, Refugee Action, the Equality and Human Rights Commission, the Commission for Racial Equality, the Information Centre for Asylum Seekers and Refugees, the Media Wise Trust and the Press Complaints Commission.

The key lesson of this research is that one way of dispelling myths about asylum is by juxtaposing them with the facts, drawn from accurate data, and by viewing them alongside real personal stories and experiences of asylum seekers and refugees. This revelation, which informed much of the discussion of this chapter, seeks to address the weakness, identified in the research reports of Rutter and Latore (2009) and of Lewis (2006), of focusing just on the myth – which is dangerous because it will reinforce it.

The facts outlined in the personal testimonies of refugees and asylum seekers who participated in the two focus groups of this research suggest that most people seek sanctuary in the UK because they are fleeing either political persecution or instability. They are looking for somewhere safe, and they are not necessarily in search of a better life; they would be happy to return if things returned to normal in their country of origin. There is no evidence that asylum seekers come to the UK seeking health care, or that they are carriers of deadly diseases such as HIV, TB or swine flu. The reality is that they often have some complex health needs caused by trauma in their home countries, which are compounded by the deprivation they suffer in the UK.

Despite dwindling financial assistance for asylum seekers and the decreasing number of those in receipt of asylum support,[5] most of them are making positive economic contributions, through paying high taxes or National Insurance contributions, staffing public services, or working long hours in potentially undesirable jobs (IPPR Report, 2007); this dismisses the myth that they are taking more than they pay back.

Finally, by contextualising why people seek sanctuary and how they are coping with the new challenges of life away from home, and by drawing on people's personal testimonies and on accurate data, the media can potentially avoid myths about asylum seekers, and hence prevent hostility towards them. This is what I conceptualised in this book as human rights journalism. With this type of journalism, hostile perceptions and actions by host communities against people seeking sanctuary would be considerably reduced, or even curtailed, as people are provided with the facts rather than the myths of the asylum system. This will proactively reduce the chances of cultural violence, which promotes the language of exclusion, and in this way it will prevent direct and indirect physical and verbal violence against immigrants.

12
Conclusion: A Case for Human Rights Journalism and Future Directions

Drawing on the Kantian cosmopolitan principle of global justice, I have made a strong case throughout this book for human rights journalism as a more radical alternative to mainstream journalism because of its more pro-active approach in prioritising the deconstruction of indirect structural and cultural violence as the best way of preventing or minimising the incidence of direct political violence. Kant (1963) believed in both peace and human rights, and indeed saw very clear overlaps between the two concepts. He preferred peace to war because he argued that war, or even making preparations for it, encourages attitudes and behaviours that undermine the realisation of human rights. Kant advocated a lawful form of international association based on the cosmopolitan condition of interdependence (1963: 18). I have above all argued that, despite some progress made since the Universal Declaration of Human Rights (UDHR) in 1948, the world is still far away from becoming a better place in the context of Kant's cosmopolitan global justice, largely because of the dominance in political and media landscapes of what I have called 'human wrongs journalism', and that human rights journalism, as presented in this book, is the way to reverse this trend. This concluding chapter takes the following structure: a case for human rights journalism; principles of the human rights-based approach to journalism; and future directions for human rights journalism.

12.1 A case for human rights journalism

Because there is little or no scholarly work directly focusing on journalism theory and practice on the basis of the human rights approach, I decided to dedicate all four chapters (Chapters 2–5) in the first part to constructing a critical theoretical and conceptual framework for what I have called human rights journalism. Since I have included conclusions in all the chapters in this book, I will avoid recapping the main points and arguments in a chronological order here; I will instead briefly refer to some of the key theoretical and empirical justifications of human rights journalism and offer some directions for its future in normative journalism praxis.

While in Part II, I dedicated three chapters to case studies of conflicts in Sierra Leone, Somalia, Rwanda and Kosovo in the context of direct political violence, in Part III, I dedicated three chapters to the 2007 EU–Africa Summit in Lisbon, poverty eradication and social movements, and refugees and asylum seekers in the context of indirect structural and cultural violence. In all six case studies, I looked at how the lack of human rights journalism undermined humanitarian intervention within the just peace framework to prevent violence, and, by extension, human rights violations. My reason for electing to look at forms of direct physical violence in Part II and at indirect forms of cultural and structural violence in the final part was informed by the aim of the book to present positive rights (economic, social and cultural rights) and positive peace (peace from structural and cultural violence), as opposed to just negative rights (civil and political) and negative peace (peace from direct violence), in order to help the reader to gain a holistic understanding of the dichotomies of these two main forms of violence. The idea is not only to underscore the importance of both sets – human rights and peace – but also to show how they overlap by supporting or undermining each other and, perhaps more importantly, how human rights journalism can mobilise humanitarian interventions to promote and protect a holistic set of human rights based on global justice.

As I discussed in Chapters 1 and 4, Norwegian founder of peace research Johan Galtung is very critical of the simple and common interpretation of peace as the absence of war or direct physical violence. He referred to this type of peace as 'negative peace' (Barash and Webel, 2002). Galtung dismisses this interpretation of peace as too narrow and argues that peace means more than just the absence of direct violence or war. He therefore develops the alternative conception of 'positive peace', which he describes as 'the best protection against violence' (Galtung, 1996: 32). Galtung distinguishes between *direct* physical violence, such as wars and acts of genocide, and structural violence, such as exploitation, inequality, misery, poverty and forced migration. By developing the phrase 'structural violence', Galtung demonstrates that it is not only the harm inflicted by the pain of direct physical violence that needs to be deconstructed but also, and perhaps more importantly, that inflicted by those indirect forms of political, repressive and economic exploitative structures. Galtung argues that, to create a complete peaceful society, both these forms of violence must be eliminated (Galtung, 1996). Despite this distinction along negative and positive lines, however, peace and human rights reinforce each other in many ways. They are so mutually dependent that peace cannot be achieved if human rights are not protected and realised, while at the same time human rights cannot be protected if peace is absent. The human rights–peace nexus, which reinforces human rights journalism and makes it complement peace journalism as counter-hegemonic journalism praxis, resonates with Schirch's justpeace framework, which prioritises preventive or pro-active peacebuilding (Schirch, 2002).

In this book I have argued that mainstream journalism has failed to pro-actively report peace and human rights in ways that have the potential not only of illuminating the important nexus between them but also of focusing on the deconstruction and promotion of positive peacebuilding and positive human rights so as to match the dominant negative peace and negative rights within the cosmopolitan context of global justice. What is more, apart from the growing body of peace studies and peace journalism research (Galtung and Vincent, 1992, 1994, 1996; Lynch and McGoldrick, 2005; Lynch 2008), which at least in recent times attempted to illuminate the failure of the media in positive peacebuilding initiatives, there is little or no scholarly work focusing on the journalism–peace–human rights nexus and critically engaging in the discussion of the failure of mainstream journalism in promoting and protecting positive peace and positive rights with the view of addressing the above problems.

Lynch and McGoldrick (2005: 59) argue that the painful effect of suffering caused by direct physical violence can equally be felt in situations of cultural and structural violence forms of violence, which form important parts of the 'conflict picture' that can easily be ignored when focusing only on situations of direct violence. However, fundamentally lacking in the Lynch and McGoldrick's (2005) study is a conceptualisation of journalism in the context of the links or overlaps between peace and human rights, and by extension between positive peace and negative peace on the one hand, and between positive rights and negative rights on the other hand. This book has attempted to fill these gaps by proposing human rights journalism as a complementary strand of peace journalism within the justpeace framework advocated by Schirch (2002), Ury (2001) and Frank (2007) and discussed in Chapters 1, 3, 4, 5 and 7. I argue that it is when violence is allowed to canalise at will, from the indirect cultural and structural forms of violence (positive peace) to direct physical violence (negative peace), that it becomes more measurably biting and destructive, and that human rights journalism can be the effective alternative strand of journalism to prevent this canalisation.

As I argued in this book, especially in Chapters 1–4, human rights journalism can serve as a complementary strand to peace journalism because it seeks to fill all the above gaps. Moreover, human rights journalism complements the four orientations of the peace journalism model advanced by Galtung (1992, 1996) and supported by Lynch/McGoldrick (2005), namely:

Peace journalism

win–win rather than win–lose oriented

truth rather than propaganda

people rather than elite

solution rather than victory.

Human rights journalism complements peace journalism by four other orientations, namely:

global (triple-win) rather than just selective (win–win) or win–lose

biased in favour of, rather than against, vulnerable voices

pro-active (preventive) rather than reactive (prescriptive)

attached rather than detached to victims of violence and justice.

With these complementary attributes of human rights journalism, peace journalism, I argue, will be justified to lay claims to the four clear values of 'humanitarianism, truth, holism and empowerment' identified by Lovasen (2008) in support of the Galtung model. These four values in a way resonate with the principles of the rights based-approach to journalism: linkages to human rights standards, participation, accountability, non-discrimination and empowerment, informed by both negative and positive rights on the one hand and negative and positive peace on the other hand (Galtung, 1992, 1996; Nowak, 2005; Beman and Calderbank, 2008).

If there are problems with mainstream journalism largely informed by the western liberal democracy model, and above all if the public, citizen and peace journalisms, as I discussed in Chapter 4, cannot sufficiently serve as the panacea, then it stands to reason that an alternative, or rather, complementary strand such as human rights journalism is required as a way forward in tackling these problems. This is the case I have made as best as possible throughout this book. Having touched on some of the key conceptualisations underpinning the key arguments justifying the need for a human rights journalism, I will now summarise some of the key findings and lessons of this study within the framework of the five principles of the rights-based approach to journalism: participation, accountability, non-discrimination, empowerment, and linkages to human rights standards informed as they relate to the values of 'humanitarianism, truth, holism and empowerment' that support human rights journalism and peace journalism.

12.2 Principles of the human rights-based approach to journalism

The human rights-based approach *Training Manual* (Beman and Calderbank, 2008) published in Bangkok in 2008 by UNESCO identified five human rights principles on which the human rights-based approach to journalism are founded. Although this training manual was made in Vietnam, ostensibly targeting Vietnamese journalists and others in developing countries, the principles of human rights-based journalism apply globally. These principles, around which I am going to highlight some of the key findings of this book, are linkages to human rights standards, participation, accountability, non-discrimination and empowerment.

Linkages to human rights standards: *The human rights approach is linked to international human rights law and standards, which outline the minimum standards required to respect and fulfil human rights. International human rights conventions, treaties, declarations and reports are the guidelines that define what basic human rights are and whether a country is meeting those rights. When reporting on social (I will add political, economic and cultural) issues, journalists should refer to the human rights conventions that have been signed by their government and the UN reports on whether the country is meeting these rights in order to get a good understanding of some of the key rights issues in the country*[1]

Yet going by the findings of this book, this principle can only be taken seriously by journalists if human rights, as an academic subject, or an aspect of it is embedded in the journalism studies curricula or training programmes. The fact that mainstream journalism prioritises aspects of negative rights (first-generation civil and political rights), and hence 'negative peace' (peace from direct violence), over those of positive rights (second-generation rights), and hence positive peace (peace from structural and cultural violence), speaks volumes about the lack of consideration and of apparent awareness of the basic human rights standards on the part of most journalists, as this book has demonstrated. This also explains why concerns about human rights based on cosmopolitan global justice are almost always traded off by the mainstream media for of political realism such as national and geo-strategic interests, as Chapters 6–11 of this book have illustrated.

Moreover, an awareness of the UN 1951 Geneva Convention on the rights of refugees and asylum seekers would help journalists to avoid the use of myths – such as reflected in calling refugees or asylum seekers 'illegal' or 'bogus'. The facts juxtaposed with these myths (as illustrated in Chapter 11) show that a refugee is someone whose asylum has been legally granted by the host government, and so cannot be said to be 'illegal' or 'bogus', while an asylum seeker cannot be saddled with the these stereotypes because, when he/she comes seeking sanctuary, he/she makes him-/herself known to the authorities of the host country. Surely, journalists' awareness and recognition of human rights standards will reduce their chances of falling prey to the use of culturally violent language, which can potentially lead to violent hostilities such as those referred to in Chapter 11. Moreover, as explored in Chapter 4, awareness of human rights standards would help them to carry out their social responsibility role of helping to right societal wrongs while at the same time upholding ethical principles of truth-telling and fairness.

Participation: *A human rights-based approach entails a high degree of participation from all the affected parties, individuals, men and women, communities, civil societies, indigenous populations and others. Participation must be active free and meaningful. It is stated in the UN Declaration on the Right to Development at the Vienna Conference in 1986 that participation must be 'active, free and meaningful', so that mere formal or 'ceremonial' contacts with beneficiaries are not sufficient. The participation of the most disadvantaged and marginalised communities should always be a priority.*

Of resonance here to the thesis of this book is the focus on participation at the grassroots level in order to achieve global poverty eradication within the context of global justice. Poverty eradication has been identified by the United Nations as the largest challenge facing international society in the search for a global society based on cosmopolitan justice (Pogge, 2005). It is for this reason that I have tried as best I could to demonstrate two main scenarios in Chapter 9: first, that, for global poverty to be eradicated, the controversies or obstacles that stand in the way of the realisation of the right to development must first be removed or resolved, and, second, that the best way to remove or resolve them is by employing human rights journalism instead of human wrongs journalism, which is dominant in the mainstream media. I have tried to show that it is impossible to talk about global poverty eradication without talking about the need to realise the right to development for all Moreover, it is impossible to be serious about averting direct physical violence without talking about some of the root structural causes (indirect invisible forms of violence) such as global poverty (against which the Seattle demonstrations were organised, for example), as well as about the forms of economic injustice that perpetuate this violence. These invisible forms of violence are the positive economic, social and cultural rights (first-generation rights) which Stammers (2009) refers to as 'non-legal' and 'pre-legal' rights, and which he also urges us to take seriously if we are to obtain a better and more holistic understanding of the human rights doctrine.

The role of the Seattle Independent Media Channel (IMC) in facilitating the historic demonstrations against the exclusive policies of the global economy embedded in the so-called free trade also provides a fine example of how human rights journalism in the context of open space and participatory media can address human wrongs journalism evident in the exclusion and silencing of the narratives of the demonstrators by the mainstream media. The participation of all, including disadvantaged and marginalised communities and societies, in the process of development is crucial. This is why, in Chapter 9, I also made a case for the more pragmatic and pro-active 'economic development/institutional development model' advocated by Pogge (2005) and Kuper (2002) as the human rights-based one, instead of the more normative and reactive 'economic growth/development as charity' model advocated by Singer (2002) in discussing the best approach to eradicate extreme global poverty.

Accountability: *A human rights-based approach identifies the 'rights holders', as well as the 'duty bearers' (those who are responsible for protecting, respecting and fulfilling these rights), to highlight who has responsibility/accountability for ensuring that the rights holders' rights are realised. This principle assists by focusing on increasing the capacity of duty-bearers, including governments, individuals, local organisations and authorities, private companies, aid donors and international institutions, to meet their obligations. As noted in human rights law, duty bearers have an obligation to progressively realise social, cultural and economic rights.*

The accountability principle resonates with the social responsibility role of the journalist as a duty bearer to report, interpret and disseminate information honestly to fellow global citizens, in ways that would make them understand not only the 'how', 'when', 'where' and 'what' of events, issues and processes but, as Lasswell (1927) put it, the 'why' – so that they would be able to make informed decisions when holding the state (national and global) and other duty bearers to account. Unfortunately, however, as this book shows, journalists have not been living up to these expectations because of their focus on the values of human wrongs journalism instead of on those of human rights journalism, such as accountability and social responsibility. Human rights journalism cares for all human beings, especially the more vulnerable people of global society. It is a humane form of journalism, that relies more on advocacy and attachment to the problems and challenges of global society. We saw how, as discussed in Chapter 3, former BBC correspondent Martin Bell showed preference for this form of advocacy/attachment journalism while addressing the News World Conference in 1996 (Carruthers, 2000: 240–41) because he would rather favour the good against the evil, the right against the wrong, and the victim against the aggressor than stay neutral in the name of objectivity. Bell's concern is to use journalism to influence things so as to make them better. We also saw in Chapter 8 how the alternative journalists of the Seattle Indy media Channel used advocacy/attachment journalism to try to influence policies in order to change the situation of the global poor. The accountability principle of the human rights-based approach to journalism therefore provides a strong conceptual support for the proactive and interventionist role of the human rights journalists, and by extension peace journalists, as change agents.

Non-discrimination: *The human rights requirement for non-discrimination demands that particular focus be given to the status of vulnerable groups, which are to be determined locally, such as minorities, indigenous peoples, impoverished groups, within the context of a rights-based approach. In order to successfully abide by this principle, there is a high need for disaggregated data by race, religion, sex, ethnicity, language and other associated areas of concern in human rights.[2] In carrying out this principle, a journalist must include safeguards to protect against threats to the rights and well-being of these vulnerable and marginalised groups, while guarding against reinforcing any existing power imbalances. Who is interviewed, where they are interviewed, how they are interviewed and what information is reported should all prevent any power imbalances.*

However, this novel principle of non-discrimination was not factored in the reporting of the Sierra Leone civil war by the mainstream British media. As I argued in Chapters 6 and 8, the lack of sustained interest in Sierra Leone by the British government was informed by political, economic and cultural empathy/distance frames rather than by empathy/critical frames in the media, and above all this framing contributed to the 'other side of the CNN factor' in Sierra Leone', as opposed to the 'CNN factor' in the case of the NATO intervention in Kosovo. We also saw how these problematic human wrongs journalism empathy/distance frames contributed to the withdrawal of humanitarian interventions in Somalia and Rwanda, as discussed in Chapter 7, and we saw above all the British government's failure to support the global partnership for development at the Lisbon EU–Africa Summit, as discussed in Chapter 10. Moreover, as I emphasised in Chapter 11, the principle of non-discrimination was not considered in the reporting of asylum seekers and refugees by a representative section of the British media that used many media myths about their situation. These myths have the potential to reinforce rather than address the imbalances of global society. Within the human rights journalism framework, every individual must enjoy his/her fundamental human right of living without fear of suffering from mass killings, humiliation or torture, protected and promoted by all, including the media.

Empowerment: *A human rights-based approach requires that interventions contribute to the enhancement of the capacities of rights holders to claim and exercise their rights. Rights holders must be placed at the centre of the process. In reporting on any issue, the interview process and the reporting should, where possible, give voice to the marginalised, allow them to express their concerns or their needs in a safe environment.*

Empowering people so that they are able to claim and exercise their rights is central to the idea of human rights education, which is the key tool available to the human rights journalist in providing a context for the issues, events and processes they report or write about. I argued in Chapter 9 that media activism can provide tremendous support for critical social movements by exposing and challenging societal imbalances, as we saw in the case of the IMC and of the battle for Seattle. Moreover, I argued in Chapter 9 that journalists have a moral responsibility to write in favour of the empowerment of societies that are economically disadvantaged in the global economy by following the roadmap of institutional development, which is proposed by Pogge (2005) and Kuper (2002), and underpinned by a global partnership for development, as outlined in the eighth Millennium Development Goal (MDG) target. However, as I noted in Chapter 10, going by the findings of the study on the reporting of the EU–Africa Summit, this empowerment principle is still a far cry from the reality. The quantitative analyses of six British quality newspapers, as well as the qualitative discourse analyses of some of the articles from these newspapers, juxtaposed with others from the African, French and US media, show that issues of national interest and human rights excuses framed the British news media discourse of the historic Africa–EU Lisbon Summit of 7–9 December 2007 more than concerns about a global partnership for development – which was in fact the main theme of the event.

12.3   Future directions of human rights journalism

Having sounded pessimistic about the challenges and failures of journalism throughout this book, I want to end on a positive note by briefly discussing some of the very good ongoing initiatives taken by some media stakeholders to improve the quality of journalism, most of which, I believe, will support the human rights-based approach to journalism I have discussed in the pages of this book. But before I do that, I would like to say that all hope is not yet lost, as even in the analyses of this book – which, as I said, sounded more pessimistic about journalism – there were, albeit very few, some examples that point to human rights journalism at work. Two of these readily come to mind. First, in my case study of the coverage of the Sierra Leone civil war in Chapter 6, the picture was not all gloom, as there were at least two exceptions. The most notable was the American journalist, Steve Coll of the *Washington Post*, whose reporting stands out as a true reflection of the peace/human rights journalism frames: intellectual–context–diagnostic as opposed to war/human wrongs journalism frame: routine–fact–evocative. The latter frame, the problematic one, was more or less employed by the three British journalists in the study: Alex Duval Smith (*Independent*), Sam Kiley (*The Times*), and Anton La Guadia (*Daily Telegraph*), although the first, Alex, did better than the last two in terms of reaching out to the peace/human rights journalism frame. Second, my study of the media myths and facts about refugees and asylum seekers in Chapter 11 recognised an improvement since the publication of the last myth-busting booklet in 2003, especially in regional papers as like the *Bristol Evening Post* and the *South Wales Evening Post*. The fact that this improvement was apparently largely attributed to the impact of awareness-raising projects of refugee rights campaigns and support organisations – for instance the Refugee Council, Refugee Action, the Equality and Human Rights Commission, the Commission for Racial Equality, the Information Centre for Asylum Seekers and Refugees, the Media Wise Trust and the Press Complaints Commission – shows that small, but concerted and sustained efforts can bring about positive change in the way journalists work. What these few optimistic notes indicate is that at least human rights journalism as advocated in this book is possible if some pro-active actions are undertaken.

Finally, I will go to outline some of the few ongoing initiatives, and some of my recommendations, which have the potential to raise the hopes for the realisation of human rights journalism as a more pro-active and viable journalism paradigm.

12.3.1 The human rights-based approach to journalism: Training Manual, Vietnam

This manual provides a guide for both media training institutions and journalists in Vietnam wishing to understand and embed human rights into their educational programmes and practices. The handbook explains human rights concepts and provides background on the international, regional and national human rights systems. It also offers practical advice on how to undertake a human rights-based approach during the investigative and reporting cycle. The final section of the manual contains a basic course outline and examples of lesson plans and exercises for trainers to support the creation of stand alone or integrated human rights training programmes for the media in Vietnam (UNESCO website, accessed 20 April 2009).

My recommendation: This training manual, though specifically targeting Vietnam, could be developed and adapted by UNESCO and other media stakeholders to be used globally to address the problems of human wrongs journalism identified in this book, and to help to spread the alternative ideals and practices of human rights journalism.

12.3.2 Journalists for Human Rights training on rights-based approach

Journalists for Human Rights (JHR) was set up in Canada, in 2002, by Ben Peterson, with the main aim of making 'everyone in the world fully aware of their rights'. Now recognised as Canada's largest international media organisation, JHR has focused its training activities in post-conflict countries on developing the journalism skills required to produce rights media that incorporates elements of the rights-based approach. The rights-based approach to journalism encompasses the rights-based principles of the Vietnam training manual discussed above, namely linkages to human rights standards, participation, account-ability, non-discrimination and empowerment (JHR website, accessed 07 August 2010).

My recommendation: Again I would encourage JHR to develop and adapt the training developed here to be used globally, especially in the West, where it would help address the problems of human wrongs jour-nalism such as those identified in this book, and promote human rights journalism. JHR can work in partnership with UNESCO and higher education institutions, offering journalism courses as well as for other media stakeholders working to improve the quality of journalism in the promotion of peace and human rights.

12.3.3   Peace Journalism Training Workshops

Since the publication of their seminal book *Peace Journalism* (2005), Jake Lynch and Annabel McGoldrick have led training workshops in peace journalism for professional editors and reporters in many coun-tries, including Indonesia, the Philippines, Nepal, Armenia and Jordan, and for clients including the British Council, Council of Europe and the Australian Department of Foreign Affairs and Trade (Lynch, 2008).

My recommendation: These training workshops have the potential to improve the quality of journalism, especially in the reporting on vio-lence, peace and human rights. However, this training mostly targets developing and post-conflict countries, whereas, going by the findings of this book (and in fact by those in the Lynch–Mcgoldrick book), it is equally needed in the West (if not more), to help it to address the problems of human wrongs journalism and war journalism.

12.3.4   The Ethical Journalism Initiative

In response to the impact the recent global financial crisis has been hav-ing on the media industry in the West by way of job cuts, dwindling sizes of papers and news programmes, and above all to the waning pub-lic confidence in news media reporting, the Brussels-based International Federation of Journalists (IFJ) launched the Ethical Journalism Initia-tive (EJI). Adopted at the 2007 Moscow World Congress of the IFJ, the EJI is a global campaign of programmes and activities to support and strengthen quality in the media.

My recommendation: While this initiative recognises 'the demo-cratic deficit caused by the lack of access by citizens to reliable, useful and accurate information' (IFJ/EJI website, accessed 20 April 2009), to quote the IFJ General Secretary Aidan White, it lacks a clear roadmap on how this is to be achieved. I would therefore encourage the IFJ/EJI to look at the possibility of embracing the ideals and practices of journalism in the promotion of peace and human rights such as those proposed in this book.

12.3.5 Media diversity and better journalism training workshops

The London-based Media Diversity Institute (MDI) works internationally to encourage and facilitate responsible media coverage of diversity. It aims to prevent the media from intentionally or unintentionally spreading prejudice, intolerance and hatred, which can lead to social tensions, disputes and violent conflict. MDI encourages instead fair, accurate, inclusive and sensitive media coverage in order to promote understanding between different groups and cultures. MDI's work includes organising journalism workshops that provide theoretical and practical training for journalists on covering diversity, minority and human rights issues (MDI website, accessed 7 August 2010).

The Bristol-based Media Wise Trust (MWT), set up in 1993 as an independent charity, has devised and delivered training on media ethics for media professionals to help them tackle problematic issues such as child abuse, diversity reporting, health issues and suicide coverage, in the UK and internationally (MWT website, accessed 7 August 2010).

My recommendation: The work of MDI and MWT, especially in the area of diversity reporting training, is quite important, and should be supported if we are to improve the quality of journalism theory and practice in the UK and globally. I would, however, encourage them to increase the geographical spread of their work to include journalists in the mainstream media in the UK and other western countries, as for now the focus of their work seems to be on developing and post-conflict transition countries.

12.3.6 Alternative media: Public journalism and citizen journalism

A number of very good initiatives have emerged in academic, policy and civil society circles to promote alternative media to challenge the inconsistencies and inadequacies of the mainstream media as we saw them in this book.

My recommendation: In order to make alternative media improve the quality of mainstream journalism within the context of human rights journalism, I would like to encourage innovative projects that would improve collaborative working between the mainstream media and alternative media. There are already a few examples of mainstream media using very good reports and feature articles from freelance travel journalists and bloggers, which are based on their first-hand account of events they have witnessed. More of this, in my opinion, should be encouraged.

Afterword

War reporting is quintessential journalism, but it is often, paradoxically, unpopular. Phillip Knightley, in his classic history *The First Casualty*, dubbed William Howard Russell, the first authentic war correspondent, 'the miserable parent of a luckless tribe'. In recent years the media have been blamed for escalating wars, as witness the indictments of news executives at the Arusha war crimes tribunal on the Rwandan Genocide and the front-page apologies published by the *Washington Post* and *New York Times* for recycling unfounded claims about the 'menace' supposedly confronting America from Saddam Hussein's 'weapons of mass destruction'.

Such have been the concerns underpinning the rise and spread of peace journalism (PJ) as a factor in journalism education and training, and latterly in scholarly research. The ideas of PJ, developed originally by Johan Galtung, were applied to journalistic practice and taken up by social movement activists seeking to 'pull the lever' of media in order to create resources and constituencies for peace.

At particular times and places, this call attained considerable traction and enabled significant agency over responses to conflict in media domains: in regions of Indonesia, following the fall of the Suharto regime, and in the southern Philippines entering peace processes after the two long-running insurgencies besetting the country, to name but two. Elsewhere, though, journalists tended to bridle at the word 'peace', as redolent of calls, now familiar, for them to go beyond its remit.

What about human rights? Journalists often feel themselves to be aligned with the cause of human rights and share a keen awareness that they are both the ones charged with maintaining them, and among their chief beneficiaries.

Human rights may, therefore, be a more promising starting point than peace for advocacy of a change in the media. In this book, Ibrahim Seaga Shaw sets out and explores the contours and distinctions of a form he calls human rights journalism. The reporting of human rights issues is often conceived in terms of naming and shaming the alleged perpetrators, and of highlighting calls for them to be brought to justice. The human rights organisations, notably Amnesty International and Human Rights Watch, have evolved to this characteristic response and – it is sometimes pointed out – to do some of the investigative work that some journalists used to do themselves.

But that is far from sufficient, according to Shaw. Such familiar reporting patterns have become associated with the overlapping concepts of the 'CNN effect', humanitarian intervention and the responsibility to protect. Indeed, the eponymous report by the International Commission on Intervention and State Sovereignty, which raised the responsibility to protect concept in the first place, named 'media organisations with a global reach' as capable of ensuring that decisions on how to respond to impending human rights emergencies not only took place before a worldwide audience, but were capable of 'adding items to the agenda' in their own right.

This phenomenon brings journalists to the brink of an ethical dilemma already familiar to policymakers: that of selectivity. Why enforce a no-fly zone to protect civilians in Libya, and not Bahrain? Why not Côte d'Ivoire (to name but a few examples receiving sharply differential degrees of media attention at the time of writing).

Indeed the last case, being located, as it is, in sub-Saharan Africa, emphasises the potential for injustice and relative deprivation in the wake of activist reporting and policy agendas for responding to infringements, underway or in prospect, of human rights.

Ibrahim's own background is as a journalist from Sierra Leone, who sought asylum in France and then moved to London. I met him at the Freedom Forum, the venue for our series of reflective discussions for journalists covering conflict, titled Reporting the World; he was running, from exile, a net-based news service (www.expotimesonline.net) for readers in his home country and abroad. British troops were still in Sierra Leone at that stage, having played a decisive role in quelling a revolt by the 'Revolutionary United Front' – which had brutalised the population in areas under its sway – and effectively ending the civil war.

It (British intervention) came 'too little, too late', Ibrahim says, in part because of the way UK media represented it, and not in time, certainly, to save thousands of lives. Even to that modest extent, as a robust response to protect civilians by armed force – one that worked largely, though not entirely, through a deterring effect – it remains, in important ways, an exception. Elsewhere in Africa, notably in Rwanda, where the UN drew down its peacekeeping mission despite warnings and entreaties from its commander, and in the Congo, where it intervened only after millions had perished, the story is grim.

The experience speaks of structural injustices that see the poorest people in the poorest countries persistently deprived of any practical access to human rights, even where these are notionally provided for. And this is the extra dimension the concept of human rights journalism acquires in Ibrahim's hands. Global justice should inform journalistic practice if it is to be truly an agent for the promotion and strengthening of human rights.

This is a rallying cry for what Ibrahim calls the 'social responsibility role' of journalism, and a welcome one. It calls for 'diagnostic reporting', he declares, explaining that reporters have a duty not only to expose abuses but to explain to readers and audiences how and why they come about; the frameworks within which they take place.

There is a hunger for change in the media, and it has drawn a great many editors, reporters, trainees, students and activists to peace journalism. Academic research has spent recent years 'catching up'. Human rights journalism represents an important additional dimension to its repertoire, one that seems capable, potentially, of inspiring many more exponents in the increasingly interdependent world we inhabit, and of providing them with reasons to carry on reporting it.

*Jake Lynch, Associate Professor and Director, Centre for Peace and
Conflict Studies, University of Sydney, Australia*

Notes

2 Human Rights Journalism: A Critical Conceptual Framework

1. Spielman, 13 November 2008: article accessed online from America.gov on 20 April 2009.
2. Edward Behr died in Paris, in May 2007, according to a *Herald Tribune* report of 30 May 2007, (accessed 6 June 2010).
3. International News Safety Institute.
4. UNESCO declaration adopted by acclamation on 22 November 1978, at the 20th session of the General Conference of UNESCO held in Paris.
5. Article 1 of the 1948 UN Universal Declaration of Human Rights. G.A. res. 217A (111), UN. Doc A/810 at 71.

3 Critical Comparative Analyses of Human Rights Journalism, Peace Journalism, Global Journalism and Human Rights Reporting

1. Most of the information in this account was taken by the author of this book from an article he contributed to the Canada-based online Sierra Leone paper *The Patriotic Vanguard*. The article was a report of the author's participation at a press freedom event organised by the National Union of Journalists in London in January 2008. The present author was publisher and editor in chief of the Expo Times newspaper in Sierra Leone between 1995 and 1998.

4 Citizen, Public and Peace Journalisms: Towards the More Radical Human Rights Journalism Strand

1. Article 1 of the 1948 UN Universal Declaration of Human Rights. G.A. res. 217A (111), UN. Doc A/810 at 71.
2. The full list of this Galtung model is reproduced in the introductory chapter of this book.
3. These five principles were identified in the human rights-based approach *Training Manual* (2008) published in Bangkok in 2008 by UNESCO. Although this training manual was made in Vietnam, ostensibly targeting Vietnamese journalists and others in developing countries, the principles of human rights-based journalism apply globally.
4. For more on this just war theory criteria, see Michael Walzer's *Just and Unjust Wars: A Moral Argument with Historical Illustrations* (1992).

5 The Dynamics and Challenges of Reporting Humanitarian Interventions

1. Cosmopolitan is a characterisation that involves the enjoyment of rights beyond one's nation-state. Apolitical means non-political or outside of the sphere of politics; an apolitical intervention is one not influenced by politics.
2. Riffenburgh, 1993, cited Knight, R.P. (1805) An analytical inquiry in the Principles of Taste, London.
3. Ibid., cited Hussey, C. (1927) *The Picturesque: Studies in a point of View*, London.
4. For more historical and theoretical discussions of the Westphalia norm, see Walzer (1992); Brown (2002); Paul Robinson (2002a); Howe (2002); Dower (2002); Caney (2000).
5. More of this discussion of Brown's argument can be found in the Chapter 7 of this book.
6. Reproduced from the OECD magazine, observer accessed on line 08 August 2010.
7. Emphases attributed to Piers Robinson (2002b).

6 The 'us only' and 'us + them' Frames in Reporting the Sierra Leone War: Implications for Human Rights Journalism

1. Working as a journalist in Sierra Leone for most of the period of the civil war until 1998, when I was forced into exile, I experienced and reported at first hand the unfolding events. I found it difficult to maintain neutrality in conducting the research for this study. However, in order to enhance the quality of my findings, I have endeavoured to avoid bringing my personal judgement in the study.
2. The following question was asked in the interview: What can you say were the main causes of the war in Sierra Leone based on your experience working in the region?
3. A Human Rights Watch Report documented the atrocities carried out by the rebels as well as by the Nigerian ECOMOG soldiers.
4. The Lome Peace accord signed in the Togolese capital Lome on 7 July 1999 indeed set the stage for ending the Sierra Leone civil war in 2001.

7 'Operation Restore Hope' in Somalia and Genocide in Rwanda

1. This happens when all the media are following the same angle of a story.
2. Cultural subjectivity frames are historical frames, which I identified in my earlier study (Shaw, 2007: 356) and cited in Chapter 4 of this book.
3. IISS, Strategic Survey 1996/97 (New York, Oxford University Press for the IISS, 1997), p. 223; cited in Paul D. Williams, 2008, Keeping the Peace in Africa: Why African Solutions Are Not Enough. *Ethics and International Affairs*. Vol. 22, issue 3, P.309–329.

4. US Department of Defence and Department of State, Congressional Presentation for Security Assistance Programmes, Fiscal Year 1993 (1992): 291, cited in the Human Rights Watch Report.

8 The Politics of Humanitarian Intervention and Human Wrongs Journalism: The Case of Kosovo versus Sierra Leone

1. For more on the justification of military humanitarian intervention, see Walzer's 'Just and unjust wars'.
2. Robin Cook made this distinction on 19 July 2000 in his speech to the American Bar Association, London. See www.fco.gov.uk/news/speechtext.asp?3989.
3. For more on this, see Hawkins(2003: 226–27). See also Lippmann's Public Opinion (1922), Bernard Cohen (1963) and McCombs and Shaw (1972) for detailed discussions of the agenda-setting model.
4. Charles Taylor has been facing trial in the Special Court for Sierra Leone in The Hague since 2008, being charged for his alleged role in the crimes against humanity in Sierra Leone committed by rebels he allegedly supported.
5. Coll was interviewed by the author of this book.
6. In her interview with this author on 15 August 2003, Leridon disclosed that this dispatch scored the highest demand mark, above all others she wrote on the Sierra Leone civil war, which shows the market value justification for hyping the humanitarian angle of war reporting.
7. The Krukenberg procedure was used by foreign doctors working with the International Committee of the Red Cross to operate hundreds of amputees at the Netland hospital in Freetown. The name of the procedure is that of the German doctor who first used it to operate wounded soldiers in the Second World War.
8. Sam Kiley and Mark Doyle, in interviews with this author in November 2003.
9. Francois Picard and Alison, in interviews with this author in April 2003.
10. Coll, in an interview with this author.

11 Reporting Asylum Seekers and Refugees in the UK: The Myths and the Facts

1. Home Office Asylum Statistics (2009).
2. Department of Health Press Release accessed.
3. Ibid.
4. Brown announced this slogan during the 2010 campaign, which many liberal critics saw as a dramatic U-turn by a Labour desperate to win over extreme right conservative voters supporting the British National Party (BNP), whose campaign leaflet carried a similar slogan: 'British Jobs for British People'. This, like the Brown slogan, could not be strictly speaking a myth but could easily pass as one, because it fails to take into consideration the fact that there are many EU and Organisation of Economic Cooperation and Development (OECD)citizens living and working in the UK, just as many British are living and working in other EU countries and beyond.
5. Home office (2009 Asylum statistics).

12   Conclusion: A Case for Human Rights Journalism and Future Directions

1. This author acknowledges the reproduction of the five human rights-based principles to journalism (highlighted in italics) adapted from the *Human Rights-Based Approach to Journalism Training Manual* edited by Gabrielle Beman and Daniel Calderbank, UNESCO, 2008.
2. Human Rights in Development: Rights-based Approaches', copyright 1996–2002, office of the United Nations High Commissioner for Human Rights – Geneva, Switzerland; retrieved (by the authors of *Human Rights-Based Approach to Journalism, A Training Manuel Vietnam*, 2008) on 01 June 2008, from http://www.unhcr.ch/development/approaches-04.html.

Bibliography

AFP (*Agence France Presse*) (14 January 2010) "Liberia's Taylor 'Gave Naomi Campbell a Blood Diamond'", http://www.google.com/hostednews/afp/article/ALeqM5iqgtCcIuDKUxtj90-lYmobtNNDfw. Accessed on 16 January 2010.

Adorno, T.W., Frenkel-Brunswik, E., Levinson, D.J. and Nevitt Stanford, R. (1950) *The Authoritarian Personality*. New York: Harper.

Alagiah, G. (1998) '"Transcripts of Interventions": Dispatches from Disaster Zones'. *Reporting Humanitarian Disasters Conference*. London. 27–28 May.

Alagiah, G. (2001) *A Passage to Africa*. London: Little, Brown and Company.

Allan, S. (1997) 'News and the Public Sphere: Towards a History of Objectivity and Impartiality', in M. Bromley and T.O'Malley (Eds), *A Journalism Reader*. London: Routledge. pp. 296–329.

Allan, S. (2006) *Online News*. England: Open University Press, McGraw-Hill Education, Berkshire.

Allan, S. and Zelizer, B. (Eds) (2004) 'Rules of Engagement: Journalism and War', *Reporting War: Journalism in War Time*. London: Routledge.

Allard, K. (1995) *Somalia Operations: Lessons Learned*. Washington, DC: Institute for National Strategic Studies/National Defense University Press, www.au.af.mil/au.awc/awcgate/ndu/allard_somalia/allardcont.html. Accessed on 18 March 2008.

Allen, K. (2008) 'The Perils of Human rights Journalism', *The Guardian*. Accessed on 09 July 2009.

Allen, T. and Seaton, J. (1999) *The Media of Conflict: War Reporting and Representation of Ethnic Violence*. London: Zed Books.

Alexander, L. (2005) *Is There a Right of the Freedom of Expression?* New York: Cambridge University Press.

Amin, S. (1990) *Maldevelopment: Anatomy of a Global Failure*. Tokyo: United Nations University Press, Zed Books Limited.

Annan, K. (19 June 2006) UN Secretary General Address to the Newly Created HRC in Geneva.

Anderson-Gold, Sharon (2001) *Cosmopolitanism and Human Rights*. Cardiff: University of Wales Press.

Anderson, R., Dardenne, R. and Killenburg, G.M. (1994) *The Conversation of Journalism: Communication, Community and News*. Connecticut and London: Greenwood Press.

Ankomah, B. (2001a) *New African*. July/August, p. 21.

Ankomah, B. (2001b) 'Four Things that Drive the British and the Western Media', in Jake Lynch and Annabel McGoldrick (Eds), *Is Coverage of Africa Racist? And Why Are We Ignoring the DRC Crisis*. Reporting the World Round Table on 16 May 2001, Freedom Forum European Centre, p. 2. London.

Arendt, H. (1985) *The Origins of Totalitarianism*. San Diego: Harcourt.

Arno, A. (1984) 'The News Media as Third Parties in National and International Conflict: Duobus Litigantibus Tertius Guandot', in A. Arno and W. Dissanayake (Eds), *The News Media in National and International Conflict*. Boulder, CO: Westview Press.

Article 19 (2002) Virtual Freedom of Expression Handbook: Case Briefs. www.article19.org.

Article 19 Report (2003) What Is the Story?. www.article19.org.

Atton, C. (2001) *Alternative Media*. London: Sage.

Atton, C. (2002) *Alternative Media*. London: Sage.

Atton, C. (2003) 'What is "Alternative" Journalism?'. *Journalism*, Vol. 4, No. 3, pp. 267–272.

Atton, C. and Wickenden, E. (2005) 'Sourcing Routines and Representation in Alternative Journalism: A Case Study Approach'. *Journalism Studies*, Vol. 6, No. 3, pp. 347–359. Reporters without Borders financed by CIA. http://www.spinwatch.org/component/content/article/164-cuba/3275-reporters-without-borders-financed-by-cia. Accessed on 17 March 2010.

Bagdikian, B. (2004) *The New Media Monopoly*. Boston: Beacon Press.

Baker, R. (1984) 'Protecting the Environment Against the Poor'. *Ecologist,* Vol. 14, No. 2, pp. 1–4.

Barash, D.P. and Webel, C.P. (2002) *Peace and Conflict Studies*. California: SAGE Publications.

Bardin, L. (1996) *L'analyse de contenu*. Paris: PUF.

Barnetson, D. (9 December 2007) EU Leaders Admit Trade Talks with Africa Difficult. Agence France Presse *(AFP)*.

Barry, B. (1994) 'The Interdependence of Security and Economic Issues in the "New World Order"', in R. Stubbs and G.R.D. Underhill (Eds), *Political Economy and the Changing Global Order*. London: Palgrave Macmillan. pp. 94–95.

Batumike, C. (2000) *Presse Écrite africaine d'Europe francophone* Éditions des Ecrivains. Paris.

Becker, J. (2002) 'Medien im Krieg', in U. Albrecht and J. Becker (Eds), *Medien Zwisschen Krieg Und Frieden*. Baden-Baden. Nomos. pp. 13–26.

Beatie, L., Miller, D., Miller, E. and Philo, G. (1999) 'The Media and Africa: Images of Disaster and Rebellion', in G. Philo (Ed.), *Message Received*, Harlow: Longman.

Behr, E. (1992) *Anyone Here Been Raped and Speaks English? A Correspondent's Life Behind the Lines*. Harmondsworth: Penguin.

Bell, M. (1995) *In Harm's Way: Reflections of a War Zone Thug*. London: Hamish Hamilton.

Bell, M. (1997) 'TV News: How Far Should We Go?' *British Journalism Review*, Vol. 8, No. 1, pp. 6–16.

Bell, M. (1998) 'The Truth Is Our Currency'. *Press/Politics*, Vol. 3, No. 1, pp. 102–109.

Bellamy, A.J. (2006) 'Wither the Responsibility to Protect: Humanitarian Intervention and 2005 World Summit'. *Ethics and International Affairs*, Vol. 20, 143–169.

Bellamy, A.J. (2010) 'Responsibility to Protect: Five Years on'. *Ethics and International Affairs*, Vol. 24, No. 2, Summer, pp. 143–169.

Bellamy, A. (2008) 'The Responsibility to Protect and the Problem of Military Intervention'. *International Affairs*, Vol. 84, No. 4, pp. 615–639.

Beman, G. and Calderbank, D. (Eds) (2008) *The Human Rights-Based Approach to Journalism: Training Manuel Vietnam*. Bangkok: UNESCO. Accessed on 12 July 2009.

Bennett, L.W. (1990) 'Toward a Theory of Press – State Relations in the United States'. *Journal of Communication*, Vol. 40, No. 2, pp. 103–127.

Berglez, P. (2007) 'For a Transnational Mode of Journalistic Writing', in Birgitta Hoijer (Ed.), *Ideological Horizons in Media and Citizen Discourses. Theoretical and Methodological Approaches*. Göteborg: Nordicom. pp. 147–161.

Berglez, P. (2008) 'What Is Global Journalism? Theoretical and Empirical Conceptualisations'. *Journalism Studies*, Vol. 9, pp. 6, 845–858.

Berlin, I. (1969) *Four Essays on Liberty*. London: Oxford University Press.

Berlin, M. (12 December 2007) 'G2: Sarkozy May Sacrifice Human Rights for Commerce, and Let's Not Kid Ourselves that We're Any Different'. *The Guardian*. Accessed on 7 December 2009.

Barrosso, M. (2007) 'Barrosso Defends Decision to Invite Mugabe to Conference'. *The Independent*. London. Accessed on 7 December 2009.

Bayefsky, A. et al. (2002) 'Protection under the Complaint Procedures of the United Nations Treaty Bodies', in Joan Fitzpatrick (Ed.), *Human Rights Protection for Refugees, Asylum-Seekers, and Internally Displaced Persons: A Guide to International Mechanisms and Procedures*. New York, USA: Transnational Publishers.

Beattie, L., Miller, D., Miller, E. and Philo, G. (1999) 'The Media and Africa: Images of Disaster and Rebellion' in G. Philo (Ed.), Message Received, Harlow: Longman.

Biltereyst, D. (2001) 'Global News Research and Complex Citizenship. Towards an Agenda for Research on Foreign/International News and Audiences', in Stig Hjarvard (Ed.), *News in a Globalized Society*. Göteborg: Nordicom, Göteborg University. pp. 41–62.

Booth, K. (1995) 'Human Wrongs and International Relations'. *International Affairs*, Vol. 71, pp. 103–126.

Booth, K. (1999) 'Three Tyrannies', in Tim Dunne and Nicholas Wheeler (Eds), *Human Rights in Global Politics*. Cambridge: Cambridge University Press.

Bounds, A. and William, W. (10 December 2007) 'Spectre of Colonialism vies with the Spirit of Lisbon'. *Financial Times*.

Bourghault, L.M. (1995) *Mass Media in Sub-Saharan Africa*. Bloomington: Indiana University Press.

Boyd-Barett, O. (2004a) 'Judith Miller, The New York Times, and the Propaganda Model'. *Journalism Studies*, Vol. 5, No. 4, pp. 435–449.

Boyd-Barrett, O. (2004b) 'Understanding: The Second Casualty', in Stuart Allan and Berbie Zelizer (Eds), *Reporting War: Journalism in Wartime*. USA, Canada: Routledge.

Boyd-Barrett, O. (2009) 'Global Crisis Reporting: Journalism in the Global Age'. Book Review in *Journalism and Mass Communication Quarterly*.

Boyd-Barret, O. and Rantanen, T. (1998) *The Globalisation of News*. London: Sage.

Brecher, J., Costello, T. and Smith, B. (2000) *Globalisation from Below*. Cambridge Mass: South End Press.

Bugge, A. and Henrique, A. (09 December 2007) 'Ambitious EU–Africa Summit Ends in Trade Deadlock'. *The Guardian*. London. Accessed on 15 September 2008.

Bull, H. (1984) 'Introduction', in Hedley Bull (Ed.), *Intervention in World Politics*. Oxford: Clarendon Press.

Brauman, R. and Backmann, R. (1996) *Les Médias et l'humanitaire: Ethique de l'information ou charité-spectacle*, CFPJ Editions Paris.

Bristol Evening Post (16 June 2005) 'Refugee Week'. Bristol: Western Press.

Brown, C. (2002) 'Humanitarian Intervention and International Political Theory', in Alexander Mosley and Richard Norman (Eds), *Human Rights and Military Intervention*. Aldershot: Ashgate Publishing.

Brown, G. (12 November 2009) 'British jobs for British Workers'. *Yorkshire Post*.

Brugidou, M. (1993) 'L'Affaire du sang contaminé: la construction de l'évènement', in *Le Monde* (1989–1992). *Rhétoriques du journalisme politique*. MOTS. Les Langues. N° 37. December, p. 40.

Caliendo, S.M. (2009) 'Media', in David P. Forsythe (Ed.), *Encyclopedia of Human Rights*. Oxford: Oxford University Press.

Campbell, D. (1998) *National Deconstruction: Violence, Identity and Justice in Bosnia*. London and Minneapolis, MN: University of Minnesota Press.

Cameron, J. (1967) *Point of Departure: Experiment in Biography*. London: Barker.

Caney, S. (2000) 'Humanitarian Intervention and State Sovereignty', in A. Valls (Ed.), *Ethics in International Affairs*. New York: Rowman and Littlefield.

Carroll, B.A. (1972) 'Peace Research: The Cult of Power'. *The Journal of Conflict Resolution*, Vol. 16, No. 14, pp. 585–616.

Carey, J. (1989) *Communication as Culture. Essays on Media and Society*. Boston, MA: Unwin Hyman.

Carruthers, S.L. (1995) *Winning Hearts and Minds: British Governments, the Media and Colonial Counterinsurgency, 1945–60*, Leicester: Leicester University Press.

Carruthers, S.L. (2000) *The Media at War: Communication and Conflict in the Twentieth Century*. London: Palgrave Macmillan.

Carruthers, S.L. (2004) 'Tribalism and Tribulation: Media Constructions of "African savagery" and "Western humanitarianism" in the 1990s', in Stuart Allan and Barbie Zelizer (Eds), *War Reporting: Journalism in Wartime*, pp. 155–169. London: Routledge.

Castells, M. (2006) *The Power of Identity, The Information Age: Economy, Society and Culture*. Oxford: Blackwell Publishing.

Cassara, C. (1998) 'US Newspaper Coverage of Human Rights in Latin America, 1975–1982'. *Journalism and Mass Communication Quarterly*, Vol. 75, No. 3, pp. 478–486.

Cater, D. (1957) *The Fourth Branch of Government*. Boston: Houghton Mifflin.

Chambers, R. (1995) *Poverty and Livelihoods: Whose Reality Counts?* Falmer, Brighton: Institute for Development Studies. University of Sussex.

Chandler, David (2000) 'Western Intervention and the Disintegration of Yugoslavia, 1989–1999', in Philip Hammond and Edward S. Herman (Eds), *Degraded Capability: The Media and the Kosovo Crisis*. London: Pluto Press. pp. 19–30.

Chandler, D. (2002) *From Kosovo to Kabul: Human Rights and International Intervention*. London: Pluto Press.

Chomsky, N. (1999) *Latin America: From Colonialisation to Globalization*. Melbourne: Ocean.

Chopra, J. and Weiss, T. (1992) 'Sovereignty Is No Longer Sacrosanct: Coding Humanitarian Intervention'. *Ethics and International Affairs*, Vol. 6, pp. 95–117.

Chouliaraki, L. (2006) *The Spectatorship of Suffering*. London/Thousand Oaks/New Delhi: Sage Publications.

Clarke, W. and Herbst, J. (1996) 'Somalia and the Future of Humanitarian Intervention'. *Foregin Affairs*, Vol. 75, No. 2, http://www.mtholyoke.edu/-jwestern/ir317clark.htm.

Cohen, B.C. (1963) *The Press and Foreign Policy*. New Jersey: Princeton University Press.

Cohen-Almaghor, R. (2001) *Speech, Media and Ethics: The Limits of Free Expression*. New York: Palgrave Macmillan.

Coll, S. (2000) 'Peace without Justice: A Journey into the Wounded Heart of Africa'. *Washington Post Magazine*, 9 January.

Coll, S. (4 May 2004) Interview by author on the telephone from Washington.

Commission for Racial Equality/Ipsos MORI (2007) *Race Relations 2006: A Research Study*. London: Commission for Racial Equality.

Copson, R. (1996) 'Africa's Internal Wars', in I. William Zartman (Ed.), *Collapsed states in Africa*. Boulder: Lynn Reinner.

Cottle, S. (2006) *Mediatised Conflict. Issues in Cultural and Media Studies*. Maidenhead: Open University Press.

Cottle, S. (2008) *Global Crisis Reporting: Journalism in the Global Age*. Berkshire, UK: Open University Press.

Creelman, J. (1901) *On the Great Highway*. Boston: Lothrop Publishing Company.

Crisp, J. (2003) 'Refugees and the Global Politics of Asylum', in Sarah Spencer (Ed.), *The Politics of Migration: Managing Opportunity, Conflict and Change. The Political Quarterly*. Oxford: Blackwell Publishing.

Crocker, C.A. (2004) *The Breaking of Nations* (revised edition). London: Atlantic Books.

Dadge, D. (2004) *Casualty of War: The Bush Administration's Assault on a Free Press*. New York: Prometheus Books.

Dadge, D. (2006) *The War in Iraq and Why the Media Failed Us*. Westport, CT: Praeger.

Damrosch, L.F. (2000) 'The Inevitability of Selective Response? Principles to Guide Urgent International Action', in Albrecht Schnabel and Ramesh Thakur (Eds), *Kosovo and the Challenge of Humanitarian Intervention*. New York: United Nations University. pp. 405–419.

Davidson, W.P. (1974) *Mass Communications and Conflict Resolution*. New York: Praeger.

Department of Health Press Release (08 August 2009). www.refugeecouncil.org.uk.

De Beer, A., Merrill, S. and John, C. (Eds) (2004) *Global Journalism. Topical Issues and Media Systems*. Boston: Pearson.

De Bonville, J. (2000) *L'Analyse de contenu des médias: de la problématique au traitement statistique*. Quebec, Canada: De Boek Université.

De Burgh, Hugo (2003) 'Skills Are Not Enough: The Case for Journalism as an Academic Discipline'. *Journalism: Theory and Practice*, Vol. 4, No. 1, pp. 95–112.

Dempsey, J. (14 December 2007) 'For EU, Rights Falling Victim to Convenience: Letter from Europe.' New York Times Media Group reproduced in the International Herald Tribune. Accessed on 31 January 2008.

Dershowitz, A. (2004) *Rights from Wrongs: A Secular Theory of the Origins of Human Rights*, New York: Basic Books.

Deuze, M. (2001) 'Understanding the Impact of the Internet: On New Media Professionalism, Mindsets and Buzzwords'. *EJournalist*, Vol. 1, No. 1, http://www.ejournalism.au.com/ejournalist/deuze.pdf (not accessed directly online but taken from a secondary source).

Deuze, M. (2002) 'The Internet and Its Journalisms'. *Online Journalism Review* (11 July), http://www.ojr.org/ojr/future/1026407729. Php (consulted on 30 August 2002).

Deuz, M. (2006) 'Global Journalism Education: A Conceptual Approach'. *Journalism Studies*, Vol. 7, No. 1, pp. 19–34.

de Waal, F. (1990) *Peacemaking Among Primates*. London: Harvard University Press.

de Waal, A. (1994) *African Encounters*, Index on Censorship.

Donnelly, J. (1989) *Universal Human Rights in Theory and Practice*. New York: Cornell University Press.

Dorman, A.M. (2010) *Blair's Successful War. British Military Intervention in Sierra Leone*. London: Ashgate Publishing.

Dowden, R. (2001a) *The Independent*, 28 March, p. 5.

Dowden, R. (2001b) Interview by Author 28th September 2001.

Dower, N. (2002) 'Violent Humanitarianism – An Oxymoron?', in Alexander Mosley and Richard Norman (Eds), *Human Rights and Military Intervention*. England, Aldershot: Ashgate Publishing.

Doyle, M. (03 July 1999) Sierra Leone: Worse than Kosovo? BBC online. Accessed on 17 November 2003.

Dunne, T. and Wheeler, N. (1999) 'Introduction: Human Rights and the Fifty Years' Crisis', in Tim Dunne and Nicholas Wheeler (Eds), *Human Rights and Global Politics*. Cambridge: Cambridge University Press.

Economist, 24 February 2001, Editorial p. 17.

Eliasoph, N. (1988) 'Routines and the Making of Oppositional News'. *Critical Studies in Mass Communication*, Vol. 5, No. 4, pp. 313–334.

Elliot, C. (1975) *Patterns of Poverty in the Third World*. pp. 1–2.

Elliott, L. and Cheeseman, G. (Eds) (2005) *Forces for Good? Cosmopolitan Militaries in the 21st Century*. Manchester: Manchester University Press.

Entman, R. (1993) 'Framing: Towards Clarification of a Fractured Paradigm'. *Journal of Communication* Vol. 43, No. 4, pp. 51–58.

Entman, R. (2004) *Projections of Power*. Chicago, IL: University of Chicago Press.

Everett, R. (1962) *The Diffusion of Innovations*. New York: Free Press.

Farah, D. (02 November 2001) 'Al Qaeda Cash Tied to Diamond Trade: Sale of Gems from Sierra Leone Rebels Raised Millions, Sources Say'. *Washington Post*.

Ferguson, R.B. (2002) 'The History of War: Fact vs. Fiction', in William L. Ury (Ed.), *Must We Fight?* San Francisco, CA: Jossey-Bass.

Fairclough, N. (2006) *Language and Globalisation*, London and New York: Routledge.

Finnmore, M. (1966) 'Constructing Norms of Humanitarian Intervention', in P. Katzeinstein (Ed.), *The Culture of National Security*. New York: Columbia University Press.

Finney, N.R. (2003) *Asylum Seeker Dispersal: Public Attitudes and Press Portrayals around the UK*. Swansea: University of Wales.

Fish, S. (1994) *There Is No Such Thing As Free Speech and It Is a Good Thing Too.* Oxford: Oxford University Press.

Fisher, W.F. and Ponniah, T. (Eds) (2003) *Another World Is Possible: Popular Alternatives to Globalisation at the World Social Forum.* London: Zed Books.

Foreign Broadcast Information Service, FBIS-AFR-93-193, 7 October 1993, p. 2, cited in HRW Arms project report.

Foucault, M. (1980) *Power of Knowledge: Selected Interviews and other Writings 1972/77,* in Colin Gordon (Ed.), Brighton: Harvester Press.

Foucault, M. (1982) 'The Subject and Power', in H.L. Dreyfus, P. Rabinow, and Michel Foucault (Eds), *Beyond Structuralism and Hermeneutics.* Chicago: University of Chicago Press. pp. 208–226.

Fowler, R. (2001) *Language in the News: Discourse and Ideology in the Press.* London: Routledge, Taylor & Francis.

Frank, T. (2007) 'Idealist and Realist Aspirations for Just Peace: An Analysis of Ethics of Military Force and the Discursive Construction of an Ethic of International Policing within the Framework of Just Peace and the Contemporary Hegemony of International Law'. Unpublished PhD Dissertation Submitted to the Theological Faculty, University of Aarhus.

Frankel, G. (2007) *Human Rights Journalism Course.* USA: Standford University.

Fraser, N. (1990) 'Rethinking the Public Sphere: A Contribution to the Critique of Actually Existing Democracy'. *Social Text,* 25/26 (1990), pp. 56–80 Duke University Press Stable, http://www.jstor.org/stable/466240. Accessed: 10/08/2009 12:48.

Galtung, J. (1969) 'Violence, Peace and Peace Research'. *Journal of Peace Research,* Vol. 6, No. 3, pp. 167–191.

Galtung, J. (1996) *Peace by Peaceful Means – Peace and Conflict, Development and Civilization.* PRIO – International Peace Research Institute, Oslo, London: SAGE Publications.

Galtung, J. (2004) Violence, War, and Their Impact: On Visible and Invisible Effects of Violence. Transcend: Peace and Development Network for Conflict Transformation by Peaceful Means. http://them.polylog.org/5/fgj-en.htm. Accessed on 27th April 2009.

Galtung, J. and Ruge, M. (1973) 'Structuring and Selecting News', in S. Cohen and J. Young (Eds), *The Manufacture of News: Social Problems, Deviance and the Mass Media.* London: Constable. pp. 62–72.

Galtung, J. and Vincent, R.C. (1992) Global Gasnost: Toward a New World Information and Communication Order? Cresskill New Jersey: Hampton Press.

Gameson, W. and Modigliani, A. (1989) 'Media Discourse and Public Opinion: A Constructionist Approach'. *American Journal of Sociology,* Vol. 95, No. 1, July pp. 1–37.

Gans, H. (1979) *Deciding What Is News: A Study of CBS Evening News, NBC Nightly News, Newsweek, and Time.* New York: Pantheon Books.

Ginneken, J.V. (2001) *Understanding Global News: A Critical Introduction.* London: Sage.

Gilpin, R. (2001) *Global Political Economy: Understanding the International Economic Order.* Princeton: Princeton University Press.

Gitlin, T. (1980) *The Whole World Is Watching: Mass Media in the Making and Unmaking of the New Left.* Berkeley, CA: University of California.

Glasser, T. (1999) 'The Idea of Public Journalism', in Theodore Glasser (Ed.), *The Idea of Public Journalism*. New York. Guildford press. pp. 3–18.

Glover, S., Gott, C., Loizillon, A., Portes, J., Price, R., Spencer, S., Srinivasan, V. and Willis, C. (2001) Migration: An Economic and Social Analysis RDS Occasional Paper 67. London: Home Office, http://www.homeoffice.gov.uk/rds/pdfs/occ67-migration.pdf.

Goldsmith, E. (1996) 'Development as Colonialism', in Jerry Mander and Edward Goldsmith (Eds), *The Case against the Global Economy and for a Turn Toward the Local*. San Francisco: Sierra Club Books. pp. 253–272.

Guardian, leading article (8 December 2007) 'Britain's Empty Chair. EU–Africa Summit', *The Guardian*.

Haas, T. and Steiner, L. (2002) 'Fears of Corporate Colonization in Journalism Reviews' Critiques of Public Journalism'. *Journalism Studies*, Vol. 3, No. 3, pp. 325–341.

Haas, T. and Steiner, L. (2006) 'Public Journalism: A Reply to Critics'. *Journalism*, Vol. 7, No. 2, pp. 238–254.

Habermas, J. (1989) *The Structural Transformation of the Public Sphere: An Inquiry Into a Category of Bourgeois Society*. Cambridge, MA: MIT Press.

Hackett, R.A. (2007) 'Is Peace Journalism Possible?', in Dove Shinar and Wilhelm Kempf (Eds), *Peace Journalism: The State of the Art*. Berlin: Regener. pp. 75–94.

Hackett, R.A. and Carrol, W.K. (2006) *Remaking Media: The Struggle to Democratise Public Communication*. New York, Abingdon, Oxon: Routledge.

Hackett, R.A. and Zhao, Y. (1998) *Sustaining Democracy? Journalism and the Politics of Objectivity*. Toronto, Canada: Garamond Press.

Hallin, D. (1986) *The 'Uncensored War': The Media and Vietnam*. Berkeley, CA: University of California Press.

Hallin, D. (1992) 'The Passing of the "High Modernism" of American Journalism'. *Journal of Communication*, Vol. 42, No. 3, pp. 14–25.

Hammond, P. (2000) 'Reporting Humanitarian Warfare: Propaganda, Moralism And Nato's Kosovo War'. *Journalism Studies*, Vol. 1, No. 3, pp. 365–386.

Hammond, P. (2007a) *Media, War and Post-Modernity*. Oxford: Routledge.

Hammond, P. (2007b) *Framing Post Cold War Conflicts: The Media And International Intervention*. Manchester: Manchester University Press.

Hammond, P. and Herman, E. (Eds) (2000) *Degraded Capability: The Media and the Kosovo Crisis*. London: Pluto Press.

Hampton, M. (2001) ' "Understanding Media" Theories of the Press in Britain, 1850–1914'. *Media, Culture and Society*, Vol. 23, pp. 213–233.

Hanitzsch, T. (2004) 'The Peace Journalism Problem', in Thomas Hanitzsch, Martin Loffelholz and Ronny Mustamu (Eds), *Agents of Peace: Public Communication and Conflict Resolution in an Asian Setting*. Jakarta: Friedrich Ebert Stiftung. pp. 185–206.

Hanitzsch, T. (2007) 'Situating Peace Journalism in Journalism Studies: A Critical Appraisal'. *Conflict and Communication Online*, Vol. 6, No. 2, pp. 1–9.

Hardt, H. (1999) 'Reinventing the Press for the Age of Commercial Appeals: Writings on and about Public Journalism', in Theodore Glasser (Ed.), *The Idea of Public Journalism*. New York: Guilford Press. pp. 197–209.

Hartley, J. (2008) 'Journalism as a Human Right: The Cultural Approach to Journalism', in M. Loffelholz and D. Weaver (Eds), *Global Journalism Research: Theories, Methods, Findings, Future*. Oxford: Blackwell. pp. 39–51.

Hawkins, V. (2002) 'The Other Side of The Cnn Factor: The Media and Conflict'. *Journalism Studies*, Vol. 3, No. 2, pp. 225–240.

Hawkins, V. (2008) *Stealth Conflicts: How the World's Worst Violence Is Ignored*. Aldershot: Ashgate.

Heffer, S. (5 January 2008) 'Brown shows how to deal with Butcher'. *Daily Telegraph*.

Held, D. and McGrew, A. (2007) *Globalisation/Anti-Globalisation: Beyond the Great Divide*. Cambridge: Polity.

Herbamas, J. (1999) 'Bestialitat und Humanitat'. *Die Zeit*, Vol. 18, 29 April.

Herbert, J. (2001) *Practising Global Journalism: Exploring Reporting Issues World Wide*. Oxford; New Delhi: Focal Press.

Herman, E.S. (2002) 'The Media and the Markets in the United States', in *The Role of the Mass Media in Economic Development*. Washington: World Bank Institute.

Herman, E. and Chomsky, N. (1988) *Manufacturing Consent: The Political Economy of the Mass Media*. New York: Pantheon Books.

Himelboim, I. and Limor, Y. (2008) 'Media Perception of Freedom of the Press: A Comparative International Analysis of 242 Codes of Ethics'. *Journalism*, Vol. 9, No. 3, pp. 235–265. London.

Hjarvard, S. (2001) 'News Media and the Globalization of the Public Sphere', in Stig Hjarvard (Ed.), *News in a Globalized Society*. Göteborg: Nordicom, Göteborg University. pp. 17–39.

Hoey, K. (2007) 'Standing up to Mugabe'. *Daily Telegraph*. Letter.

Hohenberg, J. (1978) *The Professional Journalist*. New York: Holt Rinehart Wilson.

Hoijer, B. (2004) 'The Discourse of Global Compassion: The Audience and Media Reporting of Human Suffering'. *Media, Culture & Society*, July 26, pp. 513–531.

Hoijer, B., Nohrstedt, S.A. and Ottosen, R. (2002) 'The Kosovo War in the Media – Analysis of a Global Discursive Order'. *Conflict & Communication Online* Vol. 1, No. 2. www.cco.regener-online.de.

Holm, H. (2001) 'The Effect of Globalization on Media Structures and Norms Globalization and the Choice of Foreign News', in Stig Hjarvard (Ed.), *News in a Globalized Society*, Göteborg: Nordicom, Göteborg University. pp. 113–128.

Home Office (2008) *Asylum Statistics 2007*. London: Home Office.

Home Office (2009) *Asylum Statistics 2008*. London: Home Office.

Home Office Report (2003) www.homeoffice.gov.uk.

Howe, B. (2002) 'On the Justifiability of Military Intervention: The Kosovan Case', in Alexander Mosley and Richard Norman (Eds), *Human Rights and Military Intervention*. England, Aldershot: Ashgate Publishing.

Huband, M. (2001) 'Influence of TV on Public Opinion and Newspaper Coverage', in Jake Lynch and Annabel McGoldrick (Eds), *Is Coverage of Africa Racist? and Why Are We Ignoring the Drc Crisis*. Reporting the world round table on 16 May 2001, London: Freedom Forum European Centre.

Human Rights and Journalism from www.rightsreporting.net. Accessed on 24 April 2009.

Human Rights Watch (24 January 2010) 'Egypt and Libya: A Year of Serious Abuses Human Rights Messengers Remain Particularly Vulnerable in Both Countries'. Accessed on 17 March 2010.

Human Rights Watch Arms Project Report (January 1994) Vol. 6, No.1, http://www.hrw.org/en/reports/1994/01/01/arming-rwanda Accessed on 20 October 2009.

Human Rights Watch World Report 2005 – Sierra Leone. http://www.unhcr.org/refworld/publisher, HRW, SLE, 421da31a19,0.html.

Huntington, S.P. (1996) *The Clash of Civilizations and the Remaking of World Order.* New York: Simon & Schuster.

Huysmans, J. (2006) *The Politics of Insecurity: Fear, Migration and Asylum in the EU.* Routledge: Taylor & Francis.

ICHRP Report (2002) 'Journalism, Media and the Challenge of Human Rights Reporting'. Geneva, Switzerland.

Ife, J. (2007) 'Human Rights and Peace', in Charles Webel and Johan Galtung (Eds), *Handbook of Peace and Conflict Studies.* London & New York: Routledge. pp.160–172

Ignatieff, M. (1998) *Isaiah Berlin: A Life.* New York: Henry Holt and Company.

Information Centre about Asylum and Refugees (ICAR) (2004) *Media Image, Community Impact: Assessing the Impact of Media and Political Images of Refugees and Asylum Seekers on Community Relations in London.* London: ICAR, Commissioned by the Mayor of London.

International Commission on Intervention and State Sovereignty (ICISS) (2001) 'The Responsibility to Protect', Ottawa. Paragraph 2, p. 30.

International News Safety Institute (INSI) (2003) *Dying to Tell the Story: The Iraq War and the Media: A Tribute.* Brussels, 29 July.

Ishay, M. (Ed.) (1997) *The Human Rights Reader.* London/New York: Routledge.

Iyengar, S. and Kinder, D. (1987), *News that Matters: Television and American Opinion.* Chicago: University of Chicago Press.

Journalists for Human Rights (JHR) www.jhr.ca/en/int_impact.php. Accessed on 20 April 2009.

Jacoby, E. (1983) 'Agrarian Unrest in Southeast Asia', in G.L. Beckford (Eds), *Persistent Poverty.* London: Zed Books.

Jones, B. (2005) 'Foreword', in Rich Cookson and Mike Jempson (Eds), The RAM Report: A Review of the MediaWise Refugees, Asylum-Seekers and the Media (RAM) project, 1999–2005. Mediawise Trust. Bristol. p. 4.

Jones, L. (2000) 'The European Press Views the Middle East: Sharon's Temple Mount Visit "Unprecedented Act of Provocation" Says Germany's Suddentsche Zeitung'. *The Washington Report on the Middle East Affairs,* Vol. xix, No. 9, p. 47.

Jones, L. (2001a) 'The European Press Views the East: Clinton's Last Push for Peace'. *The Washington Report on Middle East Affairs,* Vol. XX, No. 9, p. 47.

Jones, L. (September 30, 2001b) 'The European Press Views the Middle East: European Press; Mitchell Report Offers Little Hope'. *The Washington Report on Middle East Affairs,* Vol. XX, pp. 6, 29.

Kampfner, J. (2004) *Blair's Wars.* London: Free Press.

Kampfner, J. (14 December 2007) You Can Agree or Disagree, But You Can't Hide Away. *Daily Telegraph.*

Kant, I. (1963) 'Idea for a Universal History from a Cosmopolitan Point of View', seventh thesis *On History,* translation by Lewis White Beck. New York: Macmillan.

Kaplan, R. (1994) 'The Coming Anarchy: How Scarcity, Crime, Overpopulation, Tribalism and Disease Are Rapidly Destroying the Social Fabric of Our Planet'. *Atlantic Monthly*. February 1–8

Keane, F. (1996) *Season of Blood a Rwandan Journey Fergal Keane*. London: Penguin.

Keeble, R. (2009) 'War and The Journalistic Imagination: The Reporting of George Orwell and Robert Fisk'. *Literary Journalism: Newsletter of the International Association of Literary Journalism Studies*, Summer pp. 4–8.

Keeble, R.L. (2010) 'Peace Journalism as Political Practice: A New, Radical Look at the Theory', in Richard Lance Keeble (Ed.), *Peace Journalism, War and Conflict Resolution*. New York: Peter Lang Publishers.

Kelley, N. and Stevenson, J. (2006) *First Do No Harm: Denying Health Care to People Whose Aslyum Claims Have Failed*. A Report Commissioned by Refugee Council and OXFAM.

Kempf, W. (2002) 'Conflict Coverage and Conflict Escalation', in Wilhelm Kempf and H. Luostarinen (Eds), Vol. 2, *Journalism and the New World Order: Studying War and the Media*, Göteborg: Nordicom. pp. 59–72.

Kempf, W. (2007) 'Peace Journalism: A Tightrope Walk between Advocacy Journalism and Constructive Conflict Coverage'. *Conflict & Communication Online*, Vol. 6, No. 2, www.cco.regener-online.de. 25 January 2009.

Khosravi, S. (2007) 'The 'Illegal' Traveller: An Auto-Ethnography of Borders'. *Social Anthropology*, Vol. 15, No. 3, pp. 321–334. European Association of Social Anthropologists.

Khosravi, S. (2010) *The 'Illegal' Traveller: An Auto-Ethnography of Borders*. Hampshire: Palgrave Macmillan.

Kieh, G.K. (2000) 'Humanitarian Intervention in Civil Wars in Africa', in A. Valls (Ed.), *Ethics in International Affairs*, Rowman and Little Field, New York. (see also Chopra and Weiss 1992; Hehir 1995; Smith 1998).

Kiley, S. (11 May 1998) 'Sandline Weapons Still Being Used to Crush Rebel Force'. *The Times*.

Kiley, S. (22 January 1999) 'Send in the Mercenaries, Mr Cook'. *The Times*.

Kiley, S. (15 January 1999) 'Rough Justice Stalks Streets of Freetown'. *The Times Overseas News*.

Kiley, S. (10 November 2003) Interview.

Ki-moon, B. (2010) 'UN Secretary-General calls on leaders to attend Millennium Development Goals summit next September', http://www.un.org/millenniumgoals/. Accessed on 02 February 2010.

Klahr, M.L. (2008) 'In Defence of Human Rights-Based Journalism' (Interview).

Knightley, P. (2000) *The First Casualty: the war correspondent as hero and myth-maker from the Crimea to Kosovo*. London: Prion Books.

Krinjer, G.J. (1987) *Development through Liberation: Third World Problems and Solutions*. Basingstoke and London: Macmillan.

Kuper, A. (2002) 'Debate: Global Poverty Relief. More than Charity: Cosmopolitan solutions to the "Singer Solution" '. *Ethics and International Affairs*, Vol. 16, No. 1, pp. 107–120.

La Guadia, A. (14 January 1999) 'Sandline Should Have Been Left to Finish the Job'. *Daily Telegraph*.

La Guadia, A. (09 May 2000) 'The Brutal Rebel Leader with a Lust for Diamonds', *Daily Telegraph*.

La Guadia, A. (13 November 2003) Interview at the Telegraph press in London.

Lambeth, E. (1998) 'Public Journalism as Democratic Practice', in Edmund Lambeth, Phillip Meyer and Esther Thorston (Eds), *Assessing Public Journalism*. Missouri: Columbia University of Missouri Press, pp. 15–34.

Laramee, A. and Vallee, B. (1991) *La Recherche en communication: Éléments de méthodologie*. Quebec: Presse de l'Université de Quebec.

Larsen, I. (2009) 'Peace and Human Rights: A Comparative Analysis on the Role of Human Rights in Norwegian Peace Processes in Sudan'. Unpublished Master of Philosophy in Peace and Conflict Transformation thesis. Faculty of Social Sciences University of Tromsø.

Lasner, T. (2005) 'Media and Human Rights', in Rhoda Smith and Christien van den Anker (Eds), *Essentials of Human Rights: Everything You Need to Know About Human Rights*. London: Hodder Arnold.

Lasswell, H.D. (1927) 'The Theory of Political Propaganda'. *The American Political Science Review*, Vol. 21, No. 3, August, pp. 627–631.

Lederach, J.P. (1995) *Preparing for Peace: Conflict Transformation Across Cultures*. Syracsuse, New York: Syracuse University Press.

Lee, S.T. and Maslog, C. (2005) 'War or Peace Journalism in Asian Newspapers'. *Journal of Communication*, Vol. 55, No. 2, pp. 311–329.

Lee, S.T., Maslog, C. and Kim, H.S. (2006) 'Asian Conflicts and the Iraq War – A Compassionate Framing Analysis'. *International Communication Gazette*, Vol. 68, No. 5–6, pp. 499–518.

Leridon, M. (30 September 1998) 'Sierra Leone-Violence: Réparer l'horreur'. Agence France Presse *(AFP)*.

Leridon, M. (10 March 1999) 'Historic Visit of British and French Foreign Ministers to Ghana'. Agence France Presse *(AFP)*.

Leridon, M. (11 March 1999) ' "Good Bye Fashoda": Paris and London Put an End to Their Rivalry in Africa'. Agence France Presse *(AFP)*.

Levinson, N. (2003) *Outspoken: Free Speech Stories*, California: University of California Press.

Lewis, M. (2005) *Asylum: Understanding Public Attitudes*. London: Institute for Public Policy Research.

Lippmann, W. (1922) *Public Opinion*. New York. Free Press Paperback.

Limor, Y. and Nossek, H. (2002) Economic Censorship: The 'Invisible Hand', paper presented at a conference on capitalism and communication in the twenty-first century, Centre for communication and information studies of the University of Westminster (CCIS), London, 13–14 June/research_papers/ R18.pdf.

Livingston, S. (1997) Clarifying the CNN Effect (Research Paper R-18). Cambridge, MA: Joan Shorenstein Centre on the Press, Politics and Public Policy. HarvardUniversity, http://ksgwww.harvard.edu/shorenstein/researc_ publications/papes.

Livingston, S. and Eachus, T. (2000) 'Rwanda: U.S. Policy and Television Coverage' in Adelman, H. and Suhrke, A. (eds.) *The path of a genocide: the Rwanda crisis from Uganda to Zaire*, pp. 209–228. New Brunswick: Transaction Publishers.

Loffelholz, M. and Weaver, D. (Eds) (2007) *Global Journalism Research: Theories, Methods, Findings, Future*. London: Blackwell.

Lovasen, L. (2008) 'Journalism and Power: The Role of Media in Building Human Rights and Culture of Peace', www.humanrightsdefence.org/journalism-and-power-the-role-of-media-in-build. Accessed on 20 April 2009.

Loyn, D. (2003) 'Witnessing the Truth', http://www.opendemocracy.net .adapted from Jake Lynch's Debating Peace Journalism (2008).

Loyn, D. (2007) 'Good Journalism or Peace Journalism?'. *Conflict and Communication Online*, Vol. 6, No. 2, pp. 1–10.

Luttwak, E.N. (2000) 'No-score War'. *Times Literary Supplement*, 14 July 2000, http://tls.timesonline.co.uk/article/0,25368_1,00.html (consulted 12 March 2010).

Lynch, J. (1998) *The Peace Journalism Option*. Taplow: Conflict and Peace Forums.

Lynch, J. (2007) Peace Journalism and Its Discontents. Conflict & communication online, Vol. 6, No. 2, www.cco.regener-online.de. 1–13.

Lynch, J. (2008) *Debates in Peace Journalism*. Sydney: Sydney University Press.

Lynch, J. and Galtung, J. (2010) *Reporting Conflict: New Directions in Peace Journalism: New Approaches to Peace and Conflict*. Australia: University of Queensland.

Lynch, J. and McGoldrick, A. (2005) *Peace Journalism*. Stroud: Hawthorn Press.

Lye, A. (28 February 2010) Sunday Blog Western Telegraph (imported from Blog Module).

Maisokwadzo, F. (2005) 'Kick 'em out – They Can't Be Trusted', in Rich Cookson and Mike Jempson (Eds), *The RAM Report: A Review of the MediaWise Refugees, Asylum-seekers and the Media (RAM) Project*, 1999–2005. Bristol: Mediawise.

Malone, N. (2004) 'From Just War to Just Peace: Re-Visioning Just War Theory from a Feminist Perspective'. Unpublished MA thesis, Department of Political Science, College of Arts and Sciences, University of South Florida.

Mamdani, M. (2001) *When Victims Become Killers*. Princeton, NJ: Princeton University Press.

Mann, M. (1986) *The Sources of Social Power: V.1 History of Power from the Beginning to AD 1760*, Cambridge: Cambridge University Press.

Manokha, I. (2008) *The Political Economy of Human Rights Enforcement*. Global Ethics Series. Hampshire: Palgrave Macmillan.

Mathaba (13 March 2008) 'UNESCO Withdraws Patronage to Reporters Without Borders', http://www.mathaba.net/news/venezuela. Accessed on 17 March 2010.

Maren, M. (1997) *The Road to Hell*. New York: Free Press.

Marks, S.P. (2005) 'The Human Rights Framework for Development: Seven Approaches', in Arjun Sengupta et al. (Ed.), *Reflections on the Right to Development. Centre for Development and Human Rights*. New Delhi, Thousands Oaks, London: Sage Publications.

Marshall, R. (1991) 'Nothing without US pressure on Israel'. *The Washington Report on Middle East Affairs*, Vol. x, pp. 4, 14.

Masmoudi, M. (1992) 'Media and the State in Periods of Crisis', in Marc Raboy and Bernard Dagenais (Eds), *Media, Crisis and Democracy Mass Communication and the Disruption of Social Order*. London, Newbury Park, New Delhi: Sage Publications.

Matheson, D. and Allan, S. (2003) 'Weblogs and the War in Iraq: Journalism for the Network Society?', paper presented to the Digital Dynamics conference Loughborough, UK.

Mathew, P. (2008) *The Week Magazine*, Vol. 26, No. 5, pp. 24–30.

M'bayo, R.T., Onwumechili, C. and Nwafo, N. (Eds) (2000) *Press and Politics in Africa*. African Studies Volume 53 New York.

McChesney, R.M. (2002) 'The Rise and Fall of Professional Journalism', in Kristina Borgesson (Ed.), *Into the BUSSSAW: Leading Journalists Expose the Myth of a Free Press*. New York: Prometheus Books.

McChesney, R.M. (2004) *The Problem of The Media: Us Communication Politics in The Twenty-First Century*. New York: Monthly Review Press.

McCombs, M.E. and Shaw, D.L. (1972) 'The Agenda-Setting Function of Mass Media'. *Public Opinion Quarterly*, Vol. 36, pp. 176–185.

McGoldrick, A. (2006) 'War Journalism and "Objectivity" '. Conflict & communication online, 5/2. Retrieved 10 February 2010, http://cco.regener-online.de.

McLaughlin, G. (2002a) *The War Correspondent*. London: Pluto Press.

McLaughlin, G. (2002b) 'Rules of Engagement: Television Journalism and NATO's faith in bombing during the Kosovo crisis, 1999'. *Journalism Studies*, Vol. 5, No. 2, pp. 257–266.

McLuhan, M. (1965) *Understanding Media, The Extensions of Man*. New York: Mcgraw Hill.

McManus, J. (1995) 'A Market-Based Model of News Production'. *Communication Theory*, Vol. 5, No. 4, pp. 3331–3339.

McNair, B. (1995) *An Introduction to Political Communication*. Routledge. London (First edition).

McNair, B. (2003) *An Introduction to Political Communication*. Routledge. London (Third edition).

McNulty, M. (1999) 'Media Ethnicization and the International Response to War and Genocide in Rwanda', in T. Allen and J. Seaton (Eds), *The Media of Conflict: War Reporting and Represenations of Ethnic Violence*. London: Zed Books.

McQuail, D. (1994) *Mass Communication Theory*. London: Sage Publications.

MDG Task Force Report (2009) http://www.un.org/millenniumgoals/pdf/Press release MDG Gap 2009.pdf. Accessed on 27 May 2009.

Megwa, E.R. (2001) 'Democracy without Citizens: The Challenge for South African Journalism Education – Debate: Journalism Education'. *Journalism Studies*, Vol. 2, pp. 281–299.

Melucci, A. (1989) *Nomads of the Present*. London: Century Hutchinson.

Melvern, L. (2000) *A People Betrayed: The Role of the West in Rwanda's Geneocide*. London: Zed.

Melvern, L. (2001) 'Contribution on 'Is Coverage of Africa racist? And Why are We Ignoring the DRC Crisis?', in Jake Lynch and Annabel McGoldrick (Eds), *Report of the Reporting the World Round Table*. London: Freedom Forum European Centre, 16 May.

Mermin, J. (1997) 'Television News and American Intervention in Somalia'. *Political Science Quarterly*, Vol. 112, No. 3, pp. 385–403.

Mermin, J. (1999) *Debating War and Peace*. Princeton, NJ: Princeton University Press.

Mertes, T. (Ed) (2004) *A Movement of Movements*. London: Verso.

Mill, J.S. (1859) *On Liberty*. New York: Collier.

Moritz, F.A. (1997) 'American Human Rights Reporting Born in Yellow Prose'. www.worldlymind.org/creelover.htm. Accessed on 20 April 2009.

Meredith, M. (2005) *The State of Africa: A History of 50 Years of Independence*. London and New York: FP Press.

Morgenthau, H. (1967) 'To Intervene or Not to Intervene'. *Foreign Affairs*, Vol. 45, pp. 425–436.

Muhlmann, G. (2008) *A Political History of Journalism*. Cambridge: Polity.

Myers, G., Klak, T. and Koehl, T. (1996) 'The Inscription of Difference: News Coverage of the Conflicts in Rwanda and Bosnia'. *Political Geography*, Vol. 15, No. 1, pp. 21–46.

Nafziger, E.W. (2006) 'Development, inequality, and war in Africa'. *The Economics of Peace and Security Journal*, Vol. 1, No. 1, pp. 14–19.

Nardin, T. (2002) 'The Moral Basis of Humanitarian Intervention'. *Ethics and International Affairs*, Vol. 16, No. 1, pp. 57–70.

Nussbaum, M. (1997) 'Kant and Cosmopolitanism', in James Bohman and Matthias Lutz-Bachman (Eds), *Perpetual Peace: Essays on Kant's Cosmopolitan Ideal*. Cambridge, MA: The MIT Press. p. 33.

New Times (Kigali) (12 December 2007) President Mwanawasa Back from Portugal. Accessed on 31 December 2008.

Newman, N. (2007) *Communicating Asylum*. London: Institute of Public Policy Research (IPPR).

Nohrstedt, S., Kaitatzi-Whitlock, S., Ottosen, R. et al. (2000) 'From the Persian Gulf to Kosovo-War Journalism and Propaganda'. *European Journal of Communication*, Vol. 15, pp. 3, 383–404.

Nordenstreng, K. (2001) 'Something to be Done: Transnational Media Monitoring'. *Transnational Broadcasting Studies Journal*, Spring edition, http://www.tbsjournal.com/Archives/Spring01/nordenstreng.html. Accessed on 8 February 2011.

Norton-Taylor, R. and McGreal, C. (08 May 2000) 'UK Troops for Sierra Leone. Flight from Freetown: Britons Evacuated as Civil War Worsens'. *The Guardian*.

Norstedt, S.A. and Ottosen, R. (Eds) (2004) *U.S. and the Others. Global Media Images on 'The War on Terror'*. Göteborg: Nordicom.

Norstedt, S.A. and Ottosen, R. (Eds) (2005) *Global War Local Views*, Göteborg: Nordicom.

Nossek, H. (2007) 'Our News and Their News: The Role of National Identity in the Coverage of Foreign News', in Hillel Nossek, Annabelle Sreberny and Prasun Sonwalker (Eds), *Media and Political Violence*. Creskill, New Jersey: Hampton Press. pp. 41–64.

Nossek, H., Sreberny, A. and Sonwalker, P. (2007) *Media and Political Violence*. Cresskil, New Jersey: Hampton Press.

Nowak, M. (2004) *UN Covenant on Civil and Political Rights – CCPR Commentary*, 2nd edn, Kehl/Strassbourg/Arlington.

Nowak, M. (2005) 'The Internaitonal Covenants on Civil and Political Rights and on Economic, Social and Cultural Rights', in Smith and van den Anker (Eds), *Essentials of Human Rights*. London: Hodder Arnold.

Observer, OECD magazine. Accessed on 08 August 2010.

Olausson, U. (2005) Medborgarskap och globalisering. Den diskursiva konstruktionen av politisk identitet [Citizenship and Globalization: the discursive construction of political identity], Örebro: Örebro Studies in Media and Communication.

Onana, C. (2001) *Les Secrets du Genocide Rwandais: Enquete sur les mysteres d'un president*. Paris: Minsi.

Osabu-Kle, D. (2000) *Compatible Cultural Democracy: The Key to Development in Africa*. London: Broadview Press.

Ottosen, R. (2002) 'Pressfriheten under press after 11 September', in S. Finslo (Ed.), *Norsk Redakorforenings Arkbok 2001*. *Kristiansand*, Norway: Hoyskoleforlaget.

Oxfam and Refugee Council Report, 2004. http://www.oxfam.org.uk/resources/ukpoverty/downloads/ICESC_submission_2007.pdf. Accessed on 24 November 2009.

Palmer, M. (2003) *Quels Mots pour le dire? Correspondents de guerre, journalists et historiens face aux conflits Yougoslave*. Paris: Harmattan.

Parekh, B. (1997) 'Rethinking Humanitarian Intervention'. *International Political Science Review*, Vol. 18, pp. 49–69.

Parsons, T. (1965) *Social Structure and Personality*. New York: Free Press.

Parenti, M. (1993) *Inventing reality: The Politics of the Mass Media*. (Second edition). New York: St Martins Press.

Partant, F. (1982) *La Fin du Developpement*. Paris: Francois Maspero.

Patriotic Vanguard, Sierra Leone online news portal based in Vancouver. www.patrioticvanguard.com. Accessed on 27 March 2008.

Pattison, J. (2010) *Humanitarian Intervention and the Responsibility to Protect: Who Should Intervene?* Oxford: Oxford University Press.

Pedelty, M. (1993) *War Stories: The Culture of Foreign Correspondents*. London: Routledge.

Peters, J. (1999) 'Public Journalism and Democratic Theory: Four Challenges', in Theodore Glasser (Ed.), *The Idea of Public Journalism*, New York: Guilford Press. pp. 99–117.

Peterson, S. (2000) *Me against My Brother*. London: Routledge.

Philo, G., Hilsum, L., Beattle, L. and Hollman, R. (1999) 'The Media and Rwanda Crisis: Effects on Audiences and Public Policy', in Greg Philo (Ed.), *Message Received*, Harlow: Longman. pp. 213–228.

Philippe, J. (2001) 'La Légitimation de la cause humanitaire: un discours sans adversaires', in Éditions *Humanitaire en discours*. MOTS. Les Langages du politique. N°6 mars 2001. p. 15.

Plaissance, P.L. (2002) 'The Journalist as Moral Witness: Michael Ignatieff's Pluralistic Philosophy for a Global Media Culture'. *Journalism*, Vol. 3, No. 2, pp. 205–222.

Platon, S. and Deuze, M. (2003) 'Indymedia Journalism: A Radical Way of Making, Selecting and Sharing News?'. *Journalism*, Vol. 4, No. 3, pp. 336–355.

Pillai, R. (2007) *The Reception and Integration of New Migrant Communities*, Institute for Public Policy Research report for the CRE London: Commission for Racial Equality, http://www.cre.gov.uk/downloads/newmigrantcommunitiesresearch.pdf. Accessed on 12 October 2009.

Pilger, J. (1993) 'The West Is Guilty in Bosnia'. *New Statesman and Society*, 7 May, pp. 14–15.

Pogge, T. (1992) 'An Institutional Approach to Humanitarian Intervention'. *Public Affairs Quarterly*, Vol. 6, pp. 84–103.

Pogge, T. (2005) 'World Poverty and Human Rights'. *Ethics and International Affairs*, Vol. 19, No. 1, pp. 1–7.

Preston, A. (1996) 'Television News and the Bosnian Conflict, Distance, Proximity, Impact', in J. Gow, R. Paterson and A. Preston (Eds), *Bosnia by Television*. London: British Film Institute. pp. 112–116.

Puddephatt, A. (2005) 'Freedom of Expression', in Rhona Smith and Christien van den Anker (Eds), *The Essentials of Human Rights: Everything You Need to Know About Human Rigthts.* London: Hodder Arnold.

Pupavac, V. (2008) 'Refugee Advocacy, Traumatic Representations and Political Disenchantment'. *Government and Opposition,* Vol. 43, No. 2, pp. 270–292.

Ramonet, I. (13 January 2008) Africa says 'No'. *Le Monde Diplomatic/Mail & Guardian Online.* South Africa. Accessed on 31 January 2008.

Rantanen, T. (2007) 'The Cosmopolitanization of News'. *Journalism Studies,* Vol. 8, No. 6, pp. 843–861.

Reese, S.D. (2007) 'Theorising a Globalized Journalism', in Martin Loffelholz and David Weaver (Eds), *Global Journalism Research: Theories, Methods, Findings, Future.* London: Blackwell. pp. 240–252.

Richards, P. (1996) *Fighting for the Rain Forests: War, Youth and Resources in Sierra Leone.* Oxford: James Curry.

Riffenburgh, B. (1993) *The Myth of the Explorer.* London: Scott Polar Research Institute, University of Cambridge.

Robinson, P. (2002a) 'Humanitarian Intervention and the Logic of War', in Alexander Mosley and Richard Norman (Eds), *Human Rights and Military Intervention.* Aldershot: Ashgate Publishing.

Robinson, P. (2002b) *The CNN Effect: The Myth of News, Foreign Policy and Intervention.* London: Routledge.

Robinson, P. (2004) 'Researching US Media–State Relations and Twenty-First Century Wars', in Stuart Allan and Berbie Zelizer (Eds), *Reporting War: Jounalism in War Time.* London: Routledge.

Rodriguez, C. (2001) *Fissures in the Mediascape: An International Study of Citizens' Media.* Cresskill, NJ: Hampton.

Rosenblum, M. (1993) *Who Stole the News: Why We Can't Keep Up with What Happens in The World and What We Can Do about It?* Sydney: University of Western Sydney.

Ross, S.D. (2006) '(De) Constructing Conflict: A Focused Review of War and Peace'. *Journalism. Conflict & Communication Online,* Vol. 5, No. 2, www.cco. regener-online.de. Accessed on 24 September 2009.

RSF (12 October 2006) Homage to Journalist slain in Moscow – 'Anna's Voice is Stronger than Ever' article accessed on 24 July 2010 online www.rsf.org.

Russell, B. (6 December 2007) 'EU Leaders say Mugabe's Presence Will Not Derail Talks'. *The Independent.*

Rutter, J. and Latorre, M. (2009) 'Social Housing Allocation and Immigrant Communities'. IPPR Report commissioned by Equality and Human Rights Commission.

Ryfe, D. (2006) 'News, Culture and Public Life: A Study of 19th Century American Journalism'. *Journalism Studies,* Vol. 7, No. 1, pp. 61–77.

Sachs, J. (2005) *The End of Poverty: How We Can Make It Happen in Our Lifetime.* London: Penguin Books.

Sahnoun, M. (1994) *Somalia: The Missed Opportunities.* Washington DC: United States Institute of Peace Press.

Schaefer, B. (22 August 2002) 'Libyan Fox in the Human-Rights Henhouse'. *Heritage Foundation,* website Accessed on 17 March 2010.

Schirch, L. (2002) 'Human Rights and Peacebuilding: Towards Justpeace', paper presented to *43rd Annual International Studies Association Convention*. New Orleans, Louisiana, 24–27 March 2002.

Schramm, W. and Lerner, D. (Eds) (1976) *Communication and Change: The Last Ten Years and the Next*. Honolulu: University of Hawaii Press.

Schudson, M. (1995a) 'The Politics of Narrative Form'. The Emergence of News Conventions in Print and Television'. *Doedalus*, Vol. 111, pp. 97–112.

Schudson, M. (1995b) *The Power of News*. Cambridge: Harvard University Press.

Schudson, M. (1998) *The Power of News*. Cambridge, MA: Harvard University Press.

Schudson, M. (1999) 'What Public Journalism Knows about Journalism, but Doesn't Know about the Public', in Theodore Glasser (Ed.). *The Idea of Public Journalism*. New York: Guilford Press. pp. 118–133.

Seib, P. (2002) *The Global Journalist: News and Conscience in a World of Conflict*. Lanham. MD: Rowman & Littlefield.

Selm, J.V. (2003) 'Global Solidarity: Report of a Plenary Session', in Joanne van Selm et al. (Eds), *The Refugee Convention at Fifty: A View from Forced Migration Studies*. Maryland, USA: Lexington Books.

Sen, A. (1999) *Development as Freedom*. Oxford: Oxford University Press.

Sen, A. (2003) 'Principles on Freedom of Information Legislation', al-Bab.com (cited in Himelboim and Limor (2008)).

Sen, A. (2006) *Identity and Violence*: *The Illusion of Destiny*. London: Penguin Books.

Sen, J., Anand, A., Escobar, A. and Waterman, P. (Eds) (2004) *World Social Forum: Challenging Empire*. New Delhi: The Viveka Foundation.

Shah, R. (2005) 'The Right to Development', in Rhoda Smith and Christien van den Anker (Eds), *The Essentials of Human Rights: Every Thing You Need to Know about Human Rights*. London: Hodder Arnold.

Shaw, M. (1994) *Global Society and International Relations*. Cambridge: Polity Press.

Shaw, M. (1996) *Civil Society and Media in Global Crises*. London: St Martin's press.

Shaw, M. (2003) *War and Genocide*. Cambridge: Polity Press.

Shaw, I.S. (2006) Re-branding Africa, in *Africa Week Magazine*, London.

Shaw, I.S. (2007) 'Historical Frames and the Politics of Humanitarian Intervention: From Ethiopia, Somalia to Rwanda'. *Globalisation, Societies and Education*, Vol. 5, No. 3, November 2007, pp. 333–349.

Shaw, I.S. (2009) 'Towards an African Journalism Model: A Critical Historical Perspective'. *International Communication Gazette*, Vol. 71, No. 6, pp. 491–510.

Shaw, I.S. (2009) 'The "Us Only" and "Us+Them" Frames in Reporting the Sierra Leone War: Implications for Peace Journalism and Global Justice'. *Ethical Space: The International Journal of Communication Ethics*, Vol. 6, No. 1, pp. 39–47.

Shaw, I.S. (2011) 'Human Rights Journalism: A Critical Conceptual Framework of a Complementary Strand of Peace Journalism', in Ibrahim Seaga Shaw, Robert Hackett and Jake Lynch (Eds), *Expanding Peace Journalism: Critical and Comparative Perspectives*. Sydney: Sydney University Press.

Shoemaker, P.J. and Reese, S.D. (1996) *Mediating the Message: Theories of Influences on Mass Media Content* (Second Edition). White Plains, New York: Longman.

Scheufele, D. (1999) 'Framing As a Theory of Media Effects'. *Journal of Communication*, Vol. 49, No. 1, pp. 103–122.

Siebert, F., Peterson, T. and Schramm, W. (1963, 1956) *Four Theories of the Press*. Urbana: University of Illinois Press.

Sierra Leone Web (24 March 1997) Accessed on 08 August 1999.

Simeant, J. (2001) 'Urgence et développement, professionnalisation et militantisme dans humanitaire', in ENS éditions revue, *l'Humanitaire en discours*. MOTS. Les Langages du politique. N° 65, March. 28.

Singer, M. (2008) 'Drugs and Development: The Global Impact of Drug Use and Trafficking on Social and Economic Development'. *International Journal of Drug Policy*, Vol. 19, No. 6, pp. 467–478.

Singer, P. (2002) 'Poverty, Facts, and Political Philosophies: Response to 'More than Charity'. *Ethics and International Affairs*, Vol. 16, No. 1, pp. 121–124.

Smith, A.D. (10 January 1999) 'Britain Continues to Back Sierra Leone – But for How Long?'. *Sunday Independent* (UK).

Smith, A.D. (25 January 1999) 'Sierra Leone Aid May be Wasted'. *The Independent*.

Smith, A.D. (30 May 2000) 'Nostalgia Rises from Smoking Ruins of Graham's Hotel'. *The Independent*.

Smith, A.D. (22 September 2001) 'Without a Conflict to Fuel, Diamond Miners Still Work for Just 12p a Day'. *The Independent*.

Smith, A.D. (03 March 2004) Interview.

Spielman (13 November 2008) Article accessed online from America.gov on 20 April 2009.

Shinar, D. (2003) Peace Process in Cultural Conflict: The role of the Media, Conflict and Communication Online 2(1). at www.cco.regener-online.de. Accessed on 25 May 2010.

Schramm, W. and Lerner, D. (Eds) (1976) *Communication and Change: The Last Ten Years and the Next*. Honolulu: University of Hawaii Press.

Sonwalker, P. (2005) 'Banal Journalism: The Centrality of the "Us-Them" Binary in News Discourse', in Stuart Allan (Ed.), *Journalism: Critical Issues*. Maidenhead and New York: Open University Press.

Sonwalker, P. (2007) Disturbing the Banality of Journalism: Political Violence, Gujarat 2002 and the Indian News Media, in Hillel Nossek, Annabelle Sreberny and Prasun Sonwalker (Eds), Media and Political Violence. Creskill, New Jersey: Hampton Press. pp. 247–267.

Spivak, G.C. (2004) 'Righting Wrongs in South Atlantic Quarterly'. pp. 523–581.

Spurr, D. (1993) *The Rhetoric of Empire: Colonial Discourse in Journalism, Travel Writing and Imperial Administration*. Durham, NC and London: Duke University Press.

Sriskandarajah, D., Cooley, L. and Kornblatt, T. (2007) Britain's Immigrants: An economic profile. *A report for Class Films and Channel 4 Dispatches*. September. Institute of Public Policy Research.

Stammers, N. (2009) *Human Rights and Social Movements*. London: Pluto Press.

Starkey, G. (2007) *Balance and Bias in Journalism: Representation, Regulation and Democracy*. London: Palgrave Macmillan.

Statham, P. (2003) 'Understanding Anti-Asylum Rhetoric: Restrictive Politics or Racist Publics?', in Sarah Spencer (Ed.), *The Politics of Migration: Managing Opportunity, Conflict and Change. The Political Quarterly*, Oxford: Blackwell Publishing.

Strobel, W. (1997) *Late Breaking Foreign Policy*, United States Institute of Peace. Washington D.C.

South Wales Evening Post (27 December 2005) Cardiff. Wales Survey of Zimbabwe Refugee skills, Refugee Council. www.refugeecouncil.org.uk. Accessed on 08 August 2009.

Tan, Kok-Chor (2004) *Justice without Borders: Cosmopolitanism, Nationalism and Patriotism. Contemporary Political Theory.* Cambridge: Cambridge University Press.

Terlingen, Y. (2007) 'The Human Rights Council: A New Era in UN Human Rights work?' *Ethics & International Affairs*, Vol. 21, No. 2, pp 167–178.

Tharoor, S. and Daws, S. (2001) 'Humanitarian Intervention: Getting Past the Reefs'. *World Policy Journal*, Vol. 18, No. 2, pp. 21–30.

The Sun (4 July 2003) 'Swan Bake: Asylum-Seekers Steal the Queen's Birds for Barbecues'.

The Sun (2 February 2008) 'We Must Bust Bank to Pay for Baby Boom'. *The Sun*. London.

Tester, K. (2001) *Compassion, Morality and the Media.* Buckingham: Open University Press.

Thussu, D.K. (2000) 'Legitimizing "Humanitarian Intervention"? CNN, NATO and the Kosovo Crisis'. *European Journal of Communication*, Vol. 15, No. 3, pp. 345–361.

Tivona, E. (2011) The Globalization of Compassion: Women in the Foreground of Cultures of Peace, in Ibrahim Seaga Shaw, Robert Hackett and Jake Lynch (Eds), *Expanding Peace Journalism: Critical and Comparative Perspectives.* Sydney: Sydney University Press.

Tribe, L. (1988) *American Constitutional Law.* United States: Foundation Press.

Tuchman, G. (1978) *Making News: A Study in the Construction of Reality.* New York: Free Press.

Tumber, H. (2007) 'The Media and International Conflict: A Theoretical Overview', in Nossek et al. (Eds), *The Media and Political Violence.* London: Routledge, Taylor & Francis.

Underwood, D. (1993) *When MBAs Rule the Newsroom: How the Marketers and Managers Are Reshaping Today's Media.* New York: Columbia University Press.

United Nations Declaration of Human Rights (UDHR) (1948) United Nations General Assembly. New York.

Unesco(1980) The Macbride report *Communication and Society Today and Tomorrow, Many Voices One World, Towards a New More Just and More Efficient World Information and Communication Order.* London/Uniput, New York/Unesco, Paris: Kogan Page.

Unwin, T. (2007) 'No End to Poverty'. *Journal of Development Studies*, Vol. 43, No. 5, pp. 929–953.

UNHCR (2005) Report on Refugee Numbers.

Ury, W. (2001) *Must We Fight? From the Battlefield to the Schoolyard: A New Perspective on Violent Conflict & Its Prevention.* New York: John Wiley & Sons.

US Department of Defence and Department of State, Congressional Presentation for Security Assistance Programmes, Fiscal Year 1993 (1992), p. 291, cited in the Human Rights Watch Arms Report.

Uvin, P. (1998) *Aiding Violence: The Development Enterprise in Rwanda*. Bloomfield, CT: Kumarian Press.

Uvin, P. (2004) *Human Rights and Development*. USA: The Kumaran Press.

Van den Anker, Christien (2005) 'Cosmopolitanism and Human Rights', in Rhoda Smith and Christien Van den Anker (Eds), *Essentials of Human Rights: Everything You Need to Know about Human Rights*. London: Hodder Arnold.

Van der Gaag, N. and Nash, C. (1987) *Images of Africa: The UK Report*. Rome, Oxfam FAO Freedom From Hunger Campaign.

Vann, C. (2008) United Nations Heading for Failure on 60th Anniversary of the Universal Declaration of Human Rights. Accessed on RSF web site 19 July 2009.

Verghese, B.G. (1998) 'Freedom of Expression', in Asad Latif (Ed.), *Walking the Tight Rope: Press Freedom and Professional Standard in Asia*. Asian Media Information and Communication Centre. Jurong Point.

Volkmer, I. (1999) *News in the Global Sphere. A study of CNN and Its Impact on Global Communication*. Luton: University of Luton Press.

Volkmer, I. (2001) 'International Communication Theory in Transition. Parameters of the new global sphere of mediation', in Stig Hjarvard (Ed.), News in a Globalized Society, Göteborg: Nordicom, Göteborg University, pp. 65–76.

Volkmer, I. (2002) 'Journalism and Political Crisis in the Global Network Society', in Barbie Zelizer and Stuart Allan (Eds), *Journalism after September 11*. New York: Routledge, Taylor & Francis.

Weaver, D. (1987) 'Media Agenda-Setting and Elections. Assumptions and Implications', in D.L. Paletz (Ed.), *Political Communication Research*. Norwood, NJ: Ablex. pp. 211–224.

Weaver, D. (with the assistance of Wei Wu) (1998) *The Global Journalist: News People around the World*. Cresskill, NJ: Hampton Press.

Wenden, A. (2007) 'Educating for a Critically Literate Civil Society: Incorporating the Linguistic Perspective into Peace Education'. *Journal of Peace Education*, Vol. 4, No. 2, pp. 163–180.

Walker, R.B.J. (1988) *One World, Many Worlds: Struggles for a Just World Peace*. Boulder: Lynne Reinner/London Zed Books.

Walker, T. (2001) 'Is Coverage of Africa Racist? Why Are We Ignoring the DRC', in Jake Lynch and Annabel McGoldrick (Eds), Reporting the World Roundtable in London Report.

Walzer, M. (1992) *Just and Unjust Wars: A Moral Argument with Historical Illustrations*. 2nd Edition. London: HarperCollins.

Weissman, R.(1999) Democracy is in the streets, *Multinational Monitor*, December.

Wheeler, N. (1999) 'Enforcing Human Rights', in Tim Dunne and Nicholas Wheeler (Eds), *Human Rights and Global Politics*. Cambridge: Cambridge University Press. pp. 169–199.

Wight, M. (2005) 'Western Values in International Relations', in Herbert Butterfield and G. William (Eds), *The Voice of the Street*. London: George Allen and Unwin. pp. 89–131.

Williams, P.D. (2008) 'Keeping the Peace in Africa: Why African Solutions Are not Enough'. *Ethics and International Affairs*, Vol. 22, No. 3, pp. 309–329.

Wolfsfeld, G. (1997) *Media and Political Conflict.* New York: Cambridge University Press.

Wood, Leanne (23 September 2004) *Morning Star. UK.*

Zelizer, B. (1999) 'Making the Neighbourhood Work: The Improbabilities of Public Journalism', in Theodore L. Glasser (Ed.), *The Idea of Public Journalism.* New York: Guilford.

Index

CPSIA information can be obtained at www.ICGtesting.com
Printed in the USA
LVOW090042271112

308951LV00015B/732/P